Francine Pascal's

SWEET VALLEY High

SUMMER DANGER COLLECTION

including
A STRANGER IN THE HOUSE
A KILLER ON BOARD

BANTAM BOOKS
TORONTO • NEW YORK • LONDON • SYDNEY • AUCKLAND

Visit the official Sweet Valley Web Site on the Internet at:
http://www.sweetvalley.com

SWEET VALLEY HIGH
SUMMER DANGER COLLECTION
A BANTAM BOOK : 0 553 81282 3

Individual titles originally published in U.S.A. by Bantam Books
First published in Great Britain as individual titles in 1996
Collection first published in Great Britain

PRINTING HISTORY
Bantam Collection published 1999

Copyright © 1999 by Francine Pascal

including
A STRANGER IN THE HOUSE
First published in Great Britain, 1996
Copyright © 1995 by Francine Pascal

A KILLER ON BOARD
First published in Great Britain, 1996
Copyright © 1995 by Francine Pascal

The trademarks "Sweet Valley" and "Sweet Valley High"
are owned by Francine Pascal and are used under license by
Bantam Books and Transworld Publishers Ltd.

Conceived by Francine Pascal

Produced by Daniel Weiss Associates, Inc,
33 West 17th Street, New York, NY 10011

All rights reserved.

Cover photo by Oliver Hunter

Cover photo of twins © 1994, 1995, 1996 Saban – All Rights Reserved.

Condition of Sale

This book is sold subject to the condition that it shall not,
by way of trade or otherwise, be lent, re-sold, hired out
or otherwise circulated without the publisher's prior consent
in any form of binding or cover other than that in which it is
published and without a similar condition including this
condition being imposed on the subsequent purchaser.

Bantam Books are published by Transworld Publishers Ltd,
61–63 Uxbridge Road, Ealing, London W5 5SA,
in Australia by Transworld Publishers,
c/o Random House Australia Pty Ltd,
20 Alfred Street, Milsons Point, NSW 2061, Australia
and in New Zealand by Transworld Publishers,
c/o Random House New Zealand,
18 Poland Road, Glenfield, Auckland, New Zealand.

Made and printed in Great Britain by
Cox & Wyman Ltd, Reading, Berkshire.

A STRANGER IN THE HOUSE

A KILLER ON BOARD

A STRANGER IN THE HOUSE

SWEET VALLEY High®

A STRANGER IN THE HOUSE

**Written by
Kate William**

**Created by
FRANCINE PASCAL**

BANTAM BOOKS
NEW YORK • TORONTO • LONDON • SYDNEY • AUCKLAND

To Molly Jessica W. Wenk

Prologue

Scissor blades gleamed, slicing through newsprint. The sports section of the *Sweet Valley News* fell away and floated to the cement floor, a rectangular window cut from its front page. John Marin shoved the forbidden scissors under his mattress. Then he scrutinized the newspaper photo as he thoughtfully stroked his unshaven face.

An eighteen-year-old Sweet Valley man, Nicholas Morrow, had won a local sailing race. Morrow stood on the deck of his boat, grinning for the camera as his trophy shone in the afternoon sunlight.

"Eighteen," Marin muttered, glaring at the young man's handsome, smiling face. "That's just how old I was. . . ." He allowed himself a few seconds to savor the thought of being as free as Morrow to sail on the blue Pacific. He squinted, as if peering into the California sun. He drew a long, deep breath. But the stuffy, slightly rancid odor of the prison cell blocked out all memories of the tang of salt in the air. "It doesn't matter," he told the smiling young man in the photo. "It won't be long now."

But Morrow wasn't the reason John Marin had clipped the photograph. The reason was in the background. The sailboat's crew for the race was a group of local teenagers, two of whom were visible behind Morrow.

A beautiful blond girl was on the right. As she climbed from the rigging a tall, dark-haired guy reached for her hand. The girl's hair was pulled back in a windblown ponytail; her slim legs showed tanned and shapely beneath a pair of loose white shorts. The boy was identified as Todd Wilkins, but it was the girl who interested Marin.

He stared at her face, feeling a familiar rush of hatred. "Elizabeth Wakefield," he whispered, sneering. "Daddy's number-one girl."

Marin taped the newspaper clipping on the wall over his cot, next to a color photograph snipped from the front page of a gossip tabloid a few months earlier.

"And there's Daddy's number-two baby, playing *Lifestyles of the Rich and Famous*," he said, shifting his gaze to the tabloid photo. In this one a radiant, golden-haired teenager in red sequins stood between a rock star and an actor. A man who didn't know any better would have thought the blonde in the tabloid and the girl on the sailboat were one and the same. The long legs, the golden tans, and the heart-shaped faces were identical. But Marin did know better. He had studied the twins for ten long, empty years.

Marin studied Jessica Wakefield's face. A glamorous makeup job complemented the loose, sexy waves of her elaborately tousled blond hair.

"You do love hanging out with the Hollywood crowd, don't you, Jessica?" he asked. "I'm sure I can find a way to make use of that information."

The photo had been taken while the twins guest-starred briefly on a popular soap opera. Marin had watched every one of the twins' episodes, sitting with the other inmates in the crowded common room of the state prison. Normally, watching soaps was an excuse for good-natured ribbing and raunchy comments about actresses. But Marin had demanded silence on the first day of the twins' appearance on *The Young and the Beautiful*. And silence was what he got. Despite Marin's youthful appearance, the other prisoners had learned to comply when he gave an order.

He scanned the other clippings on the cinder-block wall. The twins and their older brother, Steven, beaming at their father, a candidate for town mayor . . . Jessica winning a beauty pageant . . . Elizabeth placing first in an essay contest . . . Elizabeth modeling jungle-print clothes, as part of a promotion to save the rain forest . . . Jessica chosen to appear on a talk show . . . Elizabeth kidnapped and then returned, unharmed . . . Jessica at the wedding of her best friend's parents . . . Elizabeth acquitted of manslaughter after a boy died in an accident in the Jeep she was driving. . . .

"I should have been acquitted too, ten years ago," Marin muttered, glaring again at the girl on the rigging of the sailboat. But finally, that wrong would be righted. He would be as free as Elizabeth and her sister. "It won't be long now," he said again, narrowing his eyes. "Not long at all."

Chapter 1

Elizabeth was halfway through her cereal Monday morning when Jessica skipped into the bright, Spanish-tiled kitchen where the rest of the Wakefield family was eating breakfast.

"No more pencils, no more books! No more teachers' dirty looks!" Jessica sang out. She twirled around in the kitchen, as if she were wearing a tutu instead of khaki shorts and a turquoise polo shirt. Elizabeth was wearing an identical shirt, tucked into her own khaki shorts.

Elizabeth shook her head, amused. Jessica sounded as if she were half the twins' real age, which was sixteen.

Alice Wakefield smiled. "I take it you're happy about the first day of summer vacation, Jess."

"Are you kidding? This is going to be the most awesome summer in the history of the universe."

"Ah, yes," eighteen-year-old Steven Wakefield

said with a nod. "The Golden Age of Greece, the Renaissance, and the Age of Enlightenment will be merely footnotes in history compared to the summer Jessica Wakefield waited tables at the Marina Café."

"Ha!" Jessica retorted. "You're just jealous because you'll be cooped up in a boring old law office while Liz and I are collecting humongous tips and meeting cute guys who surf and own yachts."

Elizabeth grinned at her sister and passed her the milk. "Leave it to you to make serving sandwiches sound glamorous."

"Those are certainly glamorous outfits you're both wearing today," Steven commented, gesturing toward the twins' matching polo shirts. "I thought you two clones gave up dressing alike about ten years ago."

Jessica sliced a banana over her granola. "We did—unless there's something we can get out of impersonating each other, that is. But this is different."

Elizabeth laughed. "You are looking at the official waitress uniform for the Marina Café," she said. "Except for our matching necklaces, of course." She fingered the gold lavaliere she always wore around her neck, identical to Jessica's. "See? The shirts have the café's logo on them. They come directly from fashion runways of Milan and Paris."

"I think she means *airport* runways," Jessica said. "I feel like a baggage handler. Khakis aren't exactly the height of chic."

"I *like* khakis!" Elizabeth protested.

"You would." Jessica shrugged, holding a glass of cranberry juice in her hand. A few ruby droplets spattered the smooth white tablecloth. "You're such a prep, Liz. I'm just glad Mr. Jenkins said we could wear shorts. And the turquoise shirt *does* match our eyes."

"That's a relief!" Steven said. "You wouldn't want your clothes to clash with your eyes. What would people say?"

"I see that you've been taking sarcasm lessons from Elizabeth. And fashion lessons from Dad." Jessica pointed her spoon at her brother's gray suit and then at their father's. The similarity was emphasized by the fact that Ned Wakefield looked like an older version of his brown-eyed, dark-haired son. Ned sat across the table from Jessica, but he was engrossed in the morning newspaper and apparently hadn't heard a word of the conversation. Jessica shook her head in an exaggerated way. "Steven, you're dressed like you're about forty years old."

Mrs. Wakefield smiled. "I think you look quite handsome, Steven."

"You have to say that," Jessica pointed out. "You're his mother."

Elizabeth rolled her eyes. Jessica and Steven were capable of teasing back and forth all day.

"But I suppose you have to wear dull clothes if you're going to fit in at a stuffy law firm," Jessica continued. "You'd never catch me wasting a perfectly good summer doing something so *serious*."

Elizabeth shook her head. "Only you can make 'serious' sound like a disease."

"It *is* a disease."

"I happen to be excited about being an intern in Dad's office," Steven announced. "Law offices don't generally take in undergraduates."

"So why did they hire you?" Jessica asked. "Was it your overwhelming brainpower, your sterling resume, or the fact that Dad's a partner in the firm?"

"Tell her, Dad," Steven urged. "Tell her about my brilliant interview with Marianna West and the other partners."

Ned Wakefield looked up, startled, from the *Sweet Valley News*. "Sorry, Steven," he said with a weak smile. "I guess I wasn't paying attention. What were you saying?"

"That's certainly a glowing endorsement," Jessica said through a mouthful of granola. "I hope you held the other partners' attention that well in your interview."

Steven grinned. "When I'm a rich corporate attorney, you just see if I buy you a mansion in Beverly Hills."

Elizabeth sighed. The bickering was lighthearted, but it was getting on her nerves. It was definitely time for a new topic of conversation. "Speaking of mansions, Mom," she began, "you were telling us about the huge house you're working on this summer. How many bedrooms did you say it has?"

"Seven!" Mrs. Wakefield said. "But we're planning to knock out a wall and turn the three front rooms into an enormous master suite."

"It sounds great!"

"The architect I'm working with is based up in

Oakland. You should see his sketches, Liz. They're really something. He's managed to do a terrific job, despite the, uh, eccentricities of the house's owner."

Elizabeth laughed. "How eccentric are we talking? Does he want a moat around the place?"

"Not quite. But get this—in the master bathroom, the client insists on having a fireplace!"

"Cool!" Jessica exclaimed. "Can Liz and I put a fireplace in our bathroom?"

"I don't think so, Jessica." Mrs. Wakefield smiled.

Elizabeth drank the last of her cranberry juice. "So, Mom, what kind of decorating theme do you think you'll go with?"

"I've decided on a southwestern motif," Mrs. Wakefield told her. "It's a little trendier than I usually do, but the desert colors will be great with the simple lines of the architecture."

"Should be nice," Jessica said, suddenly sounding distracted. Elizabeth followed her twin's gaze to the back page of Mr. Wakefield's newspaper. A colorful ad announced the annual Summer Fun sale at Valley Mall. No doubt Jessica would spend her first week's waitressing tips before she'd even earned them.

Mr. Wakefield turned the page and refolded the paper. Jessica sighed and picked up her bagel.

"I'm keeping all the walls white," Mrs. Wakefield continued, "with accents in a muted coral tone—"

She stopped as Mr. Wakefield began choking on his toast.

"What is it, Dad?" Elizabeth asked.

Jessica raised her eyebrows. "I don't think he likes muted coral."

"Ned, are you all right? Do you want some water?"

"I'm fine," he insisted after a moment. "Everything's OK. Nothing's wrong at all."

Elizabeth and her mother exchanged a concerned look. Elizabeth glanced back at her father, but his eyes were riveted to the newspaper. He had regained his composure, but Ned Wakefield's face was as white as the tablecloth.

Mr. Wakefield took a deep breath and tried to pretend nothing was wrong. *In all likelihood,* he told himself, *there really is nothing wrong.* He was probably overreacting to the short item he'd spotted in the *Sweet Valley News*. Of course he was overreacting.

He reread the headline: PAROLE BOARD GRANTS FIFTEEN-YEAR REPRIEVE. The message was there in black and white, but Ned couldn't believe it.

Around the courthouse Ned Wakefield had a reputation for progressive views on rehabilitation. But even he was convinced that some criminals were unsalvageable. He had learned that lesson more than ten years ago, when he was a young assistant district attorney.

He held the newspaper in front of his face and closed his eyes for a few seconds, remembering. . . .

The jury members' horrified gasps were audible when Ned passed around the crime-scene photo-

graphs of the golden-haired college student and her mother. The two women had driven to Secca Lake for a picnic on a sunny June day. They'd been abducted and held in a cabin a few miles away. A week later the kidnapper dumped the bodies in the woods, stabbed a dozen times each.

There was no doubt in Ned's mind that the defendant was guilty. And only a monster could have murdered those two lovely, innocent women, even though their family had paid the exorbitant ransom he'd demanded. A man who had committed such a crime deserved to be locked up forever. . . .

Ned had thought he'd presented an airtight case. But then the defendant took the stand and almost talked his way out of a conviction—despite the fact that every bit of evidence proved he was the murderer. This guy had been slick, all right, with his baby face and innocent eyes. By the time the defendant stepped down from the witness stand, the jury was like putty in his strong, lethal hands. Ned could see it in their eyes: those twelve citizens were set to find the monster innocent. It was up to Ned to change their minds.

"A case rests on facts, not on personalities or appearances," Ned reminded the jury. "Forget the slick talk. Forget the neat haircut and the pressed suit. The defendant brutally murdered two innocent women." He paused to emphasize that point.

"You, the jury, are obligated to the truth. And the truth is that this man"—Ned gestured toward the defendant—"is guilty, beyond any reasonable

doubt. You've seen the police reports. You've heard the testimony and reviewed the evidence. You know that the defendant's alibi fell apart under questioning. You know that the victims' blood was found on his clothes and hands. And you saw the photographs of the bodies of two women whose only mistake was to choose the wrong afternoon for a picnic at Secca Lake."

Ten years later Ned shook his head behind the newspaper, remembering the horror of the crime. Those two women had been slaughtered, pure and simple. And he had never wanted to win a case so badly, before or since. Few trials seemed to hit home with Ned the way that one had. The lake was a popular spot. His own young family often picnicked there; the jurors probably spent time at Secca Lake with their own families as well. He wanted them to realize—to understand deep down—that the murdered women could have just as easily been their own wives or daughters or sisters.

Ned had felt no happiness at the guilty verdict—only relief. The twenty-five-year sentence wasn't the life term he'd hoped for, but it had seemed like enough to keep the killer off the streets for a good, long time.

Now, only ten years later, John Marin was free on parole. And the police had never recovered the ransom money, so he was probably a rich man.

Surely money and freedom would be enough for Marin. He must have forgotten the threats he'd made that day, as the police pulled him to his feet and began leading him out of the courtroom....

Handcuffs clanked as the murderer shrugged away from the officers and leaned over the prosecutor's table. "I'll get you, Wakefield," he hissed into Ned's ear. "And you can be sure I'll hit you where you live." Ned felt the color drain from his face.

The convicted man struggled against the officers, who jerked him toward the exit. "How are those three perfect children of yours, Counselor?" Marin called in a menacing tone. "I won't forget you, Wakefield!" Marin shouted back over his shoulder as they led him down the aisle. "Your precious little girls will never be safe again!"

Ned turned to watch John Marin's back retreating out the door of the courtroom. But all he could see were the chubby faces of an eight-year-old boy and two golden-haired girls—the prettiest six-year-olds in the first-grade class.

"Yo! Earth to Dad!" Jessica called to her father. She kissed him on the cheek and was amused when he jumped. "Boy, were you ever zoning!"

"What's the matter, Dad?" Elizabeth asked, pecking him on the other cheek.

"Not a thing," he said quickly, giving them a tight smile. "I'm just a little tired. But are you girls really sure you want to take jobs this summer? I mean, you won't have many carefree summers left before college and work. Maybe you should consider just staying close to home for the next few months."

"Sounds good to me," Jessica said. "If you'd consider tripling my allowance!"

"I thought you said working at the café would be good experience," Elizabeth said. "You know, teach us responsibility and all that."

Leave it to Liz to think about responsibility, Jessica thought.

"Yeah, Dad," Steven said. "I thought it was you who suggested summer jobs in the first place."

Mrs. Wakefield placed a hand on her husband's arm. "Why the cold feet all of a sudden?"

Mr. Wakefield smiled. "I guess I'm just becoming sentimental in my old age, seeing my baby daughters grown up enough to have jobs."

"Come on, Jess," Elizabeth urged. "We won't have jobs much longer if we're late to work on our first day."

Jessica drained her glass of cranberry juice. "Punctuality is next to godliness, you know," she confided to Steven in her best Elizabeth voice.

"That's cleanliness," her mother reminded her. "As in, remember that you promised to vacuum the living room by tonight. Time's running out."

Jessica sighed. She'd been hoping her mother had forgotten that promise. Vacuuming wasn't the kind of thing Jessica generally offered to do. But she'd made the promise in a weak moment, when she desperately needed an advance on her allowance to buy a cool pair of bright red sandals. "It would really make more sense to have Elizabeth do the living room," she tried. "She does a much better job of vacuuming than I do—"

"Save your breath!" Elizabeth interrupted. "I'm busy tonight." She turned to her parents. "I forgot to mention that I won't be home for dinner. I'm going out with Todd."

Mr. Wakefield stared at her, his brown eyes intense. "Be home early." Slowly he stood and walked to the window. "And I want both of you girls to be careful today," he said quietly. "Don't talk to strangers."

In the doorway Jessica grunted and rolled her eyes. "Sure thing, Dad. We'll just ask for people's orders in sign language."

Mr. Wakefield watched the twins breeze out the door. He froze when he felt a hand on his shoulder.

"Is something wrong, Ned?" Alice asked. "You seem preoccupied."

"No, no," he said, making an effort to disguise the tension in his voice. "It's just like I said—I'm a little tired. I haven't been getting enough sleep, thanks to this wrongful-dismissal suit—"

"You have been working awfully long hours, Dad," Steven said. "But never fear. Starting today, you'll have *me* in the office to help you out. Maybe you'll be able to come home a little earlier."

"Spending more time at home isn't such a bad idea," Mr. Wakefield said thoughtfully. He turned back to the window to watch the girls in the driveway as they argued about who was going to drive the black Jeep Wrangler they shared.

"I won't forget you, Wakefield," Marin had said. *But surely, after ten years . . .*

"Dammit," Mr. Wakefield swore under his breath. How could the parole board be so blind? John Marin was a dangerous criminal. And now he was free.

"He's probably forgotten all about me," he whispered to the windowpane, trying to believe it. His heart filled with love for his children.

Behind him laughter rang out, cheerful and carefree. Steven was joking with Alice as they loaded the breakfast plates into the dishwasher. Outside, the girls had resolved their argument over driving rights—as usual, by Elizabeth giving in to her more headstrong twin. Jessica glided into the driver's seat while Elizabeth climbed in on the other side. Both twins were smiling as Jessica gunned the engine.

The Jeep moved away, growing smaller in the distance. And Mr. Wakefield felt a torrent of fear as his daughters sped out of his sight.

Chapter 2

"Dad was a major space cadet this morning," Jessica commented as she steered the Jeep toward the marina.

"He did seem kind of weird," Elizabeth admitted. She rolled down her window to feel closer to the bright blue sky and the white-gold sunlight that danced on the well-kept lawns of Calico Drive. Despite the beautiful June day, Elizabeth felt troubled by her father's uncharacteristic anxiety. "What do you think is wrong with him?"

"He said something about a tough case his firm is handling, going up against some big-time corporation. Maybe he's afraid he's going to lose."

"I suppose that could be it. Or maybe it's like he says. He's just tired."

Jessica grinned. "Or he's been abducted by aliens and replaced with a Martian clone."

"I'm sure he'll be normal by tonight," Elizabeth

said, hoping it was true. "He's been so excited about having Steven in the office with him. I bet their first day of working together will make him feel more like himself."

"Well, I'm sure looking forward to *our* first day of work," Jessica said.

Elizabeth nodded. "Me too. Waitressing isn't the most intellectually stimulating summer job I might have hoped for, but it's going to be fun."

Jessica snorted. "Intellectual? Leave it to you to even suggest that a summer job should be intellectual. Think about it, Liz. We're spending the whole summer at the marina! Sunny days, huge tips, guys with yachts—"

"Heavy trays to carry, vegetables to slice, rude customers—"

"Don't be so pessimistic, Elizabeth. Just take it from me—this is going to be the most perfect summer ever."

Elizabeth shrugged. "And *you* take it from *me*— waitressing is hard work. We'll be right near the beach, but it's not as though we're spending the summer lying on a towel, scoping guys—like somebody else we know."

Jessica batted her eyelashes. "Why, whoever could you mean?" she said in a bad imitation of a southern accent.

"You know who I mean," Elizabeth said, thinking of Jessica's wealthy but spoiled best friend. "The only thing Lila Fowler's planning to work at this summer is her tan."

"But at least she'll be nearby. She can come into the café every day with reports on good-looking surfers—and spend some of her millions on big tips for me."

"Enid will be close by too," Elizabeth said, referring to her own best friend. "Did I tell you she got the lifeguard job she was after? She just called me last night with the news."

"What a waste," Jessica said. "You can see that high platform from every part of the beach—and sitting on it will be Enid Rollins, the World's Most Boring Teenager. There really ought to be a law: Lifeguards should all be hot guys with big biceps and washboard stomachs."

"I didn't think you'd be mooning over cute lifeguards this summer, Jess. What about Ken Matthews? Just because he's out of town for the month, do you plan to forget that you have a steady boyfriend now?"

"I'll miss Ken," Jessica said with a shrug. "But what can I do about it? His parents decided to take the family to Monterey to visit his uncle Frank. So I'll just have to have a good time without him."

"I thought you were in love!"

"I am. But I'm sure Ken doesn't expect me to mope around for a month alone. He wants me to have a good time while he's gone. It's like that song from when Mom and Dad were young—love the one you're with!"

"I can't believe he really meant *that*."

"Maybe not exactly. But how would *you* know?

You and boring old Todd don't understand the first thing about having fun."

"Todd's not boring—" Elizabeth began loyally, defending her longtime boyfriend, Todd Wilkins.

"Of course, Todd *is* a hunk," Jessica admitted, interrupting her. "It's his only redeeming quality. But you've been dating him for a million years!"

"That's why I'm so glad he'll be working at the marina too," Elizabeth said. "I like having him close by."

Jessica shook her head in disgust. "Exactly. And you'll probably still see him every single day, when he comes into the café between windsurfing lessons."

"What's wrong with seeing my boyfriend every day?"

Jessica shrugged. "Nothing, I guess. But it's not just your boring relationship with Todd. Face the truth. You're in serious danger, Liz. And you don't even know it."

"What are you talking about?"

"You're in danger of growing up into a nerd! You're boring! You need to take more risks in life. Do something wild and crazy for a change."

"That's ridiculous," Elizabeth protested. But she felt interested in spite of herself. "Like what?"

"Have a secret romance. Rob a bank. Take up bungee jumping. You know, get a life!"

"I have a life!" Elizabeth protested. "A very nice life." Too late, she realized how weak that sounded. As a writer, she was sure that her thesaurus omitted "nice" when listing synonyms for "wild and crazy." She started again, trying to be completely honest. "I have a very interesting, active, fulfilling life."

"Right," Jessica said, rolling her eyes. "Name me one single night in the last two weeks that you've done anything the least bit fun."

Elizabeth opened her mouth to speak, but then shut it. She *had* been working awfully hard, studying for final exams and writing several articles for the year-end edition of the *Oracle*, the student newspaper at Sweet Valley High. "Well," she said finally, "Todd and I stopped at the Dairi Burger after school Friday for a celebration milk shake."

"You party animal!"

Elizabeth sighed. "I give up! You're absolutely right. I'm a drone."

Jessica's mouth dropped open. "I'm *right*? You mean you're agreeing with me? Call the newspapers!"

"The truth is, I've sort of been reevaluating my life for the past few weeks," Elizabeth admitted.

"Then why were you arguing with me?"

"I guess I didn't realize exactly what was wrong until now. I can finally see that I'm in a serious rut. I do a lot of things that are fun. But I've been doing the *same* fun things over and over again, all year long!"

Jessica pulled the Jeep to a stop at a red light and turned to face her sister. "So you admit you're in a rut. That's the first step toward becoming a recovering dullaholic. The next step is to find a way to shake yourself out of this dismal pattern. Might I suggest skydiving?"

"Don't press your luck."

Elizabeth thought for a minute as Jessica drove through the intersection and turned down the driveway that led to the marina. "You know, Jessica, I always claim I want to be a writer when I grow up. But how will I ever think of anything to write about if I haven't *experienced* life?"

"Exactly! Didn't Mr. Collins say that Hemingway hung out in bars all the time? And that Edgar Allan Poe was a real partyer? They didn't spend their whole lives sitting behind a computer monitor, typing."

Elizabeth grinned. "They couldn't have if they wanted to. Word processors hadn't been invented yet."

"You know what I mean."

Elizabeth nodded. "Yes, I guess I do." Roger Collins, her favorite teacher, was always telling fascinating stories about authors' lives. And none of the stories included anecdotes about weekends spent studying for exams. Elizabeth took a deep breath. "I still need to work out the details, but my mind's made up," she announced. "Somehow I'm going to find a way to have a summer full of adventure, risk, and life experiences!"

Jessica pulled the Jeep to a stop in the parking lot at the marina. Then she turned and grinned at her sister. "You know what, Lizzie? There may be hope for you yet."

"Ah, the twins!" exclaimed Mr. Jenkins, the owner of the marina café, as Jessica and Elizabeth walked in. He stroked his mustache and stepped out from behind the counter that ran along the back wall of the dining room. "I hope my new waitresses are ready for a busy day."

Jessica smiled brightly. "Hi, Mr. Jenkins!" She glanced at her sister, remembering Elizabeth's resolve to seek out excitement this summer. "I think both of us are ready for just about anything."

"That's great, Elizabeth!" Mr. Jenkins said, smiling at Jessica. "Enthusiasm is one of the most important traits of a good waitress."

"Actually, I'm Jessica. She's Liz."

Mr. Jenkins scratched his nearly bald head. "Jessica? Goodness, and I thought I finally had it straight by the end of your interview last week. Well, I'm sure I'll remember from now on."

"The café opens at nine thirty, right?" Elizabeth asked. "It's almost eight forty-five now. Do you want us to jump right in and get to work? We can start getting food out, or make sure all the tables have napkins and silverware—"

Mr. Jenkins smiled broadly at Elizabeth. "It's refreshing to see a girl your age with such a sense of responsibility, Jessica."

Jessica rolled her eyes. Elizabeth's efforts to be wild and crazy this summer were definitely off to a slow start.

Mr. Jenkins checked his watch. "We'll have you both hard at work soon enough. But first, I'd like to spend a half hour on orientation for you and two other new waitresses. We'll begin in a few minutes. You can wait for me in the storage room."

"Where's that?" Jessica asked as he began to bustle away.

"Oh. See the two doors behind the counter? The one on the right leads to the kitchen. The other is to the storage room. I'll join you in there shortly."

Morning sunlight coming through the window behind Ned Wakefield cast a shadow on the folded newspaper that lay on his mahogany desk at the law office. Marianna West, another partner in the firm, sat across from him, holding a thick stack of file folders.

"Here's what I needed your help on," she said, shoving a stray lock of strawberry blond hair out of her eyes. "It's the *Stone versus West Coast Oilcam* case. You know almost everyone in town, Ned. Can you suggest someone I could call? I need an expert witness who can testify to . . ."

Mr. Wakefield tried to keep his mind on *West Coast Oilcam*, but John Marin's image hovered in front of him like the Ghost of Murders Past. Of course Marin had been bluffing when he threatened revenge against the Wakefield family. Hadn't he?

"Excuse me, Marianna." A new voice penetrated his thoughts and Mr. Wakefield jumped in his seat. But it was only Trudy Roman, the office manager. "Sorry to startle you, Ned. I just wanted to let you know that I haven't been able to locate that old case file you asked for." She consulted her clipboard. "The *Marin* case."

"What do you mean, you can't locate it?" Mr. Wakefield demanded, his voice rising.

Trudy's brown eyes widened. "Sorry, Ned. But it's a ten-year-old case. City hall keeps a lot of the really old files in off-site storage a couple miles outside of town. I'll ask one of the interns to drive over and take a look."

Ned nodded. "Good. Sorry I lost my temper." He smiled weakly. "I didn't sleep much last night."

Trudy smiled. "Don't worry about it. Who would you like me to send after that case file? Your son, Steven?"

"No!" Ned said quickly. The last thing he wanted was for anyone in his family to find out about Marin. There was no need to frighten them until he knew whether or not the man was a real threat. "I mean, it's only Steven's first day. Besides, Phil Bowen has proven to be a real whiz at ferreting out lost information. It, uh, sounds like a good challenge for him."

"I'll get him right on it," Trudy said. She turned to go, but stopped in the doorway. "By the way, I just spoke to Amanda Mason in Sacramento."

"How's her work with the subcommittee going?" Marianna asked. "That was a real coup, having someone from our firm asked to provide legal counsel to the state legislature."

"Amanda's doing well, but she's feeling overwhelmed. She's begging us to send someone to help her out for a few weeks."

Mr. Wakefield wasn't particularly interested in Amanda's personnel problems, but immersing himself in office minutia was probably the best way to keep his mind off Marin—if that was possible. The *Sweet Valley News* on his desk was folded to the story about the murderer's parole, and his eyes kept straying to the headline. He forced them to look up at Trudy instead. "We can't spare another associate right now—not with the *Oilcam* hearing starting in less than a week."

"Oh, Amanda doesn't need an attorney," Trudy said. "The work is routine, even for a paralegal—scheduling meetings, attending briefings, maybe writing an occasional first draft of a report."

Marianna frowned. "It will be hard to convince any of the assistants to go to Sacramento at this time of year. Everyone's kids just got out of school, and people are planning vacations."

Mr. Wakefield's mind was wandering again. He stared at the Marin article, silently cursing the parole board. He prayed again that he was overreacting. But he could still see the cold glint in Marin's eyes as he threatened the Wakefield children. Now he feared the worst. If only there were something—anything—he could do to keep his children safe.

"So what's the solution?" Trudy asked. "Who can we send to Sacramento?"

Mr. Wakefield leaped from his seat. "Steven!"

Marianna laughed. "I haven't seen you this animated all morning, Ned."

Mr. Wakefield felt his face turn pink. But it was

the perfect solution. At least one family member would be out of Marin's reach for a few weeks.

"It's not a bad idea," Trudy said. "It would be great experience for Steven to see the state legislature in action. And he'd be an enormous help to Amanda."

"But Ned," Marianna said. "You were so excited to have Steven home from college for the summer. Are you sure you want to send him four hundred miles away?"

Mr. Wakefield nodded. "Absolutely."

Marianna laughed. "Don't you think you ought to mention it to Steven first?"

Mr. Wakefield forced a smile. "Oh, he'll be thrilled. I can't wait to tell him about it."

"Great," Trudy said. "When should I tell Amanda to expect him?"

Mr. Wakefield slapped his hand down on the newspaper. "Tomorrow morning. Steven will be on the first plane out of town."

He turned and pretended to be interested in the scene outside the window; the sun shone brightly on the colonial-style brick courthouse across the town square. A dachshund picked its way across the emerald lawn, with two blond teenage girls strolling along behind, talking and laughing.

Mr. Wakefield pursed his lips. He had found a way to get Steven to safety. But his daughters were still in Sweet Valley. And so was John Marin.

Chapter 3

Elizabeth's foot was falling asleep. She shifted her weight on the crate of canned hams she was perched on in the storage room of the Marina Café. Luckily Mr. Jenkins seemed to be drawing his orientation session to a close.

"The last thing I want you to remember is that customer service is the key to a successful restaurant," he pronounced, gazing at each of the four new waitresses in turn. "A satisfied customer is a frequent customer. And frequent customers keep us in business."

"Does that mean we have to be nice to people all the time?" Jessica asked. "Even if they're losers?"

Mr. Jenkins's eyebrows rose halfway up his shiny expanse of forehead. "The customer may not always be right, Elizabeth, but the customer is paying the bills—not to mention your tips. So the object is to provide excellent customer service—even to, um, losers."

Elizabeth opened her mouth to say *She's Jessica; I'm Elizabeth,* but Jessica responded first. "So dropping soup on nasty customers would be out of the question?" Jessica's blue-green eyes had a mischievous twinkle.

Mr. Jenkins frowned. "Yes, Elizabeth," he said, hesitating as if he was trying to decide whether or not she was serious. "That would be an inappropriate response."

Elizabeth sighed. Jessica was enjoying this—saying outrageous things and assuming Mr. Jenkins would blame them on Elizabeth. *Oh, well,* she decided, remembering her resolution to be wild and crazy. *I'll just be on the lookout for ways to take advantage of his confusion too. Jessica shouldn't have all the fun.* Elizabeth leaned back against a metal shelving unit piled with stacks of plastic bowls for the salad bar.

"So how do we tell if customers are satisfied?" asked one of the other waitresses, a petite, dark-haired girl about the same age as the twins.

Mr. Jenkins clapped his hands. "The best indicator of excellent service is an excellent tip," he said with a grand gesture. "So I'm sponsoring my annual tip contest for the serving staff."

Elizabeth leaned forward. This sounded interesting.

"Who remembers what I told you about reporting your tips?" Mr. Jenkins asked.

"I didn't know there was going to be a pop quiz," Jessica complained under her breath.

Elizabeth spoke up. "You said we'll each be required to report our tips to you or the manager on duty at the end of each shift."

"Good job, Jessica. I'm glad to know you've been listening so attentively."

Elizabeth grimaced after he turned away. But Jessica was grinning like a jack-o'-lantern.

"For the next week," Mr. Jenkins continued, "I will be tallying that information. For each waitress I'll arrive at the average total tips earned in one shift, between now and Saturday evening. On Saturday the employee with the highest average will win an evening out—including dinner for two at the Box Tree Café, as well as movie passes for Valley Cinema."

"All right!" Jessica cheered loudly, giving a thumbs-up sign.

Mr. Jenkins glared at her for a moment before continuing. "Of course, we want you to be well dressed for your night on the town. So the winner will also receive a fifty-dollar gift certificate for Lisette's Boutique at Valley Mall."

Jessica punched the air with her fist. *"Yes!"* she yelled.

Mr. Jenkins gave her another long stare. "I hope you show as much enthusiasm for your waitressing work, Elizabeth."

"Oh, yes," Elizabeth responded, with a sidelong glance at Jessica. "Enthusiasm is her middle name."

"Good. Well, that's all you need to know right now. If you find you have questions, feel free to ask me—or Jane O'Reilly, whom you met a few minutes ago."

Elizabeth recalled the tall, red-haired woman in her mid-twenties who had popped into the storage room during their orientation. Elizabeth hadn't had a chance to speak with Jane, but she'd instantly liked her ready smile and warm brown eyes.

"Has Jane been working here a long time?" Elizabeth asked.

"This is Jane's fourth summer at the café," Mr. Jenkins explained. "She knows the job better than anyone."

Jessica pushed a stray strand of hair out of her eyes. She hated to admit it, but Elizabeth had been right, as usual. Waitressing was hard work. She'd been at it for most of the day, with only a short break for lunch with Lila. Her feet ached and her shoulders were sore from carrying the heavy trays of food. But her tips were piling up. After she won the customer-satisfaction contest, she'd take all that hard-earned cash to the Summer Fun sale at Valley Mall. A scarlet miniskirt would be perfect with her new red sandals, and she had seen a cool one at Lisette's.

She sighed and picked up a tray of drinks. Then she marched out into the crowded dining room.

A heavyset man waved impatiently. "Are those our soft drinks?" he demanded. "It's about time." He had greasy-looking hair and a bad sunburn.

"Yes, sir," Jessica assured him, as if bringing him and his family their drinks were the most important thing in the world to her. She smiled broadly, trying to pretend he wasn't a complete jerk. *It's a good thing I have a lot of experience as an actress.*

She served the glasses of milk to two grubby, sand-encrusted children who kept taking swipes at each other.

"We asked for small-size milks," the man complained.

"I'm sorry, sir, but this is the small size," Jessica said evenly, fighting an urge to pour both glasses of milk over his head. She intentionally mixed up the other glasses, placing the diet soda in front of the man and the unnaturally pink strawberry milk shake by his slim wife. *Why not?* she figured. This was one big tip she already knew she could write off. *Besides, the guy really is a fat pig. A diet soda would do him some good.* She ignored the man's glare as he pointedly switched the glasses.

Jessica turned wordlessly and began trudging back toward the kitchen.

"Oh, waitress!" a voice called from behind her. "Are you ever going to take our order?"

Jessica whirled angrily. Then she relaxed. The voice belonged to Winston Egbert, Sweet Valley High's official class clown. This summer he was also the head of beach maintenance at the marina. Winston was sitting at table two, in Jessica's section, and he was grinning broadly. Maria Santelli, Bruce Patman, and Amy Sutton were with him.

Jessica clenched her fist in a mock threat. "I swear, Winston, you don't know how close you just came to getting pushed through that picture window and right into the marina."

"Touchy, touchy, Wakefield," Bruce said smoothly. He glanced around the sunny restaurant. "You know, the service in this place used to be so friendly and efficient. But you just can't get good help nowadays. It seems like they'll hire pretty much anyone."

But Maria's brown eyes were full of sympathy. "How's it going?" she asked Jessica. "You look like you're having a rough day."

Jessica smiled. Maria was on the cheerleading squad with her at school and usually showed a lot of sense—despite the fact that she was dating a nerd like Winston. "To tell you the truth," Jessica said, "most of the day has been a lot of fun."

Winston raised his eyebrows. "If a fun day makes you want to throw me through a pane of glass, I'd hate to be here on a bad one."

Bruce flashed his handsome, smug grin. "Actually, Egbert, I often find myself wanting to push you through windows. It's a common response to your jokes."

"Tell us about your first day on the job," Amy urged, ignoring the boys' jibes.

"It's only the last hour or so that's made me feel like a punching bag," Jessica said. "Before that, it was really cool. You wouldn't believe the glamorous people I've met!"

Wealthy, well-connected Bruce leaned back and crossed his arms. "Actually, *I* probably would."

"Hadn't you heard, Jessica?" Winston asked.

"Bruce holds the patent on glamorous people around here. You're not allowed to meet any without scheduling it through his personal secretary."

"Egbert, why don't you save Wakefield and me the trouble and throw yourself through that window?"

Maria put a hand over each of the boys' mouths. "Shut up, you guys. Come on, Jess. Tell us about the people you've met."

"Well, I served one couple who just came up the coast from Mexico in a yacht as big as our whole high school—you know, slightly smaller than Bruce's bathtub." She stuck out her tongue at Bruce. "There was a man from Seattle who says he manages rock stars, but he was a crummy tipper. And I met a woman who sailed up in a strange-looking boat called a skipjack—I saw it out the window. She left me a thirty percent tip! Right after that, Lila stopped by at my break time, and we had lunch on the beach."

"Wow!" Bruce breathed. "You had lunch with *the* Lila Fowler? You said glamorous, but I thought you meant relatively unimportant people, like mere corporate moguls and world leaders. I had no idea—"

"Shut up, Bruce!" Bruce and Lila, the two richest students at Sweet Valley High, had been rivals for as long as Jessica could remember. But Jessica had more immediate concerns than whether Bruce or Lila was more deserving of the Most Rich and Snobby Award. She'd just spotted Mr. Jenkins peering out the door from the kitchen. "Be good, you guys. My boss is giving me dirty looks."

"You'd better take our order while we talk," Amy suggested, picking up her menu. "Who's first?"

"I'll have a sparkling mineral water and the avocado salad," Maria said. "Really, Jess, you look kind of frazzled. You've been at this all day. Can't you take five and sit down with us?"

Jessica did feel frazzled, at least in contrast to Amy. As usual Amy was dressed to the hilt, and not a strand of long blond hair was out of place.

Jessica shook her head. "I'd better not, although I admit my feet are killing me." She wrinkled her nose. "And that fat guy with the two bratty kids is probably the world's most obnoxious customer. I hate having to be nice to people who are jerks."

She glanced at Bruce as she said it—but not too conspicuously. Bruce could be a jerk, but he was a rich jerk. And she needed all the tips she could get.

"I'll have crab salad and an almond-flavored cappuccino," Winston said. "The crabmeat is from the *legs* of the crab, isn't it?"

Jessica raised her eyebrows. It wasn't the kind of order she had expected from Winston. "Of course it is," she assured him, though she had no idea what part of the crab it was from. She dutifully wrote his order on her pad.

"No, no, no," Winston said, shaking his head. "On second thought, I think I'll go with the salmon quiche. And mineral water. Sparkling mineral water, with lemon. But I'd like extra radishes on the salad. And instead of the ranch dressing, could you put blue cheese on it? No, let's make it half blue cheese and half Italian. You can do that, can't you?"

Jessica gritted her teeth. "Anything for you, Sir Egbert."

As soon as she rewrote the order, Winston spoke up again. "You know, Jessica, that pasta special on the blackboard sounded awfully good. Is that black pepper or white pepper on the fettuccine?"

Jessica crossed her arms and glowered at him, using her best Lila Fowler look of disdain.

Winston grinned. "OK, make it a double cheeseburger with everything on it, a big order of fries, and a chocolate milk shake."

"You might as well be at the Dairi Burger," Maria said.

"A man needs a hearty meal after a day of back-breaking work in the blazing sun."

Bruce laughed. "Come off it, Egbert. You're no more than the beach janitor."

"I prefer to think of myself as a coastal enhancement engineer."

"Oh, Elizabeth!" Mr. Jenkins's voice rang out from across the room.

"That's strange," Amy said. "I don't see Elizabeth anywhere."

Jessica shrugged. "A few minutes ago I saw her heading to the walk-in refrigerator in the back, for mayonnaise or something. But it's not my problem."

"Elizabeth!" the restaurant manager called again. Jessica realized too late that he was motioning toward her.

"Oops," she said to her friends. "I forgot. He

couldn't tell Liz and me apart if his life depended on it."

Mr. Jenkins stalked across the room and pulled her aside. "Elizabeth, the order for table five has been ready for some time. You're going to have to move a little faster."

Jessica shrugged. Table five was Mr. Obnoxious and the rest of his stupid family. "Sorry, Mr. Jenkins. I'll be finished taking this order in just a sec."

"Tut-tut," Winston said when the manager was out of earshot. "You must learn to be faster, Jessica. He's right, you know. I always prefer fast women myself."

Jessica gave him another Lila stare, wishing she could shoot arrows out of her eyes. Luckily Winston was basically a nice guy—it was one of the reasons she usually found him dull. At least he'd feel obligated to leave her a decent tip. It was more than she was expecting to get from the guy at table five—who was now tapping his watch and glaring at her.

Jessica sighed. One thing was obvious—she was infinitely better suited to giving orders than she was to taking them.

"After ten years in prison, there's not much I don't know about picking a lock," John Marin said under his breath. He slid a metal file into the crack alongside the back door of the house on Calico Drive. He smiled when he felt the lock give way. "Old Louie the Locksmith taught me well," he said, giving a silent thanks to the convict who'd had the cell next to his in the state penitentiary.

Inside, the Wakefields' dog was barking. Marin opened the door and stuck his head in. "Be quiet, you mongrel," he growled, baring his teeth. The golden retriever shrank back. "Some watchdog you are. Old Ned is awfully complacent. If he had any sense, the place would be guarded by pit bulls—" He sneered. "Not that they'd do any good against me."

Marin gazed at the Spanish-tiled kitchen, eyes narrow. "Well, Counselor. You've certainly done well for yourself since we last met," he said. "Soon it'll be time to pay the price." He grabbed a green apple from a bowl on the table, tossed it into the air, and caught it. Then he took a bite, grimaced, and left the apple on the table. "Sour."

He sauntered into the living room, with Prince Albert, the dog, following at a respectful distance. A collection of family photographs, each in a silver frame, was grouped on one shelf of the wall unit. Marin selected a framed Christmas card that showed the entire Wakefield family dressed as elves.

"Ah, Alice," he said, poking a finger at Ned Wakefield's pretty blond wife. "I could teach you all about Wonderland. Better watch yourself, dear. You wouldn't want to fall down any rabbit holes. And that Steven's a regular chip off the old block." He laughed. "Maybe later. For now, I'll stick with the twins—they bring out all those protective, paternalistic instincts that make Ned such a pathetically easy target."

Marin stuffed the photograph into his backpack and looked around the room once more.

It wouldn't do to get caught in the Wakefield house; it wasn't time yet. But Marin wasn't in a hurry—the family would be away for hours. "Information," he said to the dog. "I need more information."

Prince Albert trotted upstairs, and Marin followed. "I'm going to know everything there is to know about Jessica and Elizabeth Wakefield," he promised aloud. "And then I'll make my move. By the time I'm finished with those little girls, their daddy is going to wish he'd never gone to law school."

Chapter 4

Elizabeth balanced her tray on one arm as she jabbed at the button on the soft drink dispenser behind the counter. Ginger ale bubbled from the spigot.

"Jane!" she called as the more experienced waitress passed. "There's something wrong with the ginger ale! It's almost all foam."

"No problem, honey," Jane told her. "Each tap hooks up to two canisters—one for syrup and one for soda. See them here in back? The ginger ale syrup must be empty. I'll check it."

"I knew waitressing was hard work, but I had no idea there were so many things to learn!"

"You're doing swell for your first day, kid," Jane said. "Yep, that's it, all right. We need to replace the syrup canister. Watch and I'll show you how. There's nothing to it." She began unhooking the empty canister from the tube that connected it to the drink dispenser. "I might as well make myself useful. I don't dare set foot in the dining room until the kitchen gets me a bowl of clam chowder for table nine."

"Mr. Jenkins said you've worked here four summers in a row. Do you go to school the rest of the year?"

"Sweet Valley University, class of last week," Jane said proudly. "Pull over one of those fresh canisters, would you, Elizabeth? Make sure it says ginger ale."

"So you just graduated from college?" Elizabeth asked, surprised. She'd assumed Jane was at least in her mid-twenties.

Jane grinned. "I know, you're too polite to say it. But I don't look twenty-two. Actually, I'm an ancient twenty-six. I took a few years off after high school to work full time and save up some money."

She pressed the button on the drink dispenser and waited a few seconds until she was satisfied with the color of the ginger ale that poured out. "That looks about right," she said. "Try it now."

Elizabeth stuck the glass under the spigot and watched it fill up.

"At this rate I'll be a student until I'm old and gray," Jane said. "But I'm starting graduate school in the fall, so I figured I'd spend one last summer with Old Man Jenkins."

Elizabeth rolled her eyes. "He's kind of a strange little man, isn't he?"

Jane shrugged and wiped some syrup from the counter. "He's a boss. All bosses are strange."

"I just wish he'd get my name right for once. He's convinced that my sister Jessica is me, and that she's perfect. But he thinks I'm a total screwup."

Jane laughed knowingly as she grabbed a basket of oyster crackers from a shelf under the counter. "He called me Jean for the entire first summer I was here. The second summer it was Joan. And last year I was Jan. I had to come back a fourth summer just to give him another chance to get it straight." She nudged the kitchen door open with her shoulder and called in to the head cook. "Samantha! I'm still waiting on that bowl of clam chowder for table nine!"

"What do you like most about working here?" Elizabeth fished her order pad out of her apron pocket and began double checking the orders for who she thought would be her last few customers of the day.

"Mostly I do it for the people," Jane confided. "This place gets the most interesting customers. I'm a sociology major, so I tell myself it's research."

"I know what you mean. For some reason people who own boats almost always turn out to be fascinating."

Jane nodded. "Speaking of fascinating, look at that fine specimen who just walked in. I swear, if I were ten years younger—"

Elizabeth laughed when she saw the new customer. It was Todd. "Don't say another word. He's taken."

"Story of my life, Liz. All the good ones are. Samantha! I'm still waiting on that chowder!"

A few minutes later Elizabeth had served her

final customer. She waved good-bye to Jane and to Jessica, then greeted Todd with a smile.

"How was your first day?" he asked as he held open the door for her.

"Great!" She gave him a quick kiss. "But my feet are ready to go on strike. I think I'm getting blisters on my blisters. How are the windsurfing lessons?"

"I still can't believe people are paying me to play in the water all day!"

"Any ideas for dinner tonight after the movie?" Elizabeth asked as they walked toward Todd's black BMW.

"How about the Dairi Burger?"

Elizabeth shrugged. "If we're going to be in a rut, we might as well be consistent about it."

Todd stared at her. "What's that supposed to mean?"

"Nothing. The Dairi Burger is fine."

She climbed into the BMW and sank back gratefully into the leather upholstery. She concentrated on the colorful boats of the marina and the jazz music that Todd had slipped into the tape deck.

"Now *that* was a hot car!" he exclaimed suddenly as they pulled out of the parking lot.

"Where?" Elizabeth wrenched her gaze away from the boats, but all she caught was a flash of red that blurred by them as it sped back toward the café.

Todd glanced in the rearview mirror. "A brand-new Miata convertible, fire-engine red. The guy driving looked only a few years older than us."

"If he's going into the Marina Café, someone

ought to warn him to stay away from Jessica's section!"

"Uh-oh! Beware the wrath of the evil twin. What's Jessica's latest crisis?"

"She's dying to go home, but one customer is lingering forever over coffee. Jess won't leave without that tip. But she's totally ticked off."

Todd laughed. "In other words, anyone who asks Jessica for anything right now may just find himself staring down the sharp end of a butter knife."

"Can I, uh, get you anything else?" Jessica asked, staring expectantly at the college-age woman at table four. She gestured at the untouched bill on the table. "I can get your change for you anytime you're ready."

The woman looked up from her book. "Oh, just another coffee refill, please."

Jessica sighed and stalked back across the room to the coffeepot behind the counter. "I can't believe this!" she screeched at Jane. "She's had about sixty cups of coffee!"

Jane laughed. "Some people just like to hang out here—the scenery's good." She gestured toward the walls of windows that surrounded three sides of the dining room. Boats bobbed at the docks, their sails colored orange by the day's last hour of sunlight. Through the window Jessica could see the flash of Elizabeth's turquoise shirt as she kissed Todd and climbed into his BMW.

"Some people get to go home at a reasonable hour," Jessica complained.

Watching the warmth between Todd and Elizabeth, Jessica was surprised at how much she missed Ken. When it came to dating, she'd always said she liked being a free agent. But it would be nice to know she had someone waiting to take her out at the end of her shift.

"Cheer up," Jane urged. "You're probably scoring brownie points with Mr. Jenkins for staying late. I bet he's in the back room right now, thinking about how dedicated you are."

"Right," Jessica scoffed. "Only he probably thinks I'm Elizabeth."

"You should be counting your blessings," Jane said, pointing at the coffee-drinking college student. "Customers who read at the table are pretty undemanding. At least she's not a pain in the neck."

"What do you mean, she's not a pain in the neck? She won't leave! How long can she sit there reading?"

"Are you kidding? I caught sight of that textbook she's wading through. It's for a sociology course I took a few years back—Human Systems and Structures 101. Each chapter takes about two pots of coffee to get through."

"But I wanted to catch this last hour of sun! How am I going to keep my tan if I never get out of here until the middle of the night?"

"Why don't you go on home, kid? I'll take care of her coffee refills, and I'll save the tip for you. If you're lucky, I might not even take a cut."

Jessica hesitated. She felt a twinge of guilt at the thought of letting Jane take over for her.

"Of course," Jane continued, "college students are always broke, so they're lousy tippers."

"Well, I'm glad to know it'll be worth the wait," Jessica said glumly. Suddenly she caught sight of a shiny red convertible pulling into the parking lot. It was the kind of car that a big tipper drove. "Thanks for offering," she said quickly. "But I think I'll stick around. As long as I'm trapped here, maybe somebody else will come in. Somebody who tips really well."

Jane nodded. "Then would you mind giving me a yell if table ten seems low on anything? I've got some work to do in the storage room."

Jessica stepped closer to the window that overlooked the parking lot. "And I've got some work to do here," she said under her breath. With the sun in her eyes she didn't have a good view of the driver, but she knew that the car was a new Miata.

She willed the car's owner to walk into the café rather than out along the docks. *"Yes!"* she said aloud when he turned up the walkway.

The college student looked up from her reading. Jessica smiled an apology and set up a table for her new customer.

"Can I help you?" she asked. "I've got a lovely table, right over . . ." Jessica's voice trailed off as she looked for the first time at the driver's face. He was drop-dead gorgeous. About twenty years old, he was tall, with wavy brown hair and deep blue eyes.

"I sure hope you can," he said easily, flashing her a dazzling smile. "Just a table for one, nonsmoking."

"Um, uh, sure," Jessica stammered. "As you can see, there are plenty of tables open. Would you like to be near a window?"

"Whatever you think," he said with another grin. "I'll place myself in your hands."

Sounds good to me. The man's chiseled features had caught her attention first; now she was beginning to notice the rest of him. His purple brushed-silk shirt accentuated his broad shoulders, which practically cried out for her fingers to touch them. *Yes*, she decided. *"In my hands" would be a very fine place for him.*

"You did say a table for *one*, didn't you?" Jessica asked as she led him to her best table. "I mean, you're not meeting someone here?"

"Nope," he said. "I just got to town, and I don't know a soul. So it's just me."

Jessica smiled back. "Can I get you anything to start? A drink?"

"Mineral water, please. And maybe a little bit of information, if you don't mind."

Jessica was intrigued. Maybe this was a classy way of asking for her phone number. She slowly tucked a stray lock of hair behind her ear and gave him a flirtatious smile. "What kind of information?"

"Do you know the area well?"

Jessica shrugged. "Sure. I've lived here all my life."

The man grinned again. He had the whitest teeth Jessica had ever seen. "That's perfect," he said. "I was hoping to meet somebody just like you."

Jessica smiled. Customer service had never been so easy. "Well, you found me. What can I do for you?"

"I'm sorry. I should have started from the beginning. My name's Scott Maderlake," he said, extending a hand. When Jessica shook it, she felt a tingle like an electric current run through her body.

"I'm Jessica Wakefield. What are you in town for—business or pleasure?"

He raised his eyebrows. "I'm here on business, but I'm beginning to think this could be a pleasurable place to be." He paused. "I work for Jillian DeRiggi. You've heard of her, of course?"

"Oh, of course," Jessica lied, racking her brain to figure out who Jillian DeRiggi might be. It certainly sounded like an important name.

"Jillian is producing a new television miniseries," he explained. "It's about a southern California high school. I'm traveling up the coast, scouting possible locations."

Jessica's eyes widened. Not only was Scott gorgeous, but he might be able to get her a part in a television miniseries. She silently thanked the bookish, coffee-drinking college student for keeping her late at work.

"So you'll go back to Jillian DeRiggi and tell her where to film her miniseries?" Jessica asked. "I guess that means you would decide what local landmarks and, um, *people* should be in it."

Scott laughed. "Decide is too strong a word," he said. "Really I'm only an intern."

"But I'll bet you have a lot of influence."

"With Jillian? She does seem to trust me. But the real reason they send people like me on these advance trips is that it would cost a fortune to have someone important do the initial location scouting. After I narrow it down to a few places that meet the criteria, Jillian will visit those sites herself and make a final decision."

"She should definitely use Sweet Valley," Jessica said. "It's perfect for your miniseries. I'm sure of it."

"So far, I like the scenery just fine," Scott said.

Jessica was almost sure he was flirting with her. "Maybe I could show you more of it," she suggested.

Scott looked straight into her eyes. "That's the best offer I've had all day. Can you start by answering a few questions?"

"Sure! Ask away." She pulled out her order pad. "But if you're planning to order something, maybe you should do it now. My boss is in the back, but he could look out here anytime. He might as well think I'm hard at work."

"Your secret is safe with me," Scott said, opening his menu. "I'll have the crab salad. And the answer to the following question: When they're not serving salads, what do the really popular, attractive teenagers do around here for fun?"

Jessica smiled warmly. He was positively flirting with her. "Mostly we show television interns around town. When that gets tedious, we bring them to a place called the Dairi Burger, which is where everyone important hangs out."

"And where do they go when they want to be alone?"

Jessica pretended to consider the question thoughtfully, but her heart was racing. "Oh, I can think of a few places," she said slowly. "Secca Lake and Miller's Point come to mind."

"Secca Lake I've heard of."

Jessica nodded. "I'm not surprised. It's beautiful. I bet it would look great on film. And Miller's Point is even better—for a lot of reasons." She thought of all the nights she'd parked at Miller's Point with one boyfriend or another, kissing and gazing at the twinkling lights of the valley below. She would love to show Miller's Point to Scott Maderlake—but as more than just research for a television miniseries.

"There are also a lot of places in town for a romantic dinner," she added hopefully.

"What about the high school?"

"I suppose that's OK for a romantic dinner—if you're into mystery meat and fluorescent lighting," Jessica joked.

Scott laughed. "Forget dinner. As I said, Jillian's new miniseries is set at a high school. Tell me about Sweet Valley High."

"I've got a better idea," Jessica responded. "Why don't I take you there?"

"I thought you'd never ask. Are you free tomorrow afternoon?"

Jessica looked into his midnight-blue eyes and felt a delicious tingle run down her spine. "I can arrange to be."

• • •

Ned Wakefield sauntered into the empty house Monday evening and tossed a stack of mail onto the kitchen table. Prince Albert padded in from the living room; Mr. Wakefield stroked the golden retriever's furry head.

"Hey, boy," he said. "What were you doing in the living room? I thought I shut that door before I left this morning. I guess I was really on edge. I must've forgotten."

He pulled out a chair. The gentle scraping of wood against the Spanish-tile floor sounded loud in the empty house. Someone had left a green apple sitting on the table, with one ragged brown circle where a bite had been taken. Somebody in the house obviously needed a lecture on not leaving out food—most likely, the culprit was Steven.

Mr. Wakefield seemed to have the house to himself. He and Steven had left the law office at the same time, but Steven had driven to the mall to pick up a few things for his trip to Sacramento in the morning. And Mrs. Wakefield wouldn't be home for another hour; she had a late meeting with the fireplace-in-the-bathroom client. As for the girls . . .

Mr. Wakefield bit his lip, thinking of Jessica and Elizabeth. It was still early. They'd probably be breezing through the door at any minute, full of stories about their first day on the job.

He grabbed a soda from the refrigerator and sat at the table. "What's in today's mail, Albert?" The dog's expression looked so alert and intelligent that

Mr. Wakefield half expected him to answer. Instead he answered himself as he sifted through the stack. "Telephone bill, electricity bill, junk mail, junk mail, junk mail, letter from Steven's girlfriend . . . And what's this one?"

He held up a plain, blood-red envelope. It looked like the kind of envelope that Christmas cards came in, but nobody would send a Christmas card in June. He turned it over in his hand. No return address. It didn't even have a postmark—obviously someone had slipped it into the mailbox. He shrugged and slit open the envelope. Then he frowned. "Now why would someone send us our own Christmas card from last year?"

Mr. Wakefield remembered the photograph well. Jessica had talked the rest of the family into posing in red-and-green elf costumes. Even Prince Albert peered out from under a floppy Santa hat.

But this copy of the photograph had been ruined. Across the family's faces someone had scrawled a message in heavy black ink, using large, angular letters:

Nice family, Ned. I especially like the girls. JM

Mr. Wakefield felt the color drain from his face. Where had Marin scrounged up one of the Wakefield family's old Christmas cards? They'd sent them all to family friends—except for the print that was framed in the living room.

Suddenly Mr. Wakefield thought of Prince Albert walking in from the living room. He stared at the green apple with one bite missing.

He shook his head. "No. It's impossible," he whispered. "He couldn't have been in the house."

In a daze, Mr. Wakefield rose from his chair and walked into the living room. By the time he reached the collection of family pictures arranged on one shelf of the wall unit, Ned knew exactly what he would find—a conspicuously empty spot where the Christmas photograph had been. Moments later, his heart stopped. John Marin hadn't forgotten—not by a long shot.

Chapter 5

"What do you mean, you can't prevent him from coming after my family?" Mr. Wakefield shouted into the phone. "What good is the police department if—"

"Ned, you're an attorney," said his friend Tony Cabrini, a police detective. "You know the law. We can't seek out this guy and haul him into jail just because of a threat he made ten years ago. That doesn't constitute probable cause, and you know it."

"I've got more than a ten-year-old threat. I received another one this evening. I'm telling you, Tony, this guy is a maniac! And he was in my house today!"

"Can you prove that?"

"Sorry. He forgot to leave his signed confession."

"There's no law against sending Christmas cards. And complimenting you on your children hardly constitutes a threat—"

Mr. Wakefield felt his face turning red. "It sure as

hell does! Dammit, Tony, I know what he meant—"

"Calm down, Ned. I agree that this guy is dangerous. But *legally* 'nice family, Ned,' is not a menacing remark. I shouldn't have to tell you that. You know as well as I do that the public defender's office would have a field day if we arrested Marin without any more evidence than that."

"So what can I do about him?"

"A guy who would leave a note like that obviously enjoys making you sweat. My bet is that you'll be receiving more of them. As soon as we can establish a pattern of threatening statements, we can pick the guy up."

"You're telling me that all I can do is sit around and check my mail?"

"For now, yes," the detective admitted. "In the meantime, we'll try to locate Marin so we can keep tabs on him. I'll talk with his parole officer tonight and call you back in the morning. If this guy violates parole even once, then we can move in on him."

"And what if that's too late?"

"I'm sorry, Ned, but it's the best I can do for now. Until we can prove that Marin has done something that's against the law, we don't have a case."

Elizabeth sighed as she walked out of the movie theater with Todd that night. "What a great movie!" she breathed.

Todd took her hand. "Sure, *Roman Holiday* is a good one. But what is this—the third time you've seen it?"

"Fourth, actually. But I never identified with Audrey Hepburn the way I did this time. I can really understand how much she needed to get out and do something different."

Todd snorted. "It's rough being a princess, with everything you could ever want handed to you on a silver platter."

"Everything except adventure! And freedom!" Elizabeth cried. "The only way she could get them was to break out of her boring, oppressive life—even if it did mean shocking everybody."

Todd looked at her strangely. "You're sounding pretty intense tonight, Liz. Are you OK?"

Elizabeth smiled weakly. "Oh, I'm fine. I just envy her for having the courage to break free and find a real adventure."

"And you envy her for finding Gregory Peck."

"That too. Especially since he was playing a writer. Jealous?"

"Insanely. And hungry. Come on, let's hit the Dairi Burger."

When Jessica strolled through the door that night, her father's voice was like a thunderclap. *"Young lady, where in the world have you been?"*

He was pacing in the living room while Mrs. Wakefield sat on the couch, her hands folded.

"I asked you a question!"

Jessica stared at him. "I was at Lila's. Remember, I called and said I wouldn't be home for dinner."

"Dinner was hours ago! It's almost ten o'clock!"

"So? You knew where I was. What's the problem?"

"The problem is that your mother and I were worried. When you said you wouldn't be home for dinner, I assumed that meant you'd be home soon after dinner. You didn't say anything about staying out so late."

"I'm sixteen years old, Dad. You have no right to treat me like a baby!"

"I'm your father. And if you can't take a little responsibility for your actions, then you don't deserve to be treated like an adult. How did we know you weren't lying in a ditch somewhere—"

His voice broke off, and he sat down weakly. Jessica just gaped at him. She'd seen her father angry before, but seldom this unreasonable.

"Ned, she *did* call to let us know where she was," Mrs. Wakefield reminded him gently.

"I know," he said, staring at his hands. "You're both right. I'm overreacting. But Jessica, there have been some crimes in the neighborhood lately. It's gotten me a little anxious, especially about you and your sister."

"Crimes?" Jessica asked. "I haven't heard of any crimes. What happened?"

"There's no need to worry about anything," Mr. Wakefield said quickly.

"Honey, I hadn't heard about any local crimes either," Mrs. Wakefield said. "Was anybody hurt?"

"No, no. Of course not. I guess it hasn't been on the news. I just heard about it around the courthouse today." He jumped up suddenly. "What time is Elizabeth coming home?"

"Ned, she said she'd be here by eleven. Don't worry about her. She's with Todd. You know how responsible they both are."

Jessica gritted her teeth. People were always raving about how responsible her twin was.

"Yes, of course," Ned said. "If Elizabeth and Todd say they'll be here by eleven, then they'll be here by eleven." He scrutinized his watch. "I think I'll go upstairs to see if Steven needs help packing for his trip." He stalked out of the room, but Jessica noticed that he turned into his den instead of going up the stairs.

"What's eating him?" Jessica asked, annoyed. "It's bad enough getting in trouble all the time for doing something wrong. But I didn't break a rule or miss a curfew or anything this time. It's not fair!"

Mrs. Wakefield smiled. "Sorry, sweetheart. But your father's been tense all day. I'm sure he'll be himself after a good night's sleep."

"I hope so. He's been acting possessed since this morning."

"You're looking a little worn out yourself, Jess. I know what hard work waitressing can be. Why don't you go on and get to bed early?"

Jessica yawned. "You're right. I am tired. Good night."

A minute later Jessica skipped up the stairs, silently thanking her father for making everyone forget that she was supposed to have vacuumed the living room.

○ ○ ○

Prince Albert wagged his tail and watched as Mr. Wakefield sat down at his desk. Mr. Wakefield struggled to catch his breath. He had to control his nerves better. He didn't want to terrify the rest of the family by telling them about Marin. But if he kept acting paranoid, they would quickly figure out that something was seriously wrong.

On the other hand, he thought, *if I warned them of the danger, maybe the twins would take extra precautions. Maybe they'd be able to protect themselves.*

"No," he said aloud to the dog. "There's no way they can protect themselves against a maniac like Marin. And what kind of precautions would help? I can't lock them in their bedrooms, under guard, until Marin forgets about them."

As soon as his hands were steady Mr. Wakefield dialed the telephone.

"Tony, I'm sorry to call you at home this late, but I couldn't wait until morning. Have you found out anything else?"

Detective Cabrini's voice was full of regret. "Nothing you're going to like. The address Marin gave his parole officer was a fake. We don't know where to find him."

Mr. Wakefield felt as if he'd been pushed off a cliff. He clutched the receiver as if it were a lifeline. "So what's next?"

"The phony address constitutes a parole violation. That means we can pick him up if we find him. Unfortunately we have no idea where he is."

"How can we locate the scumbag?"

"*You* sit home and let the police take care of it. I put out an APB an hour ago. First thing in the morning, I'll have people start tracking down any known associates of Marin's. Don't worry, Ned. We'll get this guy."

"Thanks, Tony," Mr. Wakefield said in a controlled voice. "Keep me informed."

Slowly he placed the receiver in its cradle. A moment later he realized he was still gripping it. He unwrapped his fingers from the receiver and pulled out his address book. "If the police can't keep my daughters safe from John Marin, then I'll call someone who can," he said aloud. He found the entry he was looking for and dialed the home number of James Battaglia, a private investigator he knew from a case they'd worked on together the year before.

"Jim? This is Ned Wakefield. Sorry to call so late, but I have a dangerous situation on my hands."

In Todd's car on the way to the Dairi Burger, Elizabeth couldn't stop thinking about *Roman Holiday*.

"You know," she said thoughtfully, twirling a golden curl around her finger, "I'm feeling a little like that princess, trapped in a boring routine."

"How can you be trapped in a boring routine?" Todd asked. "School just ended Friday. And today was your first day in a new job."

"Well, yes," Elizabeth said. "But that's not exactly what I meant. It's kind of hard to explain. It's bigger than that. Basically, I feel as if it doesn't matter whether school is in session or not. My life stays pretty much the same. I see the same people, day in and day out." She gestured toward the lighted sign of the Dairi Burger just ahead. "I go to the same places."

"We could go to Guido's Pizza tonight, if you'd rather," Todd offered.

Elizabeth shook her head. "No, that wouldn't make any difference! I've been to every place within ten miles of here, over and over again, for my whole life."

Todd shrugged and steered the BMW into the crowded parking lot of the Dairi Burger.

And he even pulls into the same parking space he always uses, Elizabeth thought with a sigh. "Don't you ever wish that something different would happen?"

"Why? I like things the way they are." Suddenly Todd's eyes opened wider. "Elizabeth, are you trying to tell me something about our relationship? You don't want to date other people, do you?"

"Oh, no, Todd! It's nothing like that!"

"Then what brought all this on?" he asked as they walked toward the restaurant. "I just don't get it. You're talking as if seeing that movie was a life-changing experience. It was just a romantic comedy!"

Inside the restaurant Elizabeth breathed the familiar Dairi Burger aroma of french fries and hamburgers. "Have you ever wondered what it would be like to walk into this place and smell something totally different, like Indian curries or a Thai stir-fry?"

"Were we watching the same movie?"

Elizabeth laughed. "Sorry, I guess I'm sounding kind of weird."

"Look, there's a booth about to open up!" Todd said, negotiating his way through the crowded dining room. "Let's grab it."

They settled into a booth at one end of the noisy room, waving at a few friends they spotted at nearby tables. *"I see the same people, day in and day out,"* Elizabeth repeated under her breath. She wished Gregory Peck would materialize at the next booth.

"What can I get you to drink?" asked a young, gum-chewing waitress a few minutes later.

"Two root beers," Todd said.

"No!" Elizabeth interrupted, more loudly than she'd intended. "I mean, I'm in the mood for something different." She turned to the waitress. "You don't have iced cappuccino, do you?"

The waitress blew a bubble. "Nope."

"How about iced coffee, then?"

The waitress shrugged. "Sure, why not? We got coffee. We got ice cubes."

"Do you want one too, Todd?" Elizabeth asked hopefully.

"No, I'll stick with my plain old root beer." He looked up at the impatient waitress. "I'm trapped in a boring routine," he explained.

Elizabeth watched her boyfriend's strong, handsome features and knew that he didn't have the slightest idea what was bothering her. She loved

Todd, but sometimes he was so . . . *down-to-earth*. Normally she liked that about him. But right now, it was annoying. Why couldn't Todd be a little more of a dreamer? Why did he have to be so eternally *contented*? If nothing else, she wished that she could at least get him to understand what she was feeling.

"Your root beer and your iced coffee will be coming right up," the waitress told them. She turned away from the table.

"Oh, can you make my coffee with half-and-half?" Elizabeth asked.

"All right," the waitress said in the same clipped voice that Elizabeth had heard herself use with an irritating customer a few hours earlier. "That's one boring, routine root beer and one iced coffee with half-and-half."

"And three sugars."

The waitress shrugged. "And three sugars," she repeated slowly as she wrote it on her order pad.

"Oh, and I'd like a straw."

"Naturally."

Once they were alone, Todd took her hand in both of his. "So how are you, Liz, really?" he asked. "I can't believe that seeing *Roman Holiday* could make you unhappy with your whole life."

Elizabeth shook her head. "I didn't say that I'm unhappy with my life. I love my life, Todd. I love you!" She said it vehemently, but deep down, Elizabeth wondered if she had experienced enough of life to know what real love felt like. Todd was fun, but he wasn't necessarily . . . *a soul mate*. Of course, she couldn't tell him that.

"I just want an adventure," she concluded lamely. "Something different."

"Like Audrey Hepburn, escaping the palace."

"Exactly! But it's not just the movie. There was something Jessica said to me this morning—"

Todd rolled his eyes. "Oh, I get it now. It figures that your psycho sister would have something to do with this."

"She's not a psycho, and you know it! Besides, what she said made a lot of sense."

"Jessica made sense? And you said nothing unusual ever happens."

"Cut it out. All Jessica did was point out the fact that I'm in a rut, and that I'll never be a great writer if I haven't experienced anything interesting to write about."

Todd snapped his fingers. "I've got it! I'll help you overthrow the government! Then you can write one of those techno-espionage thrillers while we spend the rest of our lives in prison. Or we can rent ourselves out as assassins so you can write murder mysteries. Or I'll buy you a horse, and you can write westerns."

"That's not exactly what I had in mind."

"What then?"

"Working at the café today really opened my eyes. You wouldn't believe the fascinating people who come into a place like that. Todd, there's a whole world out there!"

"But you knew that before."

"Yes, I did. But today I talked to a woman who's just back from three months in Hawaii, studying volcanoes. One family was sailing out to Catalina to spend the whole summer camping and hiking. And another customer was on a cruise from Baja all the way up the coast to Alaska, just to see what's there!"

"You want to sail to Alaska?"

"I want to experience *life*!"

"I thought this *was* life. And you've always raved about how much you love Sweet Valley. Now you're telling me that one day of meeting yacht owners has changed all that?"

"It's not just the one day of meeting yacht owners."

"Oh, I forgot about Audrey Hepburn and Jessica. In that case, it makes perfect sense."

"Don't be sarcastic, Todd. I'm serious about this."

"I can tell you are. But Liz, I really don't get it."

Elizabeth jumped at a snapping sound just over her head. The gum-popping waitress was back. "You two ready to order?"

"I'll have a bowl of clam chowder," Elizabeth said, pointing a finger at the most exotic thing on the menu.

The waitress popped her gum again. "I suppose you want that made with half-and-half."

"No, just the regular way."

The woman pulled a pencil out from behind her ear. "OK, that's one clam chowder, made the boring, routine way. And how about you, Mr. Adventure?"

Todd began to describe what he wanted on his Dairi Burger. Elizabeth could have recited it with him—cheese, ketchup, lettuce, tomato, and mustard, with no pickles or mayo, just like always.

After the waitress left, Todd changed the subject and began telling her about his windsurfing students. Elizabeth tried to listen, but she found herself focusing on Todd's neat, conservative haircut, his wholesome good looks, and his mall-store rugby shirt. He was so ordinary.

Of course, she'd hated it when Todd cut his hair in an urban-commando look and tried to grow a mustache. But that was just it. Even when Todd played at taking a walk on the wild side, he couldn't pull it off. It was just a game, and it didn't suit him. For the first time Elizabeth realized just how unsophisticated her boyfriend really was.

She sipped her iced coffee, trying to feel exciting, cultured, and cosmopolitan—like her customer who was sailing up the coast from Baja. But it was hard to feel exciting, cultured, and cosmopolitan in a room that was full of the same wholesome, small-town, teenage faces she'd seen every day for the last several years.

Her good friend Olivia Davidson gazed into Harry Minton's eyes, holding his hand. Just behind Elizabeth sat Amy Sutton and Caroline Pearce; she could hear enough bits and pieces of the conversation to know they were gossiping about guys, as always. Across the room, Rose Jameson appeared to be telling a funny story to Andrea Slade and Sally Larson. Bruce

Patman and Kirk Anderson sprawled on vinyl-covered stools at the counter, bragging loudly to each other about their victory in the season's final tennis match against Big Mesa High School.

In fact, except for Jessica—who was probably off with Lila somewhere—the place was full of the same people as always, having the same kinds of conversations they always had while eating their usual Dairi Burger orders.

Elizabeth wanted to scream.

Then her eyes fell on someone she hadn't noticed earlier. In the back corner of the restaurant a young man sat alone in a booth. He was scribbling furiously in a small, spiral-bound notebook. Elizabeth was intrigued.

He looked about twenty. A terrific tan set off his handsome features and showed above the neckline of a white T-shirt he wore with a navy windbreaker. His brown, wavy hair was a little lighter than Todd's. And it was disheveled, as if he'd been standing in the wind.

Suddenly he looked up, and their eyes locked. Elizabeth felt a jolt run through her body, like electricity. As his gaze met hers, it seemed to Elizabeth that time froze. Then he bent his head back down to his notebook and resumed his writing. But in those few seconds of eye contact, Elizabeth knew she had found the indefinable something she had been searching for. She had found her Gregory Peck.

She might have even found her soul mate.

Chapter 6

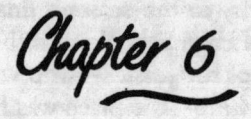

It was very early Tuesday morning, but John Marin was wide awake. Ideas raced through his mind in an intricate dance of vengeance and carefully laid plans. Finally he gave up on trying to sleep. He jumped out of bed, reached for his mini-recorder, and played back the tape of Ned Wakefield's conversation with the private investigator the evening before.

"I have a dangerous situation on my hands," Wakefield had begun, sounding terribly serious.

Marin laughed. "Much more dangerous than you imagine, Counselor," he said, sneering at the cassette tape as if it were Ned Wakefield himself. "For instance, you have no idea that I left a little present in your telephone receiver yesterday. You may not know it, Ned, but I made straight A's in the prison's wiretapping course. Of course the class was, shall we say, *extracurricular*."

He listened while Mr. Wakefield gave the private investigator the details of the case.

"You say his name is John Marin?" Battaglia asked, his voice crackling through the tape recorder as he spelled out the name.

"That's right," Wakefield answered. "What can you do?"

"If the police will cooperate, I'll coordinate with them as I begin trying to locate the guy. In the meantime, if Marin really is after your daughters, the best way to find him will be to stick close to the twins. I'll hire a man to watch them during the day while they're working at the restaurant."

"Battaglia's spy won't be the only one watching the little darlings," Marin said with a chuckle. He had already hired his own guy to keep an eye on Jessica and Elizabeth. The man was a little slow on the uptake, but very dependable—in other words, perfect for Marin's purposes.

"Good," Wakefield told the investigator. "And I'll ask Detective Cabrini to allow you access to the police files. In fact, I'll call him back right now and have him courier you over a photograph of Marin sometime tomorrow."

Marin stopped the tape machine. "Bingo!" That was exactly the bit he had wanted to hear again. Now all he had to do was replay the next conversation between Wakefield and Cabrini, and he'd know the details of the delivery of that photograph.

"Sorry, Counselor," Marin said with a smile. "But I wouldn't be surprised if a funny thing happens to that mug shot on its way to Battaglia. I have a funny feeling your private investigator is going to end up with a photograph of the wrong man."

Elizabeth was only half listening to Jessica's chatter as the twins walked from the parking lot to the café Tuesday morning.

"Lila was going on and on last night about her new bathing suit," Jessica said. "Frankly, I think yellow is unflattering on brunettes. Why spend all that time perfecting your suntan if you're going to wear a color that makes you look all washed out?"

Elizabeth didn't care if Lila's tan looked washed out. She was too busy thinking about the mysterious guy she'd seen at the Dairi Burger the night before. She'd felt drawn to him, like steel to a magnet. But she wasn't sure why. He wasn't any more handsome than Todd. And she knew nothing at all about him; he could be a real creep. Elizabeth dismissed that thought immediately. It couldn't be true. Even from across the room, she'd seen her own longing for adventure and romance mirrored in his eyes.

Elizabeth realized she had stopped walking and was standing perfectly still at the base of the pier. Jessica, a few steps ahead, turned back and tapped the side of Elizabeth's head with her knuckles. "Earth to Liz! Earth to Liz! You haven't been listening to me!"

Elizabeth smiled sheepishly. "Sorry, Jess. I guess I was busy, uh, looking at the boats." She hadn't been. But as soon as Elizabeth said it, she found her imagination caught by the streamlined white hulls, as lovely as sculptures in the morning sunlight, with their billowy sails and scarlet and blue flags that fluttered in the breeze. She wished she could be on one of the gleaming decks, with nothing but sparkling blue ocean for miles around.

Jessica shook her head. "I think you've caught Dad's spacing-out disease. I didn't realize he was contagious."

"Aren't they beautiful?" Elizabeth said, gazing at the sailboats.

Jessica shrugged. "Sure. But I've got to get inside. Remember, Mr. Jenkins said I could leave after the lunch rush if I was here in time to help set up for breakfast. Are you coming in?"

"I'll be right there," Elizabeth said. For a moment she wondered why Jessica wanted to leave work early—she'd been so adamant about winning the tip contest. *She probably has a real emergency to take care of, like buying a new bathing suit to keep up with Lila's wardrobe.*

Elizabeth stood for a minute more, watching the gently bobbing boats. She imagined herself sailing to distant ports, where tile-roofed houses lined lush hillsides and the air was filled with the fragrance of wildflowers.

Suddenly the daydream vanished. Ten yards away, a man was fishing off the dock. He wore old, patched clothes, and half of his face was hidden under a big, floppy hat. Even at that distance Elizabeth could tell that the man needed a shave. A prickly feeling ran up her spine. She couldn't see his eyes, but she was sure the man was watching her.

She hurried toward the restaurant, but she could still feel the stranger's eyes boring into her back.

An hour later Elizabeth set a tray of muffins on the counter of the Marina Café as Jessica reached for the coffeepot.

"Can you believe that guy at table five?" Jessica asked.

"The one who's dressed like he just stepped out of a bad novel about yachting?"

"That's the one. But get this—he says he started in Portugal and he's sailing around the world all by himself!"

"Sailing around the world?" Elizabeth's eyes seemed to lose focus. Her face took on a dreamy look, and Jessica stared at her curiously for a moment.

"He's stopped here for a few days to take a break from all that sailing," Jessica said. "But he's not like any sailor I've ever met."

"Right. And you've met so many. What's so different about this guy?"

"He ordered a peanut-butter-and-jelly sandwich and a Diet Coke!"

"First thing in the morning? That is kind of weird."

"I tried to tell him we don't have peanut butter and jelly on the menu. But then I figured, what the heck. So I'm making it for him myself and charging him the same price as an egg salad."

"Mr. Jenkins would be proud of you, Jessica."

Jessica laughed. "You mean Elizabeth."

"You're right," Elizabeth agreed. "He would say Elizabeth. Are you finished with that coffeepot? My customer said she'd fall asleep right at the table if I didn't get her some more caffeine, fast."

"Why don't you just give it to her intravenously?" Jessica asked, handing her the pot.

"Actually, that's how she asked for it," Elizabeth said over her shoulder. "But I'm not quite that dedicated to the theory that the customer is always right!"

"Ugh!" Jane complained, coming up behind Jessica. "Look at that guy walking in right now. What a loser!"

"Oh, great," Jessica said. "He's sitting down at my table. Hey, do you know where those little containers of half-and-half are?"

Jane pointed to a carton on a shelf behind the counter. "He sure doesn't look like he can afford much of a tip," she commented wryly.

Jessica stood on tiptoes to reach the box. "He doesn't look like he could afford a glass of water. What scruffy-looking clothes! He'll probably scare all the rich, generous customers away from my section."

"Here, let me reach that for you. I'm a couple inches taller." Jane handed her the box. Then she glanced back into the dining room and grinned. "You lucky devil! I think that creep likes you."

"Come off it, Jane."

"I'm serious. It's hard to see under that enormous hat he's wearing, but I'm almost positive that he's staring straight at you, no doubt with hunger in his eyes."

"Right, because he wants me to come and take his breakfast order. What do you wanna bet he orders a glass of water and maybe some of those little packages of oyster crackers?"

"And ketchup," Jane said with a laugh. "That'll definitely win the tip contest for you."

Jessica frowned. "I'm lousy at math, but it doesn't take a genius to know that fifteen percent of nothing is nothing."

"Cheer up. Maybe he's a filthy-rich codger who slinks around in rags because he wants to see who'll treat a poor man right. There could be an inheritance in it for you."

"I won't hold my breath—except maybe when I'm taking his order. He looks like he takes a bath about once every leap year." She grabbed a tray of muffins and coffee and hurried back to the dining room.

Jessica stood as far away from the haggard man as possible while she took his order for eggs and coffee. As she turned away from his table she caught sight of Lila sauntering in, her new yellow one-piece visible under a lacy white cover-up. Jessica was relieved to see her best friend; she could use some pleasant conversation. Besides, Lila could afford to tip well. Business in Jessica's section would be slow until that weird guy left.

"Hey, Lila!" Jessica called. "Sit over here. It's my section."

Lila eyed the man in the tattered hat. "Uh, I don't

know, Jess. The view is better over there." She pointed to the far side of the café.

"Lila Fowler, don't you dare!" Jessica glanced at the stranger again and sighed. She could see Lila's point. But what were friends for? She directed her to the table in her section that was farthest from her unkempt customer. "How's this?"

"I guess it'll do," Lila said uncertainly. "I still don't understand why you want to wait on people all summer. I mean, it's so tacky. It's like being a *servant*."

Jessica shrugged. "We can't all be born millionaires—present company excepted, of course. Besides, it's not that bad. I've been meeting the most exciting, glamorous people here!"

Lila raised her eyebrows. "Oh, really? Like who? Mr. Clean over there, in the hat that's ten years out of style?"

"Forget about him," Jessica said. She pointed instead to the peanut-butter lover at table five. "See the guy eating the sandwich? The tall man in the yacht club clothes?"

Lila nodded. "Too overdone. Nobody's wearing epaulets this season."

Jessica rolled her eyes. "He's on an around-the-world sailing trip from Portugal! Isn't that romantic?"

"Peachy," Lila agreed, but she was watching the scruffy stranger again. "Well, you seem to have made an admirer out of that loser. His eyes are following your every move."

"How can you tell under that big hat?"

"A woman knows these things," Lila said, as if she

were thirty years old instead of sixteen. "I'm surprised your own guy radar didn't tell you."

"My own guy radar is set for gorgeous, hunky, *clean* guys! I just wish he'd leave so I could get some customers again."

"I thought that's what I was."

"Of course you are," Jessica said, remembering the tip. "What can I get for you?"

"The fruit plate, with yogurt," Lila decided. "So are you still meeting your television intern this afternoon?"

Jessica smiled, thinking about Scott's sexy blue eyes. "I'm off at two o'clock, and I'm meeting him at four. That'll give me time to shower and change so I don't smell like french fries."

Lila grimaced. "How is your high-and-mighty sister taking the news about him?"

"Well—"

"I can't imagine Elizabeth would approve. Didn't she warn you off older men after that fiasco with Jeremy Randall? I mean, you did go after another woman's fiancé."

"That wasn't the way it was, and you know it!" Jessica insisted. "Besides, this is completely different. Scott's not engaged to anyone. And he's not that much older than we are!"

"How old is he, anyway?"

"I'm not sure," Jessica admitted. "He looks about twenty. And what my snoopy sister doesn't know won't hurt her. So keep quiet about him."

"My lips are sealed," Lila said.

Jessica sighed. "When I'm a famous television star, I'll be able to date him openly, no matter how old he is. Nobody will dare criticize me."

"I'll keep that in mind when you're a famous television star," Lila said, eyeing Jessica's apron with an air of disdain. "Until then, I assume you won't want to be seen with Scott in too public a place—at least, not in any place where there might be people who would mention it to Elizabeth. Or to Ken."

"True. But sneaking around can be fun. It kind of makes romance more exciting."

"So where are you meeting Prince Charming today?"

"In the school parking lot."

Lila wrinkled her nose. "He sure knows how to show a date a good time. Obviously he's sparing no expense."

"I told you last night. He's scouting locations for a miniseries about a southern California high school. If he recommends that they film it here, it could be my big break!"

"Just because he's looking for a California high school doesn't necessarily mean you'll end up starring in the miniseries."

"No," Jessica acknowledged. "But you never know. If he really likes me, then he just might drop a few hints to Jillian DeRiggi, the producer. And when she sees me, well, who knows? Maybe she'll think I'm perfect for a big, juicy role!"

"And maybe she won't."

"It doesn't have to be a big part, of course.

Couldn't you just see me on television, in a small but pivotal role? I could play a girl who dies tragically in the first episode, leaving behind my grief-stricken friends and throwing the whole school into turmoil. Or I could be the beautiful but untouchable girl that every boy in school worships from afar but is afraid to ask out. Or I could be—"

Lila cut in. "Or you could be the teenage waitress who gets fired from her job for hanging out with me when she's supposed to be working."

Jessica followed Lila's eyes. Mr. Jenkins was standing behind the counter, glaring expectantly at Jessica.

"Oops," Jessica said. "It's a good thing he's having so much trouble telling Elizabeth and me apart. It comes in handy when he's mad about something!"

Before Jessica slipped through the door of the storage room, she turned one last time to check on her customers. Unfortunately the guy in the floppy hat still seemed to be staring straight at her.

The door to the storage room swung open, and Elizabeth nearly crashed into her sister. Jessica was emerging from the room with a penitent expression on her face.

"Whew! Am I glad that's over!" Jessica breathed. "Jenkins was chewing me out for 'not providing excellent service.' He said I was talking to Lila for too long when I should have been serving other customers."

"He was probably right," Elizabeth told her. She

fitted a new filter into the coffeemaker. "Face it, Jess. You lose track of time when you're gossiping with your friends."

"That's almost exactly what he said," Jessica told her. She grinned. "Except that when he said it, he called me Elizabeth."

Elizabeth's mouth dropped open. "And you let him go on thinking it was *me* who was goofing off instead of working?"

"Don't worry about it. It'll be good for your reputation. If you can't be truly wild and crazy, you can at least let people think you are."

"Talking to Lila is hardly a walk on the wild side," Elizabeth said, flicking the switch on the coffeemaker. "Maybe you should get back out to your customers before Mr. Jenkins sees you again and *I* get into even more trouble."

Jessica shook her head. "What customers? Nobody will sit in my section with that filthy, disgusting-looking creep there."

Elizabeth shuddered. "That guy really makes me nervous. Every time I'm in the dining room, I can feel him watching me."

"Me too. He won't stop staring. Yuck!"

"Maybe it's our imagination," Elizabeth suggested, not really believing it. "I wonder if Jane thinks he's staring at her too."

"Nope on both counts," Jessica told her. "In fact, both Jane and Lila said they noticed that he was staring at *me*. Maybe he just likes blondes. Or maybe he thinks we're one person."

79

"I don't think so, Jessica. I'm not sure how I can tell, but I've got a very strange feeling about that man."

Elizabeth stood behind the counter of the Marina Café that afternoon, wrapping silverware in cloth napkins. Jane appeared from the kitchen with a tray. At the same time, Jessica walked up from the dining room, pocketing her latest tip.

"Is it two o'clock yet?" Jessica asked. "My feet are killing me."

"Five minutes after," Elizabeth said with a grin. "That's what you get for not wearing a watch of your own."

"Hallelujah!" Jessica cried. "I can't wait to get home and take a shower so I can—" She stopped suddenly.

"So you can what?" Elizabeth asked. "You never told me why you're leaving early this afternoon. What is it this time, an emergency trip to the mall with Lila?"

Jessica nodded vigorously. "That's exactly it. Lila's going to help me pick out a bikini." She untied her apron. "Well, guys, I'm outta here as soon as I grab something to drink. I promise I'll think about you two slaving away while I'm having fun this afternoon."

Elizabeth smiled. "Actually, it's been a really good day so far. I think I'll manage a few more hours."

Jessica poured herself half a glass of diet soda and drank it down in one gulp. "At least that spooky guy in the gross clothes finally left."

"Not completely," Jane said. "I noticed him on my break. He's out on the dock, fishing. But he really seems to be watching this place—probably hoping for another glimpse of you two." She grinned wickedly. "This guy's got it bad for you girls. It must be true love."

"Gag!" Jessica called over her shoulder as she practically sprinted toward the door. "Thanks for the warning. I'll stay away from the dock. Happy waitressing!"

A minute later Elizabeth was once again alone with the silverware. She gazed across the café. The dining room was striped with yellow bars of sunlight from the huge windows. Outside, white sails gleamed against a turquoise sky. For the hundredth time that day, Elizabeth found herself daydreaming. She saw herself balanced on the deck of one of those lovely sailboats, with the sun warm on her face. The boat bounced gently over the swells, and the ocean's surface reflected the clear blue sky and the golden sunlight. And she wasn't alone on the boat. Standing beside her, adjusting a sail, was a young man wearing a navy windbreaker, his wavy, light brown hair tossed by the wind. . . .

Moments later, Elizabeth's eyes widened. The door of the restaurant had opened, and in walked the guy from the Dairi Burger, as if Elizabeth's fantasy had conjured him up. She dropped a set of silverware with a clatter.

Jane returned to the counter. "Check out that guy," she said, nudging Elizabeth. "He can climb in my rigging anytime!"

Elizabeth couldn't stop staring at his handsome face. She'd never believed in fate before, but his timing was too perfect to be coincidence. *Maybe we are soul mates.*

"Well, what are you waiting for?" Jane asked. "That's your table, isn't it?"

Elizabeth took a deep breath and hurried out to take his order.

"What can I get for you?" she asked, her heart pounding in her chest.

"I'll have an iced coffee with half-and-half," the young man said. "With three sugars and a straw."

Elizabeth's mouth dropped open.

"Is something wrong?" he asked. His deep blue eyes were sweetly soft in his tanned face. They had tiny wrinkles at their edges, as if he'd been squinting into the wind.

"Oh, no," Elizabeth said quickly. "Everything's just fine." She walked quickly from the dining room.

"What a hunk!" Jane exclaimed in the kitchen a few minutes later. "And you should see his boat!"

Elizabeth looked at her curiously. "He only just walked in. How do you know he has a boat?"

Jane shrugged. "If there's one thing you learn in college, it's how to do efficient research. Trina, the dishwasher, says she talked to your newest customer out on the docks this morning. She told me which boat was his, and I slipped out a minute ago to take a look."

Elizabeth was still shaking because her dream guy had ordered "her" drink. She fixed the iced coffee quickly and hurried back to the dining room with it. He was still there, now writing in his spiral-bound notebook.

He looked up when she set the coffee in front of him. "Thanks." His smile was heart-stopping.

"Will there be anything else?"

"No, that's all for today."

Elizabeth ran into Jane in the storage room a few minutes later. "Tell me more," she begged. "What kind of boat does he have?"

"It's a forty-foot sloop named the *Emily Dickinson*."

Elizabeth felt faint. Emily Dickinson was her very favorite poet. "Did you happen to get the name of the guy, too—or just the name of the boat?"

Jane shrugged. "Sorry. My research methods aren't that thorough. Trina couldn't remember his name. But get this—he's just sailed in from Hawaii, all by himself. Now he's on his way to South America."

"What else did Trina say?"

"Not much. Just that he's some sort of writer."

"*A writer?*" Elizabeth was having trouble catching her breath. One little thought about soul mates the night before and this guy seemed to drop down from heaven, just for her.

"Don't just stand there, sweetie," Jane told her. "You're dying to know more, aren't you? So march yourself back out there and strike up a conversation."

Elizabeth nodded. Jane was absolutely right. She wheeled around and headed back to the dining room.

When she reached the young writer's table, her heart sank. He was gone.

But she smiled when she saw that he'd left her a twenty-five-percent tip. Somehow, she was sure they'd meet again.

"So this is the famous Sweet Valley High," Scott Maderlake said as he climbed out of his red Miata. "I can already see that it's got a lot of potential—it's very California. The visuals are great."

Jessica saw the way his blue eyes slid over her swingy yellow halter dress. He was definitely talking about more than the high school. *Lila Fowler, eat your heart out. Yellow looks terrific on some people.*

Scott had a speculative look on his face. "It looks like the kind of place where a lot of exciting things might happen."

"I could tell you some pretty intense stories!" Jessica said. "Wilder than anything your scriptwriters could dream up, I guarantee."

"How about telling me over an early dinner?" Scott asked. "It's obvious that we can't get inside the school right now, though I'd like to eventually."

"Give me a few days," Jessica said. "I'll think of a way to get you in."

"Great!" Scott said, with a sexy smile that made Jessica's knees melt. "For now, why don't you leave your Jeep here and come with me in the Miata? You suggest a place to eat, and you can show me the sights along the way."

Jessica nodded eagerly. "Sounds like a plan."

"Can you recommend a restaurant up the coast?"

Jessica slid into the front seat of his car and thought for a moment. She wondered if it would be rude to suggest Café Mirabeau, one of the most expensive restaurants in the area. She took in the airplanelike control panel, the soft leather interior, and the solid wood dashboard. *He can afford it,* she decided.

Mr. Wakefield pulled his brown LTD into the driveway of the Wakefield house on Calico Drive. "Good," he breathed. "I'm the first one home." He wanted to make sure nobody reached the mailbox before he did—just in case John Marin had made any new deliveries.

He ran to box and yanked the day's mail out of it. Then he quickly flipped through the envelopes and catalogs. "Thank goodness!" he said with a sigh. "Nothing out of the ordinary. I guess Marin decided to lay low for the day."

Prince Albert barked a greeting as Mr. Wakefield stepped into the house. Mr. Wakefield walked through the downstairs, his gaze sliding around the familiar rooms. Then he collapsed onto the living room couch, patting Prince Albert's head. "It's all right, Albert," he said. "There's no sign of an intruder. I don't think Marin's been here today."

The dog barked a cheerful reply.

"You're right," Mr. Wakefield said. "I probably overreacted. Maybe I shouldn't have called a private investigator. But if the police can't protect my family,

I have to take things into my own hands."

Then his heart skipped a beat. A sheet of lined paper lay on the coffee table, with writing on it. "What's that?" he said aloud. The golden retriever stared at him quizzically.

Ned lifted the note from the table, barely breathing. Had he been wrong? Had Marin been in the house that day after all? Was the note another threat?

Yo, Mom and Dad, the note said in Jessica's loopy scrawl. *I'm with Lila. Don't expect me for dinner. See ya later tonight. P.S. Chill out, Dad! You worry too much.*

Mr. Wakefield exhaled, relieved that the note wasn't from Marin. At the same time, he was concerned about Jessica. Did she really have to go out every single night?

Prince Albert nudged the note out of the way and licked his hand. "You're right, boy," Mr. Wakefield said. "I'm getting paranoid again. But I'm not sorry I called Battaglia. You can never be too careful."

Chapter 7

"So Winston Egbert, the nerdiest kid in the junior class, was left with his neighbor's baby girl for a whole week!" Jessica related to Scott over dessert at Café Mirabeau.

Scott was hanging on her every word. "So what does a sixteen-year-old guy do with an abandoned baby when his own parents are on vacation?"

Jessica's lips slid over a spoonful of chocolate mousse. She'd certainly outdone herself on the choice of restaurant. Dinner had been terrific, the mousse was the best she'd ever tasted, and Scott hadn't even winced at the prices on the menu.

She gestured with her spoon. "For one thing, Winston the Nerd became the most popular guy in the class. Crowds of girls showed up at his house every day to play with the baby." She laughed. "It was a good thing—he really needed the help. I've never seen anything as funny as

87

Winston Egbert trying to diaper a baby!"

"What about school?" Scott asked. "Did he stay out the whole week?"

"Oh, no," Jessica said. "He brought little Daisy with him, and we all took turns watching her during our free periods. You should've seen us, passing her off like a football, hiding her from teachers—"

"That is priceless! You know, Jessica, you're right. These stories you're telling me are better than anything Hollywood has to offer. We could use you as a consultant on the miniseries. I mean, if you'd be interested."

Jessica froze with a spoonful of chocolate mousse halfway to her mouth. She could hardly believe what she'd just heard. A slow smile spread across her face. "If I'd be interested? Are you kidding? I'd love it! But Scott, you ain't heard nothing yet. Let me tell you about the time my sister's best friend, Enid Rollins, was in a plane crash. . . ."

Elizabeth sat at the Dairi Burger with Enid that night. Her friend was talking, but Elizabeth's eyes kept straying to the corner booth where *he* had sat the night before.

She had been relieved when Todd said he'd be busy tonight. For a change of pace, he'd said, he was going to a drag race with some of the other guys from the school basketball team. A drag race! That was supposed to be exciting?

Of course I love Todd, she reminded herself. *But right now, a little distance from him is just what I need.*

"I can't wait to meet Jane," Enid was saying. "You did say she'd be here at eight o'clock, right?"

Elizabeth shook her head, trying to clear it. "I'm sorry, Enid. What was that?"

Enid took a sip of her diet soda. "What's up with you, Liz? You seem like you're a million miles away. Is everything all right?"

Elizabeth opened her mouth to tell Enid about the good-looking young stranger she couldn't get out of her mind. But suddenly there was a hand on her shoulder. She whirled around, half expecting to see her mystery man.

"Hey, Liz!" Jane said. "Sorry I'm a little late."

Elizabeth introduced her new friend to Enid, then slid over in the booth so that Jane could sit down.

"So, are you still obsessing about Sailor Boy?" Jane asked.

Elizabeth nodded sheepishly. "I can't stop thinking about him. I feel like we were meant to be together, but I don't even know his name."

Enid's eyes widened. "What in the world are you talking about?"

"I was just going to tell you about it. There's this guy I saw in here last night, when I was with Todd. It sounds weird, but we looked at each other across the room, and, I don't know. We connected."

"But you didn't even talk to him?"

Elizabeth shrugged. "Not last night. But he came into the café today—and Enid, it's like we're soul mates."

"I thought you and Todd were soul mates!"

"I don't know what to think about Todd. He's driving me crazy lately. We've been together for so long. And suddenly I'm bored. I want something . . . *different*."

"A different guy?"

"A different life! I'd love it if Todd could help me find what I'm looking for. But he doesn't understand, and he won't even try. He acts like I'm a spoiled kid who doesn't know how good I've got it." She bit her lip. "Sometimes I wonder if he's right."

Enid shook her head. "Of course he's not right. There's nothing wrong with wanting to expand your horizons. Todd should be more supportive."

Jane whistled. "You ought to see this sailor, Enid," she said in a conspiratorial tone. "He's gorgeous! And his sailboat may be even better looking than he is."

Enid stared at Elizabeth. "His sailboat?"

"Yeah, he owns a sailboat," Elizabeth said. "But Enid, it gets worse."

"How can it be worse?"

"His boat's named the *Emily Dickinson*—and he's a writer!"

"Oh, boy," Enid said, her forehead wrinkling with concern. "This is serious. This guy really does sound like your soul mate."

"What's so wrong with that?" Jane asked them both. "I say go with the flow."

Enid raised her eyebrows. "Elizabeth, I'm worried that you're going to do something you'll regret. As you just said, you and Todd have been together for a long time. Is this mystery guy of yours worth screwing up that relationship for?"

"I don't know. I just don't know."

"You sound pretty mixed up, kid," Jane said, patting her on the arm. "You're never going to know for sure until you have a conversation with Mr. Sailor that amounts to more than 'Will that be one sugar in your coffee, or two?'"

"Three, actually," Elizabeth said. She absentmindedly stirred her iced coffee with her straw.

Jane gave her a blank look. "Come again?"

Elizabeth sighed. "Never mind. It's not important."

"So what're you going to do?" Enid asked, looking at her expectantly.

"There's really nothing I can do until I actually meet this guy. I guess I'll just keep my eyes open and hope that he comes back into the café."

"Maybe he won't," Jane pointed out. "For all we know, he could be casting off for South America as we speak."

"He'll be back," Elizabeth said quietly. "I'm sure of it."

Jessica lay on her rumpled bed that night, twisting the telephone cord around her finger. "And then, Lila, he said that he could use me as a consultant on the miniseries! Can you believe it?"

Lila's bored skepticism oozed through the phone line. "Is he going to pay you?"

"Is getting paid the only thing you ever think

about?" Jessica cried. "The money isn't what's important!"

"Bite your tongue!"

"Lila, think about the opportunity! The closer I am to the production of the miniseries, the more likely I am to get cast in it. Don't you see?"

"I just can't take this very seriously, Jess. For your entire life, every two weeks you've been finding a new, surefire way to become a star."

"This is different!" Jessica said, jumping to her feet.

"You always say that!"

"You wait and see. Scott's so psyched about the stories I've been telling him that he might just convince the producer to use them in the plot. And if they've got a story line about Jessica Wakefield, why should they go any further than me to find the perfect woman for the role?"

Jessica sucked in her cheeks and watched herself in the mirror, trying to decide if she looked more glamorous that way. "So, Lila. What do you think I should wear to the Emmy Awards—something black and slinky?"

Lila's resigned sigh crackled through the phone. "I'll tell you what, Jess. You win an Emmy, and I'll let you have your pick of anything in my closet."

"Thanks, Li. And I'll be sure to thank you in my acceptance speech." She lifted her long hair off her neck to see what it would look like piled on top of her head. Suddenly she dropped it and put her hand to her mouth. "Oh, no!"

"What's wrong?" Lila asked. "Has your show been canceled already?"

"My necklace is gone! My gold lavaliere necklace, just like Elizabeth's."

"It's probably tangled up in your jewelry box."

"No, Lila. It's not. You know I hardly ever take it off. I'm sure I was wearing it earlier this evening."

"So what's the big deal? It couldn't be worth all that much. It's only fourteen karat."

"It's not the money! My parents gave us those necklaces on our sixteenth birthday. And my mom had a fit last week when I lost a bracelet my grandmother sent. She'll go ballistic if I tell her I lost the necklace too."

"Then you'll just have to find it before she notices."

Wednesday morning at the Marina Café was hectic. After a couple of hours of racing back and forth between the kitchen and the dining room, Elizabeth darted into the storage room; Mr. Jenkins had sent her back for paper towels to fill the dispenser in the ladies' room. She was determined to find the towels quickly so she could get back to the dining room and collect more tips.

Unfortunately the storage room was a mess. Elizabeth finally spotted a cardboard box marked PAPER TOWELS, but it was blocked by a half-dozen other crates. She'd have to dig her way down to it, one box at a time.

"Darn! I'll never get back to the customers at this

rate," she muttered as she began hoisting boxes. "Why did Jenkins have to pick me?"

A few minutes later she finally reached the paper towels. As she lifted the box, she tensed. All of a sudden, the tiny hairs on the back of her neck stood up straight. Someone else was in the storage room.

She dropped the box and spun around. The scary-looking guy from the dock stood facing her, still wearing the enormous hat that concealed his eyes. Up close, he looked positively sinister, especially now that she was alone with him.

"What are you doing here?" she demanded in a choked whisper.

Before she finished getting out the words, the man had disappeared.

Tears of fright blurred Elizabeth's vision as she tore open the box of paper towels and jerked out a package. She gulped for air. Then she raced out of the storage room.

As Elizabeth emerged into the dining room she collided with a tall, strong man. She nearly screamed.

"Hey, hey! It's all right," said a deep voice. Elizabeth looked up into the blue eyes of her soul mate.

She felt her face turning pink with embarrassment; he practically had his arms around her. She pulled away and tried to collect herself. "I'm sorry for crashing into you," she said finally. "There was just this man in the storage room who gave me the creeps, and I thought . . ."

"You look really rattled," he said in a soothing

voice. "Why don't you take a break, and we'll go outside for a few minutes. Some fresh air will do you good."

Elizabeth nodded. He was right—she was too frazzled to wait on customers. "Give me a minute to get someone to cover for me," she said, scanning the dining room for Jessica. "I'll see if my sister can watch my tables."

Jessica turned to the door of the kitchen in surprise. Elizabeth had just run in as if she were being chased. Her face was flushed, and her blue eyes were wide. She seemed out of breath.

"What's with you?" Jessica asked, making a peanut-butter sandwich for the around-the-world sailor from Portugal. He'd shown up again for breakfast.

Elizabeth scanned the kitchen, panting. "Good, Mr. Jenkins isn't in here."

"He's out back arguing with a seafood distributor," Jessica said, gesturing toward the back door. "Why? What's wrong?"

Elizabeth shook her head. "Nothing's wrong," she said unconvincingly. "But Jess, I need to go outside for a few minutes. Will you cover my tables?"

"No way! I've got enough work to do of my own without yours too. Ask Jane to do it."

"Please, Jessica. If *you* cover for me, Mr. Jenkins won't notice I'm gone. He'll think you're both of us. I'll be back in ten minutes, I swear."

"I'll do it on one condition," Jessica said, putting the peanut butter back on the shelf.

"What?"

"I need to leave a few hours early. I have some, uh, things to get done. I'm going shopping with Lila this afternoon. There's, uh, a fashion show at the mall at three o'clock. I'll cover for you now, but you have to cover for me then."

"You work for me for ten *minutes*, and then I cover for you for a few *hours*? That's not fair!"

Jessica shrugged. "OK, so take twenty minutes."

Elizabeth sighed, quickly untying her apron and throwing it over a hook. "All right, all right. It's a deal."

"And I want half the tips from any of your customers that I wait on!"

"That's extortion!"

Jessica smiled. "I prefer to think of it as private enterprise."

"Jessica!"

"OK, OK. No tips."

"Thanks, Jess. You're the best." Elizabeth thrust a package of paper towels into her sister's hands. "And put this in the ladies' room when you get a chance."

"Wait a minute! You still haven't told me where you're going!" Jessica protested.

But Elizabeth was already gone.

Halyards clanged in the breeze as Elizabeth walked along the docks of the marina with the sailor. His name, she'd finally learned, was Ben Morgan.

Ben touched her arm. "You're still shaking."

"I know," Elizabeth said. "It's kind of embarrassing. But that guy really freaked me out. Only restaurant employees are supposed to be in the storage room. And he was so seedy looking . . . ugh." She shook her head. "Let's talk about something else. Tell me about yourself."

Ben smiled, and Elizabeth felt breathless all over again. "Well," he said, "I've just spent a month 'on this wondrous sea, sailing silently.'"

"That's Emily Dickinson you just quoted!"

"Guilty as charged," Ben said. "Sorry. I'm kind of a poetry fanatic. Sometimes I forget that I shouldn't inflict my habit on others."

"I'm the same way," Elizabeth said. "And Emily Dickinson is my favorite!"

"No kidding? What a coincidence. I even named my boat after her!"

"Really?" Elizabeth asked, trying to sound surprised.

Ben smiled again. "A man gets a little strange sailing around by himself, with only reading and writing for company."

"Writing? What do you write?"

"Well, I'm working on a novel right now. It's a travel-adventure story. I'm taking a year off from college to sail around and collect information for it."

Elizabeth's heart pounded. "How wonderful," she breathed. "That is exactly what I'd like to do, if I weren't so . . . hemmed in."

Ben stopped walking. He turned to face her. "Hemmed in by what, Elizabeth?"

She shook her head. "By Sweet Valley,

California, I guess. By being Elizabeth Wakefield."

"I don't understand."

Elizabeth laughed. "I'm not sure I do either. It's just that everyone has all these expectations of me. I'm supposed to be a good little girl, and get good grades, and listen to my parents. And mostly I just go along with all those expectations."

Ben nodded. "I know what you mean. It's like your life is all scripted out, and you're just playing along. You're desperate to do something . . . unexpected."

Elizabeth stared into his beautiful dark blue eyes. She felt as if she could fall into those eyes as easily as she could fall off the edge of the dock and into the sparkling water below. "Yes!" she cried, startled to hear him express her own feelings. "That's it. That's it exactly!"

Suddenly Elizabeth felt embarrassed. After all, this guy was a complete stranger. "Look, I want to thank you for being so nice to me. But I'm rambling. I can't help it; you're very easy to talk to. Thanks for saving me from that creep in the storage room. But I should get back to work."

She turned and fled toward the restaurant. She could feel Ben's gorgeous blue eyes on her back, and she desperately wanted to reverse her direction and run straight back—right into his arms.

Calico Drive looked deserted this late in the morning. John Marin pulled his car to a halt in front of the Wakefield house and reached for the small, tissue-wrapped bundle on the seat beside him. He stuffed the bundle into a padded envelope and scrawled *Ned* across the front.

Then he flipped down the window visor to reveal a picture of Ned Wakefield he'd clipped there.

"Counselor, I'm holding you in contempt," he sneered at the photograph. "And your sentence will be torture."

Marin sealed the envelope. Then he leaped from the car and slid the package into the Wakefields' mailbox.

For a moment he stopped on the sidewalk and stared at the quiet house. "I wish I could stay here and wait for you, Counselor," he said, his eyes narrowed into hard slits. "I'd love to see your face when you open that package. Aw, Ned, you're so much fun to torment. It's almost too easy!" He laughed as he climbed back into the car.

"A private investigator? Really! Battaglia's a novice compared to me. He hasn't even slowed me down. I could have stuck a knife into either of those sweet young girls by now, and Battaglia too. But I'm having so much fun, keeping you on your toes, Ned. I'd like to prolong the agony just a little bit longer."

He laughed again, gunned the engine, and drove off down the street. "Besides, I can't decide which twin is prettier, Jessica or Elizabeth. Which one should I kill first, Counselor? Which one?"

Chapter 8

Elizabeth stepped warily into the café, her heart racing. She felt exhilarated by her walk along the docks with Ben. On the other hand, she expected Jessica to pounce on her any minute, demanding to know where she'd been.

She breathed a relieved sigh when she saw that Jessica had her hands full with a birthday party at table five. A half-dozen six-year-olds were arguing over a pile of paper party hats while three adults tried in vain to referee. Obviously it would be some time before Jessica got around to asking about Elizabeth's absence.

Elizabeth waved a hand at her sister to signal that she was back on duty. Jessica threw her a dirty look, taking her attention away from the table just long enough for a chubby boy to dump a glass of grape juice down the front of her shirt. Elizabeth tried to stifle her laughter. On Jessica's list of favorite things, baby-sitting ranked somewhere between algebra tests and zits.

Jane accosted her as soon as she ran back to the kitchen to grab her apron. "So tell me about Sailor Boy!"

Elizabeth felt her face coloring. She smiled weakly. "Sorry, I've got a ton of customers to serve. I'll fill you in later."

Breakfast time melted into lunch hour, and business in the café never let up. Elizabeth hardly had time to catch her breath between customers. She was happy about the volume of business. Most of the customers were pleasant and interesting. And after two days of waitressing, Elizabeth was beginning to feel in control of the job. She loved the sense of competence that came with knowing what to do and what to say. By noon she could juggle orders at five different tables at once without mixing anything up.

"I'm really getting the hang of this!" she whispered to Jane once as they slid by each other, trays held high.

Jane smiled. "I knew you would."

Waitressing took her mind off her scare in the storage room that morning. Already it seemed like a dream. Elizabeth could almost believe she'd imagined the whole incident.

But she couldn't keep her mind off Ben. Every time Elizabeth glanced out the expanse of windows—toward the sailboats bobbing in their berths—she could feel tropical breezes in her hair and see the white beaches and rugged volcanic peaks of Hawaii off the bow. In her daydreams, it was always Ben who stood beside her on the deck. Every time the bell on the door jingled, she looked up. She'd love to see Ben saunter in for iced coffee, his light brown hair disheveled by the ocean breeze.

A little after noon, Jessica left for the day. Elizabeth was preparing a salad in the kitchen when Jane stopped behind her and sang into her ear, "Lover boy's arrived!"

Elizabeth's heart jumped. She smoothed her hair and took a deep breath. Then she checked the coffeepot to make sure there was plenty in it for Ben's iced coffee. Then, grinning, she walked steadily through the swinging door to meet him.

"How's my favorite waitress?" asked a sexy voice from the counter.

Elizabeth exhaled slowly, disappointed. Todd leaned across the counter and kissed her on the cheek. "Gimme a nice cold root beer!"

Mr. Wakefield couldn't stand it any longer. He'd been sitting at his desk for half the day, going over Marianna's briefs for the *West Coast Oilcam* wrongful-dismissal case. But he couldn't keep his mind on his work. The only wrongful dismissal that interested him lately was John Marin's early release from prison.

He grabbed the telephone and dialed James Battaglia's number. "Jim? It's Ned. What have you got for me?"

"Not much," the private investigator said. "This Marin guy knows how to cover his tracks."

"Have you been able to locate him?"

"I'm sure he's nearby. But every time I think I've almost caught up with him, he throws me a curveball. I get the feeling he's toying with me."

Mr. Wakefield nodded. "That sounds like Marin."

"Have the girls noticed anyone unusual hanging around?"

"They haven't mentioned anything odd. Has your man been keeping an eye on them during the day?"

"Yeah, he's been down near the marina as much as possible, watching the café. I've dropped by the neighborhood myself a few times, in between trying to track down Marin. So far, neither of us has seen anything suspicious. Have you told the twins what to watch for?"

Mr. Wakefield shook his head. "No. They don't know anything about Marin. Until I've got more to go on, upsetting my daughters isn't going to do any good."

"All right, Ned. I'll play it any way you want."

"Have you been in touch with the police? Did you get Marin's picture from them?"

"I'm in constant contact with Detective Cabrini. And a courier dropped the mug shot by my office yesterday. I gave a copy to my hired man last night so he can watch for him at the marina. Funny, Marin doesn't look at all like you described him. You said he has a baby face and could almost pass as a teenager. I thought he looked about thirty in the photo."

Mr. Wakefield shrugged. "Well, the man's twenty-eight years old now. The last picture I've seen was taken years ago. Cabrini must have sent you something more recent."

"I guess doing time in the state pen would age anybody."

"Do the police have any new information on his whereabouts?"

"Nothing substantial. But Cabrini and I will coordinate our efforts if either of us gets a lead."

"Good," Mr. Wakefield said, but he felt a sinking sensation in the pit of his stomach. "Keep me informed, Jim."

Mr. Wakefield slammed down the receiver and jumped up from his desk. He threw the *Oilcam* papers into his briefcase, grabbed his suit jacket from the back of his chair, and stalked out of the room. "Trudy, I'm leaving early," he barked as he passed the office manager. "There's something I have to check on at home."

A half hour later he sat at his desk at home, turning a brown, padded envelope over and over in his hands. *Ned* was scribbled across the front in a large, angular hand. There was no return address, but Mr. Wakefield knew instantly who had sent it. He tore open the package. With shaking hands, he unwrapped a tissue-paper bundle.

Such a lovely young neck, the note said.

A gold lavaliere necklace fell to the desk, its chain jingling softly, like a young girl's quiet laughter.

Jessica could barely stop laughing long enough to give instructions to Scott. "Boost me up a little higher," she urged. "I can almost climb in." Her head and shoulders were inside the window of the girls' locker room at Sweet Valley High, but the rest of her was still outside. The windowsill was cutting into her solar plexus, and the cradle of Scott's hands felt wobbly through the sole of her left sneaker. The whole scene was hysterically funny.

Suddenly Jessica stopped laughing. "Shhh!" she hissed. "I think I heard something!"

"Inside the building?"

"No, back toward the parking lot. Oh, my gosh. We're going to get caught. Did you hear anything?"

"Not a thing."

Jessica remained still for as long as she could, balanced in the window. Finally she shook her head. "Maybe it was my imagination."

"Somehow I can tell you have an active one," Scott said. "Can you pull yourself in now?" He lifted her foot a little higher. "I can't keep you up in the air like this forever."

"Yep. That'll do it. I think I can make it now." She pulled herself into a crouch in the windowsill and then jumped to the tile floor of the locker room. Even in the summer the smells of sweaty gym socks, deodorant, and cosmetics blended into a heady aroma.

"Are you all right?" Scott called from outside.

"Piece of cake!" Jessica yelled back. "Come around the corner of the building and I'll let you in the back way."

"I can't believe we're really doing this," Scott said

after she'd opened the back door of the locker room for him. "You don't seem like the breaking-and-entering type."

"I didn't break a thing," Jessica said with mock indignity. "I only entered! The lock on that window's been broken for two years."

Scott dusted his hands off on his navy windbreaker. "I take it you've had occasion to use that entrance before."

Jessica shrugged. "Remind me to tell you about it sometime. You might be able to use it in your miniseries."

"We might be able to use *this* in the miniseries. But I don't know how I'll explain it to Jillian if she has to come bail me out of jail for breaking into this place."

"Just tell her you wanted your research to be thorough."

Scott shook his head. "Jessica, you're unbelievable. So, is this what the inside of a girls' locker room looks like? When I was in high school, I spent a lot of long, boring math classes dreaming about getting inside one of these places."

Jessica laughed. "Well, I hope it's everything you dreamed it would be."

"Actually, it looks just like the guys' locker room. But it smells better."

"Ugh," Jessica said with a grimace. "Hey, here's a good story for you. Do you see that football helmet and protective gear back in that storage area?"

"Yeah. What's it doing here?"

"Claire Middleton," Jessica said, as if the name explained everything. "She's a junior here, the first girl in the district to play on the boys' varsity football team. She tried out for first-string quarterback early in the year and came pretty close to making it. Now she plays second string."

"A girl playing quarterback? You're pulling my leg."

"That's what we all thought when we heard she was trying out. But she turned out to be just as good as the guys. Almost as good as Ken—" She stopped, reluctant to discuss her boyfriend around Scott.

"Ken who?"

"Uh, Ken Matthews. He's the first-string quarterback. Come on, the smell in here is choking me. Let me show you the rest of the school."

Scott shrugged. "Sure. Why not? As long as we're already trespassing, we might as well get the whole tour."

Elizabeth smiled when her best friend walked into the Marina Café that afternoon. "Enid!" she called. "I'm glad you could stop by."

"Which is your section?" Enid asked. "I wouldn't want my hard-earned tip money going to any other waitress."

"Thanks! I need all the help I can get if I'm going to win the big tip contest," she said.

"Then you should have chosen your friends better. Lila Fowler can afford to tip a lot better than I can. I think that gives Jessica the advantage."

"Maybe, but you're a much more generous person than Lila."

"Ha! So was Ebenezer Scrooge. I just saw Lila on the beach five minutes ago, arguing with a vendor about the price of a can of soda."

"That's funny. I could've sworn Jessica said she and Lila were going to a fashion show at the mall this afternoon." Elizabeth checked her watch. "Jessica should be there right about now, panting over clothes she can't afford."

"I hadn't heard about a fashion show. But believe me, I just left Lila on the beach not ten minutes ago."

Elizabeth shrugged. "Maybe I got the time wrong."

"Or maybe Jessica was using Lila as an alibi for one of her schemes." Enid raised an eyebrow.

"Well, I don't have time to worry about her schedule—especially since I'm covering her section as well as my own this afternoon. Speaking of which, what can I get you?"

Enid shook her head. "How about one of those iced coffees you've been raving about?" She grinned. "What is it, with half a sugar and three straws?"

"That's half-and-half, three sugars, and one straw," Elizabeth corrected her. "It's a never-fail recipe for breaking out of a rut."

"Will drinking it make a good-looking sailor miraculously appear and carry me onto his boat so we can sail off into the sunset together?"

"Sorry. I'm a waitress, not a fairy godmother."

"Good. I'd get seasick anyway. Seriously, has your mystery man been back?"

Elizabeth nodded. "This morning. We strolled out along the docks during my break. Oh, Enid! It was so Old World. You know, a real, old-fashioned *promenade* on the wharf, watching the sails billow in the breeze."

"Do you at least know his name now?"

"His name's Ben. And he's absolutely perfect! I couldn't have created a better match for me if I were writing it in a novel. Which, by the way, he's doing—writing a novel, I mean."

"I hate to rain on your promenade," Enid said. "But what are you going to do about Todd?"

Elizabeth frowned. "Todd was in here today, an hour after I left Ben on the docks. What a contrast! I mean, he barrels in, looking like such a . . . *high school guy*. He was full of stories about that drag race he went to last night. *A drag race!*"

Enid sighed. "I know. It can't compare with sailing around the Hawaiian Islands. Ben sounds so exotic."

Elizabeth nodded. "And Todd is just Todd."

"That used to be enough for you."

"I know. And maybe it will be again. Maybe I'm just going through a phase. Am I crazy to risk what I've got with Todd? I mean, I don't even know how long Ben will be in port! And he's still a complete stranger, really."

Enid opened her mouth to reply, but Mr. Jenkins appeared behind the counter and beckoned to

Elizabeth. "Elizabeth, I believe the order is ready for table nine," he said with a disapproving stare.

Elizabeth sighed. "What a time for him to finally get my name right," she whispered to Enid. Then she grinned. "Coming, Mr. Jenkins!" she called in a louder voice. "But I'm not Elizabeth. I'm Jessica!"

Jessica and Scott stopped outside the door of the high school auditorium. "Here's where we have assemblies and school plays and band concerts and stuff," she said, gesturing toward the door. She knew she was babbling, but Scott seemed endlessly amused by her anecdotes, so she figured she might as well keep him entertained.

"We've got a really great band—the Droids. See that poster for them on the bulletin board? Olivia Davidson designed it. She's a friend of my sister's, kind of an artsy type. Did I tell you how she met her boyfriend, Harry Minton?"

Scott smiled and held open the door for her. "No, I don't think I've heard that one."

"She had a painting in an art show, and an anonymous person offered to buy it if Olivia would speak at a stuffy-sounding arts foundation."

Scott nodded. "That sounds like a big honor for a high school student."

"Olivia thought so too," Jessica said with a laugh. "Only when she got to the place, she found out there wasn't any arts foundation. Harry made the whole thing up just to meet her."

Scott looked at her admiringly. "Is there any

square inch of this school that you don't have a story about?"

"The chess club room," Jessica said instantly. "I'm happy to say that I've never set foot in the place and never plan to."

"I don't blame you," Scott said, laughing. "I've always been nervous around people who like things as slow and complicated as chess."

"Exactly!" Jessica said with a nod. "It's amazing how much you and I have in common."

"So what about this room?" Scott asked. "We're standing in front of the stage. As naturally dramatic as you are, I'm sure you must have a story about it."

"At least a dozen," Jessica said cheerfully, happy for the chance to inform him about her acting experience. "I've been in a lot of plays in this room. A few months ago I was Lady Macbeth. But my understudy was a two-faced liar who sabotaged me and made me miss opening night."

"I hope you got to play the part eventually."

"Oh, sure. I did all the other performances, and I got rave reviews. But you should have seen Lila Fowler, my snobby millionaire friend, in that play! She was so ticked off at having to play an ugly old witch that she started adding her own lines to the script. Have you ever heard a cast member say 'Oh, gross!' onstage, in the middle of a Shakespeare performance?"

Scott laughed. "You and your friends are just too much, Jessica. I should be taking notes on all this for our scriptwriters."

"Don't worry about it," she said magnanimously. "I'll remember which stories you liked and tell them myself."

"I'm so glad you've agreed to help us out with this production. You're going to be a wonderful addition to the crew."

Suddenly the look in Scott's deep blue eyes grew serious. For the first time Jessica was acutely aware of how all alone they were in the big, empty school building. Scott smiled at her, and his sexy grin seemed to light up the dim, cavernous auditorium. Jessica's eyes caressed his broad shoulders and his strong, muscular body.

Scott leaned close to Jessica. He put a hand on Jessica's neck, pulling her close. She closed her eyes and began to relax into his arms.

Suddenly she felt a prickling at the back of her scalp. Jessica's eyes shot open. She spun around just in time to see a shadowy figure disappear through the auditorium door.

Chapter 9

The Wakefields had just sat down to dinner on Wednesday evening. Mrs. Wakefield was telling Elizabeth about the new kitchen in the mansion she was renovating, but Mr. Wakefield couldn't keep his mind on skylights, granite countertops, and ceramic tiles.

He reached into his pocket to feel the necklace he'd received in the mail. He knew that the twins wore their identical lavalieres almost all the time. His stomach lurched every time he thought about it. Marin must have been close enough to one of them to grab it away. But close enough to which one? He couldn't see a necklace on either Jessica or Elizabeth, but one of them could be wearing the gold chain under her blouse. He drummed his fingers on the table.

"Has either of you seen or spoken with anybody out of the ordinary recently?" he blurted, interrupting the conversation.

Elizabeth choked on her iced tea. Jessica glanced up quickly. Both twins recovered quickly. They glanced at each other. Then they turned to look at him, their lovely, heart-shaped faces completely blank.

Elizabeth struggled to swallow a gulp of iced tea. She wondered what her father was getting at. He couldn't know about Ben. Could he? The handsome young writer and sailor was certainly unusual. But she wouldn't dream of telling her family about him. At least, not until she had sorted out her feelings for Todd.

"Oops," she said, forcing a carefree smile. "I guess that tea went down the wrong pipe! No, I don't think I've talked with anyone unusual in the last few days—unless you mean all the interesting customers we get at the marina."

Her father scrutinized her face. "Are you sure?"

Elizabeth laughed. "Well, there *is* Mr. Jenkins, our boss. He's pretty weird. No matter how many times we tell him, he can't get our names straight. I've just resigned myself to answering to the name 'Jessica' for the rest of the summer."

Jessica raised her eyebrows. "You could do worse."

"So you haven't seen anyone doing anything strange lately?" Mr. Wakefield asked again, his eyes oddly intense on Elizabeth's face.

"Only you, Dad," Jessica pointed out. "You've got to admit, you've been acting like a total basket case all week."

Elizabeth briefly considered bringing up the scene in the storage room with the seedy-looking man. But now that she'd had time to think about it, the whole incident seemed surrealistic, almost as if she'd dreamed it. *Maybe I did dream it*, she told herself. Even if it had really happened, it probably didn't mean a thing. The poor man was probably a little unstable and just got lost.

In any case, her father was acting paranoid enough lately when it came to the twins. If she told him that a creepy, badly dressed man had bumbled into the storage room by mistake and frightened her, her father just might lock both girls in the house for the rest of the summer. And that would make it awfully hard to make good on her resolution to seek out excitement—and to see Ben again.

"What about you, Jessica?" Mr. Wakefield asked.

He won't give it up, Jessica thought. *What is with Dad this week?* She wondered if her father somehow knew about Scott, but she dismissed the idea immediately. She hadn't even told Elizabeth about him. Lila was the only person who knew about him, and her father wasn't in the habit of calling Lila for the latest gossip.

Jessica shrugged. "Sure, I've met strange people this week," she began glibly. "At the café the other day I waited on a man who started in Portugal and is sailing around the world! He said he'll be in town for a week or so to rest. The same guy was in again today. Both times he ordered a peanut-butter sandwich for breakfast! That seemed pretty geeky for someone who's sailing around the world."

"Anything else?"

Jessica thought about the glimpse she'd caught of a mysterious person in the doorway of the school auditorium.

Sure, she said to herself. *And what would I say to Dad about that? "Oh, yeah, Dad. I climbed in the window of the girls' locker room at school so I could let this twenty-year-old television guy into the building. And then, right when he was about to kiss me . . ."*

Jessica noticed that her father was drumming his fingers on the table. He stared intently from one twin to the other. "You girls aren't hiding anything from me, are you?"

"No, Dad," they answered together.

Mrs. Wakefield looked concerned. "Ned, is there something in particular you're getting at?"

"No, no, nothing at all," he insisted. "I'm just making conversation."

Jessica glanced at Elizabeth and rolled her eyes in Mr. Wakefield's direction. Elizabeth looked away quickly. Jessica studied her sister's face, curious. Elizabeth was definitely hiding something.

Jim Battaglia's voice sounded tired over the phone that night. "Calm down, Ned," he urged. "You said the package had a necklace in it that belongs to one of your girls? Are you sure it's theirs and not just something similar he bought to scare you?"

"Positive. And that note he sent—" He broke off,

shaking his head. "What have you found, Jim? Has anyone out of the ordinary been close to either of my daughters?"

"I wasn't sure if I should mention it, Ned, but Jessica—"

"What is it, Jim? Has somebody suspicious been near her?"

"No, nothing like that. This really isn't what I was hired to find out, but Jessica seems to be seeing some guy she met at the café. I'm sure it's harmless. I sneaked a look at him myself this afternoon. I was at a bit of a distance, and it was dark. But I could tell that the guy wasn't Marin."

"So who is he?"

"I can find more out if you want me to. But since it's not Marin, I don't think it's relevant to this case."

"Do you know anything at all about him?"

"A little. You know that I hired a man to keep an eye on your daughters. I didn't want him to attract their attention or Marin's. So I had him dress inconspicuously, like the kind of local color that you find around any marina."

"What does this have to do with Jessica seeing some boy I don't know?"

"My man was in the café Tuesday and overheard Jessica telling her friend Lila that the new boyfriend's name is Scott. He's an intern with a television production company."

"I wonder why she never mentioned him at home."

"Lila wondered too." Battaglia spoke as if he was

117

consulting notes. "It has something to do with Jessica knowing that her sister wouldn't approve of her dating a new guy while Ken somebody is on vacation."

Mr. Wakefield nodded. "That's Jessica all over. How old is this guy?"

"My guess is about twenty. In fact, that was Jessica's guess too."

"And when she's with this guy, is she doing anything I should be worried about?"

"Are you sure you want to know, Ned?"

Mr. Wakefield's eyebrows shot up his forehead. *"What kind of a question is that?"*

"A realistic one. As far as I know, Jessica isn't involved in anything more than the usual kinds of high school shenanigans. I'd tell you if there was anything dangerous. But I've got teenagers of my own, even if they are living with their mother for the summer. I know this from experience, Ned—sometimes it's better not to know too much about what they're up to."

"All right. I feel like a jerk anyhow, spying on my own daughters. And this guy is probably no different from the other hundred or so that she's been out with in the last year."

"Good. So you don't want me to go ahead and investigate him. That's a relief, Ned. Those kinds of cases make me feel like the scum of the earth."

"I know what you mean. But Jim, you will let me know if she's getting into, uh, anything I should know about?"

"You have my word on it, as a fellow father. But we were talking about the necklace. Do you think you can figure out which twin is missing hers?"

"Eventually. For now, I think I'll leave the necklace in my desk drawer for safekeeping."

"Let me know when you determine whether it's Elizabeth's or Jessica's. It's important."

"I bent over to pick up what I thought was a beach ball someone left behind, under a towel," Winston said at the Beach Disco that night during a break in the music. "But it wasn't a beach ball—it was a guy's head! His friends buried him up to his neck in the sand and he fell asleep!"

Todd and Maria burst into laughter. Elizabeth smiled, but she felt as if she were several thousand miles away—well, twenty-five-hundred miles, to be exact. In her mind, she was standing on the deck of the *Emily Dickinson* with the sunshine warming her shoulders as she helped Ben maneuver the boat into a lush, romantic cove of a remote Hawaiian island.

"Ah, yes," Winston said. "It was another danger-filled day in the life of a coastal enhancement engineer."

Maria slipped her arm around him. "Face it, Win. The most dangerous thing you face on the job is a bad sunburn."

"That's all you know about it. You haven't heard about the little kid who slipped a jellyfish into my swim trunks."

Todd groaned. "Ouch."

Winston leaned back in his seat and took a long swig of his orange soda. "Let me tell you, beach maintenance is about as exciting as life gets."

"That's a pretty depressing statement about life around here," Elizabeth said with a sigh. Immediately she wanted to take back her words; she hadn't intended to speak out loud. Todd glanced at her, concerned.

Winston began another story—something about a teenage girl, a bathing suit, and a dog with a Frisbee. Todd and Maria were laughing immediately. But Elizabeth was having trouble even pretending to be interested.

As exciting as life gets. That pretty much summed up the last sixteen years in Sweet Valley. Winston, Todd, and Maria were three of her favorite people. But now they seemed immature—and as boxed in as she was by the pretty suburban streets and cloudless blue skies of Sweet Valley, California. But why was she the only one who seemed to notice how little it had to offer? In its own way, Sweet Valley was a nice place to live. But *nice* wasn't exhilarating. *Nice* didn't feed her longing for something different, something both meaningful and adventurous. *Where's the romance in my life?*

She glanced at Todd, who was trying to toss pretzels into Winston's open mouth. Elizabeth sighed and turned away.

Romance . . .

Elizabeth imagined Ben in the cozy, wood-paneled cabin of his sailboat. He sat at a built-in desk, writing his novel with a fountain pen by candlelight. Outside the boat, gulls called in the night. And the lights of a tropical shoreline twinkled in the distance.

Suddenly Elizabeth was in the daydream. She stood behind Ben, almost touching him, wearing crisp navy and white. She leaned over his tousled hair to read the page he'd completed in his neat, graceful handwriting. Then his hands moved up her arms. He stood, turning to face her, and his eyes were full of love. Then he kissed her, slowly and deliciously. Under Elizabeth's feet the boat vibrated gently from the ocean's rolling swells.

A voice yanked Elizabeth off the sailboat and back to reality. "Wow! The Droids are loud tonight!" Maria yelled across the table, hands cupped in front of her mouth.

The band had returned from its break and had just started playing "Come Away with Me," the latest composition by lead singer Dana Larson.

Todd leaned toward Elizabeth and asked her to dance. Elizabeth exhaled slowly. Then she pasted a smile on her face and rose from her chair. "Sure. Why not?"

Jessica stood in the kitchen late that night, her face chilled by a blast of icy air from the freezer. The tile floor was cold and smooth under her bare feet. "Rocky road or jamocha fudge ribbon?" she asked herself aloud.

"Elizabeth?" came a deep voice from the stairs.

For a split second Jessica wondered if Mr. Jenkins was calling her. *Obviously I've been working too much,* she thought a moment later. She had gotten so used to being called Elizabeth that she wanted to reply every time someone talked to her twin. "No, Dad! It's me. Liz isn't home from the Beach Disco yet."

Ned wandered into the kitchen, his forehead wrinkled with concern. "She said she'd be home by midnight."

Jessica rolled her eyes. "I wouldn't worry if I were you. This is Elizabeth we're talking about, remember? Her idea of living it up is ordering ketchup to go with her fries. I can't believe Ms. Perfect would come home late—especially when she's out with Mr. Responsible."

"Well, they're not exactly late," her father admitted, checking his watch. "It's only ten minutes to twelve."

"See what I mean? And I bet that's Todd's car I hear pulling up outside. You want some ice cream? I can't decide between rocky road and jamocha fudge ribbon."

"No, thanks. I think I'll go to bed."

"Oh, I see. You want to pretend you weren't waiting up for her."

"I wasn't waiting up for her," he said quickly. "I, um, had some briefs to review."

"Right. And you always prowl up and down the stairs while you're going over briefs. Are you sure you don't want some ice cream?"

"I'm sure. And don't leave the freezer door open all night."

"Good night and sweet dreams to you too!"

Elizabeth entered the kitchen a minute later. "Oh, hi, Jess. I thought I saw a light on in here." She hesitated. "You didn't hear anything outside a minute ago, did you?"

Jessica shook her head. "Just Todd's car and your voices on the front step. What should I have been listening for—kissing noises?"

"No! I just thought I heard a noise from around the back of the house." She parted the curtains and glanced out the window. "But I don't see anything out there now."

Jessica shrugged. "Must have been a squirrel or something."

"I guess it must have been."

"Hey!" Jessica said suddenly, noticing the low-cut fuchsia blouse Elizabeth was wearing. "That's *my* blouse! Since when do you borrow my clothes? Especially sexy ones."

"I know," Elizabeth said with a sigh. "It's not my usual style. I figured you wouldn't mind, since you're the one who's been telling me I need more adventure in my life."

"But you didn't even ask!"

"So? You're always borrowing my things."

"OK, I can be generous. But remember this when I want to wear that funky new vest you bought. So did the blouse work?"

Elizabeth shrugged. "Not really. It seemed to catch Todd's eye at first. But then he said I didn't need to dress that way to impress him. He likes me just the way I've always been."

"He would."

Elizabeth looked as if she wasn't sure whether to take Jessica's comment as an insult or a show of support. She opted for changing the subject. "What're you doing, anyway?"

"I'm trying to decide between rocky road and jamocha fudge ribbon. Want to help?"

"I'll help eat it. But I'm too tired for a hard decision like that."

"Me too," Jessica agreed. "Let's have both."

A few minutes later the twins were sitting at the table, eating ice cream. "Except for Todd's lack of fashion sense," Jessica began, "how was your date?"

"The same as always," Elizabeth replied. "The Beach Disco doesn't change much."

"But the Droids were playing there tonight," Jessica pointed out. "I'd have gone myself, but I was too tired." *Breaking into empty school buildings can be hard work*, she thought with a chuckle.

"What's so funny?" Elizabeth asked.

"Nothing."

"Then why did you laugh?"

Jessica shrugged. "I didn't laugh."

"Yes, you did."

"Did I? I guess I was thinking about Dad," Jessica lied. "Do you know that he was down here not five minutes ago, all frantic because you weren't home yet?"

"I wish I'd been doing something exciting enough so that I wanted to stay out late." She looked away. "I'm afraid my summer of being impetuous isn't working out that way."

"I'm not so sure," Jessica said suspiciously. "You weren't very convincing at dinner tonight when you told Dad you hadn't met anyone unusual lately." Jessica's comment was a shot in the dark, but it seemed that she'd hit her target. She was sure she saw fear spring into her sister's eyes.

"Do you think he suspected anything?" Elizabeth asked.

"Dad? He's a guy, remember? That means he's got zero intuition. Your identical twin, on the other hand—"

Elizabeth's eyes went blank. "Your twin radar is picking up my wishful thinking. I only *want* something unusual to happen. You know how bored I've been."

Jessica licked a drop of jamocha fudge ribbon off her spoon. "You never told me about that mysterious break you took from work this morning. Where were you?"

"Oh, nowhere special. I was just going crazy in the café. Mr. Jenkins was ordering me around, and the customers wanted their food yesterday. I had to get outside and walk along the docks for a few minutes, that's all."

Jessica raised her eyebrows. "Then why did you look so happy when you came back to work?"

"I guess the fresh air did the trick," Elizabeth said, staring at her ice cream. "The weather was great; the sky was blue. You know how it is."

"No, I'm not sure that I do."

Elizabeth sighed and looked straight at her. "To

tell you the truth, I spent the whole morning obsessing about Todd."

"Gag me. True love can be really sickening. I've never thought of you as the mooning-around-because-you're-separated-for-eight-hours type."

"Not obsessing that way," Elizabeth explained quickly. "Just the opposite. All this talk of wanting more excitement has made me wonder if Todd and I are right for each other after all."

Jessica's mouth dropped open. "Are you serious?"

"I don't know. I still love Todd, I think. But lately I want something more."

"I can see why. He can be even more of a goody two shoes than you."

Elizabeth scowled. "That's not what I mean! It's just that sometimes he seems so small town and unworldly. I wonder if he's holding me back. Maybe I shouldn't be tied down to someone like him at this point in my life."

"That's exactly what I've been trying to tell you!" Jessica exclaimed. "You need to meet new people. So what happened on your walk on the docks that made you happy the rest of the day? Did you decide to dump Todd?"

"*No!*" Elizabeth looked shocked. "I mean—sure, I thought about it. But not really seriously. Oh, I don't know. I guess I didn't come to any decision at all. I'm more confused than ever."

Jessica crossed her arms in front of her. "You still haven't told me why you were so happy after your walk."

"Yes, I have. It was the fresh air and the sunshine. But speaking of taking breaks from work, you told me that you and Lila were going to a fashion show at three o'clock this afternoon."

Jessica gulped. Once again, she considered telling Elizabeth about Scott. But after the disastrous experience she had with Jeremy Randall, Elizabeth wouldn't approve of her dating another older man—especially behind Ken's back. *Besides, Liz is so uptight about always following rules; she'd have a fit if I told her we broke into the school.*

"We did go to a fashion show," Jessica insisted. "It was at the mall."

"Then why did Enid see Lila on the beach right around that time?"

"Enid must have just *thought* she saw Lila. Everyone looks the same when you're sitting way up in one of those lifeguard chairs with the sun in your eyes."

"Enid wasn't up in the lifeguard chair when she saw Lila. She was walking by the concession stand when Lila was getting a soda, just after three o'clock."

"Oh, that explains it! You said *three* o'clock. It turned out that I had the time wrong for the fashion show. It didn't start until later."

"Why don't I believe you?"

Jessica shrugged. "You know how rotten I am at keeping track of times. Lila had said to meet her at the mall at four, and I got mixed up and thought it was three. I don't remember what time she finally made it to the mall, but the fashion show was great.

I'm dying to buy this cute red miniskirt I saw."

Elizabeth opened her mouth as if to protest, but Jessica plunged on. This might be her only opportunity to get Elizabeth to agree to work part of a shift for her, just in case she had another chance to see Scott during the work day.

"Speaking of shopping, I may need you to cover for me at work again. Lila finally agreed that yellow isn't a good color for her. She wants me to help her pick out another new bathing suit."

"I can see why," Elizabeth said wryly. "She probably only has eight or nine to choose from. But I know the way you and Lila shop together. You won't be able to help her pick something out without buying things for yourself, too. And you can't afford to go crazy at Lisette's the way Lila can."

"I know. I should've been born rich, like Li. But I just have to have that skirt, to match my new sandals. Luckily I'll be able to buy it at the end of the week—as soon as I win the tip contest."

"No way! *I'm* going to win the tip contest. Face it, Jessica. I'm a better waitress than you any day."

Jessica tossed her hair. "You might be better than me at remembering people's orders," she admitted. "But everyone knows the most important part of customer service isn't the picky little details. It's all a matter of style. And when it comes to style, nobody stands a chance against me."

"Huh." Elizabeth looked away from her, and Jessica thought once again that her sister was hiding something. "OK, I'll consider covering for you. But only if you cover for me when I need you to," Elizabeth concluded.

"Why? What do you have to do that's more important than collecting tips?"

Elizabeth jumped up suddenly. "Did you see that?"

"Did I see what?"

"I'm not sure. Some sort of shadow outside the window."

"The Shadow knows!" Jessica sang, melodramatically but off key.

"I'm serious, Jess! And I could've sworn I heard another noise."

"You're getting as paranoid as Dad," Jessica said. "Steven was saying last week that the tree by the window needs trimming. I bet a branch just brushed against the glass."

Elizabeth glanced toward the window again. Finally she shrugged and sat down with a sigh. "I think all Dad's talk about being extra careful is putting me on edge. I'm sure there's nothing out there to be afraid of."

Chapter 10

The morning sun felt good on the back of John Marin's neck. There was nothing like ten years behind bars to make a man appreciate the simple things in life—things like the warmth of the sun, the curve of a woman's leg, and the sweetness of revenge.

Alice Wakefield certainly had a great pair of legs, he decided. He was ogling Wakefield's wife from a crouching position behind a row of large crates at the mansion Mrs. Wakefield was working on. *She ought to get herself one of those miniskirts that Jessica likes so much.* He nodded slightly, imagining.

Above Marin arched the incomplete metal frame of a greenhouse-style breakfast nook that was being created out of an old porch. The glass panes weren't set in place yet, so it had been easy to slip through the metal framework to watch her at work on the kitchen.

Mrs. Wakefield's hair gleamed gold in the sunlight

as she leaned over a crate, a young carpenter standing beside her. She carefully tore at the cardboard. "See what I mean, Frank?" she said, raising her voice to be heard over the buzz of a floor-sanding machine that was running in another part of the house. "These new kitchen cabinets are hickory, with an ivory finish. Look how light the color is. The stain on the moldings you brought is cherry. It's much too dark."

The carpenter nodded. "Yep, you're absolutely right, ma'am. I guess someone back at the shop screwed up."

Mrs. Wakefield sighed. "I really need these moldings today," she said. "I may have to fly up to Oakland in the morning to meet with the architect, and I'd like to make sure everything's in place before then."

"Don't worry. Somebody must have loaded the wrong moldings onto my truck. I'll head back there now and bring you the light-colored ones."

The carpenter left, and Mrs. Wakefield was alone. Marin couldn't help but notice how vulnerable the slender blond woman seemed as she stepped carefully across the floor, which was strewn with old plumbing fixtures and scraps of wood. Marin knew that Wakefield's wife was close to forty, but she looked at least ten years younger than that. And with her blond hair and blue eyes, she could almost be mistaken for one of her twin daughters.

Mrs. Wakefield whistled a Broadway show tune as she pulled some papers out of a portfolio. Then she sat at a makeshift table that was set up over two sawhorses. Pencil in hand, she studied the plans, glancing up now and then to compare the design on the paper with the architecture of the room around her.

Carefully Marin pulled out his Polaroid camera. He turned off the flash; luckily he wouldn't need it. Bright patches of sunlight checkered the kitchen, streaming through the greenhouse addition and the high skylight directly over his subject's head. She sat facing Marin, but she was too intent on her work to notice as he snapped several photographs. The buzz of the power sander upstairs covered the clicking of his camera.

Marin caught his breath when she raised her eyes to inspect the skylight. The sight of her bare, unprotected neck was tempting. He imagined tightening his hands around that neck, feeling the tendons under her warm, tanned skin and the vibrations of her vocal cords as she tried to scream.

No. It was too easy. Wakefield's pain would be over all too quickly. For now, Marin decided, he would concentrate on the daughters, as he'd planned. That was what he'd been leading up to all week. It was what Wakefield was expecting. Why waste all that amusing terror? After the twins were dead, there would be plenty of time for Marin to have his fun with this particular member of the Wakefield family.

Thursday night, a clean-cut young couple in polo shirts and white shorts stepped into the Marina Café. It had been a busy day, and Elizabeth was tired. But a tip was a tip. And these two looked as if they could afford a big one. So she smiled broadly and reached for two menus.

Suddenly a turquoise flash whisked between herself and the new customers.

"Wouldn't you like to sit over here by the window?" Jessica asked the couple, gesturing toward a table in her section. Both the man and the woman did a double take, looking from one identical twin to the other. Without giving them time to reply, Jessica grabbed the menus in Elizabeth's outstretched hand and led the customers to table nine.

"You jerk!" Elizabeth hissed into Jessica's ear as she passed her a minute later. "They were *my* customers! I saw them first. You're turning into a tip thief!"

Jessica smiled. "Tip thief? Well, yes, I did seat them in my section. But it had nothing to do with tips."

"Oh, sure," Elizabeth said as they walked across the room together. All day she had wished business would slow down a little. But now there were only two tables occupied. She hated to just sit around doing nothing.

Jessica grinned. "I was just providing excellent customer service, like Mr. Jenkins said. That couple really will have a better view from table nine."

"It's my own fault," Elizabeth said as they reached the counter. "I should have been faster. But I'm exhausted! What about you? Why are you so energetic?"

Jessica grabbed two bottles of mineral water.

"Because I'm looking forward to tonight."

"Why? What happens tonight?"

Jessica shrugged. "Who knows?"

Elizabeth opened her mouth to question her further, but Jessica took off for table nine with the mineral water.

Mr. Jenkins emerged from the kitchen. "Elizabeth," he said. Elizabeth had become so accustomed to being called Jessica that she almost forgot to look up. Then she realized that he really was talking to her.

"I have a job that I especially want you to take care of," he continued. Elizabeth's heart sank. She knew she didn't have the energy for one of Mr. Jenkins's special jobs. But her boss didn't seem to notice her lack of enthusiasm. "Now that the dining room isn't busy anymore, I need you to mix the special herb blend into the house salad dressing. It's all set up in the back—"

"Uh, Mr. Jenkins," Elizabeth interrupted. "I'm not Elizabeth. I'm Jessica."

"Oh!" he said, surprised. "I see. And where is your sister?"

Elizabeth pointed to table nine, where Jessica was taking orders.

"Ah. Thank you, Jessica."

Elizabeth burst into muffled laughter as Mr. Jenkins rushed toward her sister, intent on salad dressing.

"Way to go, Wakefield!" Elizabeth turned to see Jane standing near the kitchen door. The older waitress somehow managed to give Elizabeth a high five, although she was carrying a tray of sandwiches.

They watched, amused, as Jessica finished taking the order and trudged back to the storage room to make salad dressing.

"That was smooth," Jane said. "I didn't know you had it in you."

Elizabeth felt a little guilty, but she decided she could live with the guilt a lot better than she could live with mixing five gallons of salad dressing.

"It serves her right," Elizabeth decided. "Jessica just stole those two customers from me."

"All's fair in love and war. And believe me, this tip contest is war. As for love . . ."

Jane gestured with her tray, a mischievous grin on her face. Then she hurried back to the customers. Elizabeth whirled around to look where Jane had pointed. And there was Ben, sitting at the counter.

"Hi, beautiful," he said, his blue eyes crinkling at the corners.

Elizabeth grinned, feeling energetic for the first time in hours. "What'll it be? The usual?"

"Forget the iced coffee. I have a better idea. Let me show you my boat."

Elizabeth's heart skipped a beat. "You're kidding."

"Would I kid about a thing like that?"

"I can't go," Elizabeth said, checking her watch. "My shift doesn't end for another hour."

"That is a problem, isn't it? Who'll handle this standing-room-only crowd in the dining room?" He gestured around the restaurant. At table nine,

Jessica's customers sat drinking their mineral water, talking quietly. At table one, Jane was serving sandwiches to a family with three sunburned children. The other tables were empty. The fourth waitress on duty was sitting at the end of the counter, sipping a soda.

Elizabeth laughed. "I see what you mean."

"Come on, Liz. I bet you've always wished you could have known Emily Dickinson. Now's your chance. Your boss won't even miss you."

Elizabeth untied her apron. "I'll ask Jane to cover for me."

Jessica rinsed her hands in the sink behind the counter. "Yuck! I'll never eat salad again. That herb stuff we put in the house dressing smells like my brother's stinky gym socks."

Jane laughed. "At least you're off the hook for a while. Mr. Jenkins is very methodical about choosing people to mix salad dressing. Your turn won't come again for at least a week."

Jessica glanced around the dining room. In one corner the preppie people were eating their quiche. And at one of Jane's tables three noisy children were breaking potato chips into tiny slivers and grinding them into the carpeting. "I'm sure glad those kids are in your section and not mine! But thanks for taking care of table nine."

"If you want to show your gratitude by splitting the tip—"

"I'm not *that* grateful."

Jane shrugged. "Sorry to say it, honey, but it's not gonna make a bit of difference in the tip contest. I've got the prize in the bag."

"I know you have a lot more experience, but I haven't been doing too badly," Jessica said. "One guy today gave me twenty-five percent!"

"Oh, yeah? And what did he order? Lobster, with appetizers and dessert?"

Jessica shook her head sadly. "No, just a peanut-butter sandwich, like he does every morning."

"Cheer up. You'll do OK in the long run. You do have a couple of advantages over me when it comes to tips," Jane admitted. "Being sixteen and blond gives you and your sister an edge in this job. But I've won the tip contest every year I've been here. And it'll be the same this year. Wait and see."

"Speaking of my sister, where's Liz?"

"She cut out early," Jane said with an amused look. "Something came up."

"Like what?"

Jane shrugged. "What do I know? I only work here."

"Out with it, Jane. My sister's hiding something, and I want to know what it is."

"You'll have to ask her."

Jessica sighed. "It's probably not worth the trouble. After all, this is Elizabeth we're talking about. I bet she just wanted to see her boyfriend."

Jane nodded. "You don't sound as if you approve."

"Todd's a hunk, but he's a boring hunk. I keep telling Liz she needs more excitement in her life."

Jane smiled enigmatically.

"Is there something you're not telling me?"

"Just that she said she'd be back around the end of the shift. If you're not here, she'll assume you caught a ride."

"With my luck I'll be stranded here, while Liz and Todd are out reading Shakespeare or something."

"I wouldn't know about that," Jane said. "But I do know I have to start the inventory of the storage room. Mr. Jenkins is out, and the other waitress went home. Can you handle things in the dining room for a while?"

"Most of it," Jessica said. "But the kids with the potato chips are your problem!"

"OK, OK. I'll be back to check on them in ten minutes. Just give me a shout if they start hurling dishes."

Jessica poured herself an iced tea and sat at the counter. She knew she should be finding something useful and waitress-y to do, like sweeping the floor or wrapping silverware into neat little napkin bundles. But what was the point, when there was no boss around to see her doing it? Sweeping the floor wouldn't make anyone leave her a bigger tip.

A few minutes later the bell on the door jingled. Todd and Winston sauntered into the restaurant, looking considerably more tanned than either of them had been at the beginning of the week.

"Hi, Jessica!" Todd greeted her. "I'm looking for Elizabeth. Is she in the back?"

Jessica's mind raced. So Jane had been lying to

cover for Elizabeth, who was definitely not out with her boyfriend. *Unless Elizabeth has another boyfriend on the side!* It seemed absurd. *Elizabeth?* On the other hand, her twin had seemed fed up with Todd lately, and she claimed she was looking for adventure.

Jessica wondered wickedly if she should say just enough to get Todd worried, to pay Elizabeth back for keeping secrets from her. After a few moments Jessica decided against it. After all, she was keeping secrets too. If Elizabeth learned about Scott, Jessica definitely didn't want her blabbing the truth to everyone.

"No, Todd. Liz isn't in the back. In fact, she isn't here at all. We weren't busy, so Mr. Jenkins told her she could take off an hour early," she lied. "She was looking pretty ragged."

"Is she all right, Jess?" Todd asked, settling himself onto one of the vinyl-covered stools at the counter. Winston took the one next to him. "She's seemed distracted this week."

"She's fine," Jessica assured him. "She's just going through some kind of phase."

"Well, I've thought of a way to cheer her up," Todd said. "We have a date to go out Saturday night, but we hadn't decided exactly where to go. I thought of something I think she'll like a lot. I'm planning to surprise her."

"Oh, yeah?" Jessica asked. "Where are you going to take her? A fancy, sophisticated restaurant?"

Todd shook his head. "Nah. Elizabeth isn't into

that kind of stuff. But she said she wanted to do something different. You know, it's been at least six months since we went bowling!"

Jessica tried not to look too horrified. "*Bowling?* I don't think that's what Elizabeth meant by different."

"I know. That's the beauty of it. It's completely unexpected!"

Winston nodded. "I think it's a great idea. Maybe I should see if Maria wants to come along, and we can join you."

Jessica sighed. "Lucky Maria."

"I don't think so, Win," Todd said. "I want this to be just me and Liz—you know, a really special evening."

Jessica suddenly understood exactly what Elizabeth meant about wanting to meet new people.

"But Jessica, you still haven't said where Elizabeth went," Todd remembered after Jessica had taken their order and was pouring a root beer and an orange soda. "Are you sure she's OK?"

"She's just tired. It's been a hectic day here, believe it or not. Liz thought some fresh air would wake her up. She said she was going to take a walk along the docks and look at the boats."

Todd looked thoughtful. "Maybe I should run out and try to catch her."

Jessica didn't know where Elizabeth was or what she was doing. But if Todd wasn't supposed to find her, it was probably safest for him to stay in the café. "Actually, Todd, I could be wrong about that. She might have said she was going to walk along the beach. I don't remember for sure."

"Synchronize watches!" Winston ordered. "Our mission, if we choose to accept it, is to locate one missing blond waitress. You check the docks, Wilkins, and I'll check the beach. After all, I am a certified coastal enhancement engineer."

Jessica laughed. "You mean beach custodian."

"You wound me."

"No, but somebody should."

"It won't do much good to charge around searching for Liz," Jessica told Todd. "She could have gone anywhere. Besides, she said she'd be back around five o'clock. Why don't you stay here, drink your sodas, and maybe order a snack? I could use another good tip before I get off today."

"Actually, Jessica, I've got a tip for you right now," Winston told her.

"Really?"

"Sure. Are you ready?" He cupped his hand around his mouth and spoke toward her ear in a stage whisper. "Try putting on a clean apron."

"Ha ha. Very funny. Now I'm getting advice on my looks from a guy whose nose is pink and peeling. That's pretty gross."

"Injuries sustained in the line of duty, Jess. No sacrifice is too great for a—"

Jessica and Todd droned in together. "A coastal enhancement engineer!"

"I can't believe it!" Elizabeth exclaimed, gesturing around the wood-paneled cabin of Ben's sailboat. "This is exactly how I pictured it!"

"It's small, but it's home," Ben said.

Elizabeth touched the dark, glossy wood of Ben's built-in desk. "Is this where you write your novel?"

"This is the place," he said, nodding.

Elizabeth scanned the titles of the leather-bound books that lined the walls. "Coleridge's 'Rime of the Ancient Mariner'!" she said. "That's one of my favorite poems. And here are two volumes of Emily Dickinson. And *Moby Dick*. I love that book!"

"And these over here are all Russian," Ben told her. "Tolstoy, Dostoyevsky, and the others. I like a big, complicated plot I can really sink my teeth into. Especially for the long, quiet voyages by myself."

"You have some of my very favorite authors here," Elizabeth said. "It's amazing how we like to read all the same things."

Ben led her up the narrow staircase to the deck of the boat. "I just had a thought. Do you want to go for a sail?"

Elizabeth opened her mouth to say no. After all, Ben was still a stranger—even if he did like poetry. And she had to be back at the café in time to give Jessica a ride home.

"I won't take no for an answer," Ben said. "We'll just go for a quick spin—you'll be back in no time."

Elizabeth hesitated.

"Come on, Liz. It'll be an adventure."

At the word *adventure,* Elizabeth envisioned herself sailing into the picture-postcard harbor she'd been imagining.

"I'd love to go for a sail," she heard herself saying. *And why not?*

A half hour later, she scanned the harbor of her hometown from a quarter mile offshore. "Sweet Valley looks absolutely beautiful from out here!" she marveled. "It's like some Mediterranean village."

"It is lovely," Ben said. But he was staring into her eyes, not at the coastline. Elizabeth felt her face redden.

She turned away from the helm and examined the network of ropes that kept the sails in place. "This is a much bigger boat than the ones I've sailed," she said. "How do you manage it on your own?"

"Oh, it's not too difficult once you get the hang of it," Ben said. "And it's worth every bit of trouble. There's nothing like sailing out on the open sea, with nothing but—"

He grinned, and Elizabeth knew just what he was thinking. She finished the line from 'Rime of the Ancient Mariner' with him. "'Water, water everywhere!'"

"You really do read Coleridge!" Elizabeth said. "I thought maybe you just kept the book around to convince poetry lovers that you're trustworthy."

"Did it work?"

"I'm not sure yet," Elizabeth answered truthfully. "I hope so."

She gazed back at Ben as he leaned over to check an instrument. If anything, he was better looking when he was on his boat. He seemed relaxed and comfortable behind the helm. Even standing still he seemed to be in motion, more alive than anyone she normally saw in sleepy little Sweet Valley. Ben's tanned face looked alert and vital, and his eyes were bluer than the sky.

Those eyes met her own, and he smiled. "You look exactly like the goddess of the sea," he said.

"You've got to be kidding. With my hair blowing all over the place?"

"Especially with your hair blowing around you," he said, his eyes holding hers.

Elizabeth took a few steps closer. She felt mesmerized, imagining what it would feel like to have his arms around her and his lips against hers. *No!* She wouldn't give in to temptation. She had to think of Todd. As long as she and Ben could keep up a conversation, she could stay in control enough not to do anything she might regret.

"Do you often have guests on board?" she asked.

Ben shook his head slowly. "You're the first," he whispered.

Elizabeth smiled dreamily. Again she thought how easy it would be to lose herself in his dark blue eyes. Then she thought of Todd's brown eyes. Elizabeth shook her head and tore her glance away. She was still dating Todd, no matter how bored she was with him lately. And even looking at Ben, this close up, felt dangerous.

Instead Elizabeth strolled to the bow of the boat and let the wind and salt spray wash over her. She took a deep breath. The salt air rushed through her body—cold, fresh, and exhilarating. Elizabeth felt as if she'd been in prison for sixteen years and had just been set free.

"I should have had an adventure a long, long time ago," she said, her voice whipped away instantly by the wind. "Today is the start of a whole new life."

Chapter 11

A block away from the Wakefield house, John Marin chuckled as he watched Mr. Wakefield disappear through the front door on Thursday evening. "That's right, Counselor," he said with a sneer. "The mailbox is empty today. Let's see what that does to your peace of mind."

Marin set the binoculars down on the seat beside him and started up the car. His plan was working better than he had anticipated. Ned Wakefield was out of his mind with fright. And the twins had no idea who he was or how dangerous he could be. He'd been close to both of them several times now—at the restaurant, on his boat, and in the dark auditorium of the empty school building. But he'd used a tremendous amount of self-restraint. If there was one thing he'd learned about in ten years of prison, it was waiting.

He flipped down the window visor with

Wakefield's photograph on it. "The wait won't be for much longer, Ned," he said. "In fact, I've chosen my first twin. As soon as you're as terrified as I want you to be, I'll make my move. But first, how about one more package?"

From the pocket of his jacket he pulled the snapshots he had taken of Mrs. Wakefield at the remodeling site that morning. "Ned, you're a lucky man," he said, smacking his lips. "I had a pretty one of my own once. But she didn't want to wait through a twenty-five-year sentence." He narrowed his eyes. "By the time I finish with your family, you'll know what it's like to be alone too."

He picked out his favorite snapshot—a stray breeze had lifted Mrs. Wakefield's skirt a few inches above her knees. He smiled at the photograph. "Here's one to make hubby cringe, Alice. I'll write a little love note to Ned on the back of this pretty picture." He looked at her legs again. "On second thought, maybe I'll keep that particular photo for myself." Marin shoved the picture back into his pocket and pulled out his second-favorite shot instead. He scrawled a few words on the back, then sealed it in an envelope.

Soon Wakefield might have the police watching his house. So dropping the envelope in the mailbox directly was out of the question. Instead he would mail it from the post office a few blocks away. It would still arrive by Friday.

Marin rubbed his hands together, anticipating his prey's horrified reaction. He could hardly wait.

* * *

Mr. Wakefield stalked through the house that evening. There was no mail that day from Marin. Although Mr. Wakefield was glad to be spared further evidence of Marin's proximity to his daughters, the absence of a visible threat set his nerves even more on edge. The silence seemed like the calm before the storm.

Something else had upset him almost as soon as he'd walked into the house. Prince Albert's brown studded collar was missing, though Mr. Wakefield was sure the dog had been wearing it that morning. The implication hit him like a bullet in the chest. Somebody had taken off the dog's collar within the last eight hours. But Prince Albert had been locked in the house all day, alone.

At least, the dog was supposed to have been alone.

Maybe it wasn't Marin, he told himself. It was possible that the collar had slipped off by itself. He'd probably find the strip of leather lying in one of Prince Albert's favorite spots.

But the collar wasn't under the kitchen table or near the living room couch. In fact, it didn't seem to be anywhere downstairs. Upstairs, Mr. Wakefield cautiously reached for the door of Jessica's room. Prince Albert was Jessica's dog more than anyone's, and he seemed to have a special affection for her disorderly bedroom.

Snooping in his daughters' bedrooms wasn't Mr. Wakefield's usual style. He swallowed his guilt and slowly pushed open the door, feeling a sense of rising panic. He almost expected to see Marin sitting on Jessica's unmade bed, a leer on his face.

The room was empty—if any room that was perpetually covered in mounds of laundry, compact disks, and notebooks could be called empty.

If it were anyone else's bedroom, Mr. Wakefield would have been horrified at the sight, convinced that Marin had ransacked the place. But messiness came as naturally to Jessica as flirting with boys and showing up everywhere a half hour late. It was oddly comforting to stand in her room and know that it was the same as ever. Untouched.

"What's that?" he cried suddenly. Prince Albert's dog collar lay neatly in the middle of Jessica's pillow, and a piece of crumpled lavender notebook paper was attached to it. The writing was in Marin's messy scrawl.

You ought to do something about the lock on the kitchen door, Ned, the note said. *You don't want strangers in the house.*

Mr. Wakefield jumped when he heard a voice behind him.

"Hi, honey," Mrs. Wakefield said from the doorway, a puzzled look on her face. "Is there something wrong in here?"

Mr. Wakefield shoved the note into his pocket. "No, nothing at all," he said quickly. "Prince Albert's collar was missing, and I just found it here, by Jessica's bed. I guess it slipped off him during the day."

"That's strange. I didn't know that collar was loose."

Mr. Wakefield kissed his wife, wondering if the time had come to tell her about John Marin. The situation was becoming more and more serious; she had a right to know what was happening. He'd have to tell her all about it after dinner that night.

"How was your day?" he asked as they walked downstairs toward the kitchen. "Is your mansion coming together all right?"

Mrs. Wakefield laughed. "I wish it *was* my mansion! Actually, it's looking great. Except for the finishing work, the new kitchen is almost ready. And speaking of kitchens, how's pasta and pesto sound for dinner? I picked up the sauce on my way home."

"Great," he said, pulling lettuce and tomatoes out of the refrigerator. "I'll make a salad."

"Did you hear from Steven today?"

Mr. Wakefield nodded. "He called the office. Amanda's really pleased with the work he's doing. She wants him to stay at least another week."

"But surely he can come home for the weekend? I thought he was planning to see Billie."

Mr. Wakefield grinned sheepishly. "Actually, I bought him a plane ticket so that Billie could fly up to visit him. It sounded as if they could both use a mini-vacation." In truth, it had seemed like the best way to ensure Steven's safety for the next few days.

"That was sweet of you, Ned. I had no idea you were planning that."

"It was sort of a spur-of-the-moment thing," he lied.

"Well, I have some plans for the weekend that I wanted to tell you about."

"Oh?"

"It just came up today, Ned. The architect in Oakland has some revisions on the plans for the master bedroom, and he wants to go over them in detail. He can't make it down this weekend, so he's asked me to fly up to the bay area for the weekend. I called the airport, and there's a flight at seven in the morning."

Mr. Wakefield tried to keep the relief out of his voice. "So you'll be gone all weekend?"

"Well, I was hoping both of us could go."

"Both of us?" He looked down at the counter, his mind racing.

"Sure. Why don't you come with me? You've been stressed out all week, and we haven't had much of a chance to talk. We can get a hotel room in San Francisco, somewhere romantic. I'll have to work a few hours on Saturday, but besides that, it'll be our own little getaway!"

"That sounds great, Alice. But I don't think we should leave the girls all by themselves."

"They're sixteen years old, Ned. They've been by themselves for a weekend plenty of times! Besides, they've both been working so hard all week that they'll be too tired to get into trouble."

Mr. Wakefield smiled weakly. "You're right, of course. But I still don't feel good about leaving them."

"Sweetheart, they'll be fine."

"It's not just the girls," Mr. Wakefield continued. "It's this wrongful-dismissal suit we're working on. Oilcam is a heavy hitter—they've got us up against the best lawyers on the West Coast. I'm going to have to put in a lot of homework on this one." Mr. Wakefield took his wife's hand. "But I'll tell you what, Alice. In a few weeks, when, uh, *things* have settled down a little, the two of us will go on a romantic weekend together—Tahoe, Napa Valley, Palm Springs, Catalina, anywhere you want."

"That sounds wonderful," she said, ruffling his hair.

Mr. Wakefield rinsed off his hands. "Now, if you've got things under control here in the kitchen, I've got a phone call to make before dinner. I'll be in my den."

A few minutes later Mr. Wakefield sat at his desk, straining his ears for the sound of the girls' Jeep in the driveway. He'd feel a lot better when he saw that they were safely home from another day at work.

"First the Christmas card, then the necklace, and now the dog's collar," he muttered. "Three times constitutes a pattern. Cabrini has to agree that we now have probable cause to pick up Marin, if we can find him."

He slid the elf photograph out of an envelope and tossed it onto the desk, next to the lavender slip of paper he'd found with the dog collar. Then he slid open the top desk drawer, where he'd left the gold lavaliere.

The necklace was gone.

Mr. Wakefield used his fist to pound the desk drawer shut. Nobody in his family would go near his desk drawers. Marin must have taken the necklace back. *He's toying with me again.*

Through the door he heard the clatter of plates as his wife set the table. He sighed, thinking of her. She was still as beautiful as the day they were married, and she'd hardly aged at all in the ten years since Marin's trial. It was comforting to know that she would be safely out of town for the weekend. It also meant that he didn't need to say anything to her about Marin. She'd refuse to go to Oakland if she thought her daughters were in danger.

And they were definitely in danger. Mr. Wakefield had assumed that the girls needed protection only when they were away from the house. But obviously, Marin could get into the Wakefields' home anytime he wanted.

"You don't want strangers in the house," he read aloud from the lavender-colored note. He shuddered, then picked up the telephone and dialed Detective Cabrini at the Sweet Valley police department.

"Tony? It's Ned Wakefield." He waved the note in front of the receiver, as if the police detective could see it through the phone. "This Marin thing has gotten out of hand. I think I've got enough evidence now for you to make a case."

"What have you got?"

"Three threatening notes, and evidence that he's been inside my house at least three times. And I want to report a missing necklace as well. If you can't get him on anything else, maybe you can at least hold him for being in possession of stolen property, if you can find the necklace on him."

"We still haven't been able to locate the guy, Ned. We suspect he's been using several aliases since he left prison. It's making him hard to track."

"Are you saying you can't help me?"

"No, that's not what I'm saying at all," the detective answered quickly. "I think we can prove now that you're being harassed, if nothing else. I can make a case for getting your family some protection. What exactly are you asking for?"

"I want you to assign someone to watch my house, twenty-four hours a day."

"Done," the detective agreed. "I'll have at least one squad car outside your house, starting first thing in the morning. The next time Marin shows up there, he can kiss his freedom good-bye."

"Let me guess," Elizabeth said to her first customer of the day on Friday morning, "I bet you'll have a peanut-butter-and-jelly sandwich and a Diet Coke."

"You remembered," said the man, who was dressed like a yachtsman in a movie.

"It's a memorable order, for first thing in the morning," Elizabeth said, writing it on her pad. "So how much longer are you staying in Sweet Valley—I mean, before you continue your around-the-world sail?"

"I haven't decided yet," the man said. "I haven't stopped anywhere for more than a day or two since I left Portugal. And there certainly seems to be a lot to see here."

"Have you done much sightseeing since you've been in town?"

"Mostly just people watching," he answered. "It's one of my favorite hobbies."

"Well, the marina is certainly a good place for that," Elizabeth said.

"You said it!" He smiled, but something about his expression made Elizabeth uneasy. She wasn't sure why, but this man, with his epaulets and brass buttons, seemed insincere. "For example," he continued, nodding toward Jessica's section. "Take that guy sitting in the far corner, the one with the hat that covers half his face."

Elizabeth shrugged. "What about him?"

"He looks so out of place that I find myself curious. I think I saw him fishing on the docks recently. And wasn't he in here a few days ago? Now I notice that he seems to be watching you—and your twin sister. Is he a friend of yours?"

Again Elizabeth felt uneasy. The yachtsman seemed to be trying hard to appear casual about his questions, but there was a real intensity in his brown eyes. Besides, she wasn't sure if "providing excellent customer service" included gossiping with one customer about another. It didn't feel ethical, somehow. Still, she had to be polite.

"Oh, no! He's not a friend. I mean, I've waited

on him once or twice. He's been in several times this week. But I've never really met him. In fact, he hardly ever says a word, beyond placing his order."

"So you don't know anything about him?"

"Nothing," Elizabeth said.

"Do you have any idea why he would pay so much attention to you and your sister?"

Elizabeth shook her head. "None at all. One of the other waitresses says he must like blondes. Well, if that's all for now, I should get back to the kitchen. I'll bring your sandwich right out."

Elizabeth ran into Jessica in the kitchen a few minutes later. "Jess, you know that customer who looks like a yachtsman, only more so?"

"Sure, the peanut-butter man from Portugal. I notice he sat in your section today instead of mine. The dirtbag probably scared him straight to the far side of the restaurant. I never get any customers when that creep is sitting in my section."

"Has the peanut-butter guy ever said anything that seemed weird to you?" Elizabeth asked as she put two slices of bread on a plate.

Jessica shrugged. "Ordering a peanut-butter sandwich and a soda the first thing in the morning isn't exactly normal."

"I mean besides that."

"Is there something in particular you had in mind? Because if you're just making conversation, I'd really like to take this plate of eggs out to El Creepo, so that he'll eat fast and get away from my tables.

Tomorrow's the last day of the tip contest. I can't afford to lose any more business."

"Never mind," Elizabeth said helplessly. "I was just wondering."

With trembling fingers, Mr. Wakefield tore open the envelope he'd found in the mailbox Friday afternoon. A Polaroid photograph fluttered to the coffee table, facedown.

She's awfully pretty, read Marin's handwriting on the back. *But it's the girls I'm interested in.*

A sense of unreality washed over Mr. Wakefield. He couldn't believe this was happening to his family.

He felt as if his hand was moving in slow motion as he turned over the photograph. His heart stopped when he saw the picture of Mrs. Wakefield, standing in the center of an unfinished kitchen, stacks of tiles at her feet. Thoughtfully she gazed at a blueprint she held in her hands. There must have been a skylight in the ceiling directly above her: soft, warm light shone down on her, highlighting her golden hair.

Mr. Wakefield leaned forward heavily, resting his forehead in his hands. Mrs. Wakefield had left for Oakland—she was safe. But the girls were still here. And so was Marin.

"I don't know how much more of this I can take," he whispered.

Jessica glanced at Scott's profile as he drove them to Miller's Point that night. The night was a little breezy, so the top of the Miata was up. But the warmth she was feeling had nothing to do with the temperature inside the car. The thought of Scott's gorgeous smile and the memory of their interrupted kiss in the school auditorium made her tingle all over. She was looking forward to being somewhere private with him.

"Here's the turn," she murmured. They had reached the road that dead-ended in a wide clearing at the top of a cliff. "And *this* is Miller's Point."

Scott parked in a secluded spot under a pine tree. "So this is where the high school kids go when they want to be alone," he said, turning off the engine.

"See how bright the stars look from up here?" Jessica said, breathlessly. "You can hardly tell where they end and the lights of the valley begin."

"It's beautiful." He brushed a strand of hair away from her face. "I'm sure we'll find a way to use this place in the plot of the miniseries. It seems like a natural place to bring a beautiful girl."

"Then it should be a good spot to, um, do some more research for your miniseries."

Scott flashed her a smile that melted her insides. "That's me," he said softly, "a tireless researcher."

Scott looked into her eyes, and Jessica forgot everything but him. His hand felt warm against the side of her face.

"I have something for you," he said. Jessica was sure he was about to kiss her. Instead he pulled a box from his jacket pocket and handed it to her.

Jessica gasped. "Oh, Scott, a necklace! It's beautiful!" She held up a gold necklace that looked like a long tennis bracelet. Tiny, multicolored gemstones twinkled in the light from the dashboard.

"Not as beautiful as you are. I wanted to thank you for being such a wonderful tour guide."

Scott's arms reached around her shoulders, and Jessica felt delicious heat spreading through her from every point where his skin brushed against her. Slowly his warm lips touched hers. Jessica wrapped her arms around him and pulled him close, feeling a chill of excitement run through her entire body.

Then she screamed.

Chapter 12

Jessica couldn't stop screaming.

"Jess, what's wrong?" Scott asked. "What is it?"

"A face! In the rearview mirror! There was a man out there, looking in at us!" she yelled.

Scott whirled in his seat. "I see him running into the trees! Stay here, Jessica! Lock the doors until I get back."

"Scott, no!"

But Scott was gone, chasing the man into the woods. Jessica locked the doors and hunched over in the front seat, hugging herself and waiting for him to return.

What if he doesn't come back? she asked herself. *What if that awful man hurts him?*

Suddenly she realized just who the man was. It was the creepy guy from the docks, the one who kept coming into the café and following the twins around the dining room with his eyes. *Well, maybe not with his eyes,* she corrected herself. Until tonight, his eyes had always been hidden behind his hat. But it had to be him. It just had to be.

An old movie was on television—a suspenseful thriller that Elizabeth normally would have enjoyed. But even though Gregory Peck had the starring role, she couldn't keep her mind on the screen. She kept thinking of Ben on the deck of the *Emily Dickinson,* with the wind blowing through his light brown hair. She loved the old version of *Cape Fear.* But watching a movie at home with her father wasn't her idea of the adventurous life.

Apparently Elizabeth wasn't the only one who was too preoccupied to pay attention to the television. For someone who was sitting in an easy chair, her father looked curiously ill at ease as she handed him a bowl of popcorn.

"You know, Liz, it's nice spending the evening at home together," he said. His words made the evening warm and cozy, but his tense posture told a different story. "I appreciate the fact that you stayed home on a Friday night to keep your poor old dad company while your mother's in Oakland. It was nice of Todd to let me borrow you for the evening."

"Todd couldn't go out tonight anyway," Elizabeth explained. She wished she hadn't felt so relieved when Todd broke the news to her earlier that day. "His parents asked him to stay home tonight. They're entertaining a client who brought his teenage son along."

"Did anything interesting happen at the marina today?"

Normally Elizabeth and her father felt perfectly comfortable together. Tonight the conversation seemed forced. But Mr. Wakefield obviously needed a distraction from his own thoughts. And, Elizabeth had to admit, so did she.

"Enid told me there was a report of a shark sighting a little farther down the coast," Elizabeth began in a chatty voice. She absentmindedly twirled her gold lavaliere necklace in her fingers. "They closed a marina a few miles down. But the shark was too far away for an alert at Sweet Valley's beaches. It was probably a false alarm anyway. We haven't had a shark near here in ages."

"You never know about sharks," Ned said softly. "They can turn up anywhere, when you least expect it." He sounded as if he were talking to himself. "It's too bad your sister couldn't be with us this evening. I don't get a chance to spend enough time with you girls."

Elizabeth forced a laugh. "You know how she and Lila are! It's like a disease. They're physically incapable of staying home on a Friday night."

"So Jessica's with Lila?" Ned asked, as if he didn't think it was true. "Do you know where she and, uh, *Lila* were planning on going tonight?" He interrupted himself in a louder voice. *"Elizabeth, what's in your hand?"*

"Popcorn. Cheddar cheese flavor." She held out the bowl.

"The other hand!"

Elizabeth looked down to see that she was still fidgeting with her gold lavaliere. "My necklace. It's the one you and Mom bought me and Jessica for our sixteenth birthday. Why?"

He leaned forward in his chair. "Have you been wearing that necklace all week long? You haven't taken it off at all, right? Not even once?"

"No. I've even showered with it on. Dad, what's going on? What's the big deal about my necklace?"

"Nothing," he said with a sigh, leaning back into the cushions of his easy chair. "I just found one of them in the house a couple days ago and forgot to mention it. I was wondering if it was yours or Jessica's."

"It must be Jessica's. Do you want me to give it to her?"

"No! I mean, I don't have it with me right now. I, uh, think I left it in my den. I'll give it to her myself."

"Are you sure you're all right, Dad?"

"I'm fine," he said with a tight smile. "Everything's fine. But Liz, you never told me if you know where Jessica is tonight."

"I think she said something about the Beach Disco. The Droids are there through the weekend."

The phone rang, and they both jumped.

"I'll get it!" Elizabeth and Mr. Wakefield said together. But Elizabeth was faster. She raced into the living room, leaving her father sitting on the edge of his chair, a look of near panic in his eyes. Elizabeth prayed that it would be Ben's voice on the other end of the line. Her father was so jumpy; after a few minutes of talking with him, she felt as if she'd just ridden a roller coaster. Ben's soothing voice and easy conversation would be welcome relief.

Of course, Elizabeth reminded herself, she had no reason to expect that it would be Ben on the phone. In fact, it couldn't be Ben. He didn't even have her phone number.

"Elizabeth, is Jessica there?" Lila spoke in the formal tone of voice she reserved for people she wasn't particularly close to.

Elizabeth stared at the telephone receiver. "On a Friday night? Are you kidding? I thought she was out with you."

As surprised as she was, Elizabeth remembered to keep her voice low so that her father wouldn't hear her from the family room. Whatever game her sister was playing, the least Elizabeth could do was cover for her until she knew more.

Lila sighed. "Jessica was supposed to meet Amy and me at my house so we could drive together to the Beach Disco. We've been waiting for an hour for her to show up!"

"Oh, gosh!" Elizabeth said as realization hit. "I don't know why I didn't see it before!"

"Elizabeth, are you in the same conversation that I'm in?"

"Lila, it all makes sense now! Jessica's been slipping out of the café for unexplained breaks. She leaves work hours early without saying why. And now she's out for the evening, supposedly with you, but you don't know where she is."

"What's your point?"

"The point is that I'm an idiot for not seeing it sooner. This is how Jessica always acts when she's seeing some new guy and doesn't want me to know about it. Level with me, Lila. Is my sister dating somebody else while Ken's away?"

"Now whyever would you think that?"

"Come off it, Lila. We both know Jessica. And I can tell from your voice that you know exactly what I'm talking about."

"Me? I certainly don't know what you mean."

"Yes, you do. Tonight I bet Jessica finagled a date at the last minute, after you'd made plans together. And then she forgot to mention it to you. It's just like her to do something like that. Who's she seeing, Lila?"

"How am I supposed to know who your sister is dating? You're the identical twin, not me. Besides, if I did know—and if it was supposed to be a secret—what kind of friend would I be if I told?"

"We both know Jessica couldn't keep a secret if her life depended on it."

"That's a blinding flash of the obvious."

Elizabeth scowled. "Jessica wouldn't have told me about this guy if she thought I'd disapprove of her seeing someone behind Ken's back. But she would tell you."

"Well, she didn't tell me where she is tonight."

"OK. But I'm right, aren't I? My sister is dating somebody."

"You didn't hear it from me."

After a few more minutes Elizabeth was satisfied that she wasn't going to coax any more information out of Lila. She was a little hurt that her twin sister hadn't confided in her about this new boyfriend, whoever he was. On the other hand, Elizabeth hadn't told Jessica about Ben, either.

"Who was that on the phone?" her father asked as Elizabeth bounded back into the family room a minute later.

"It was Enid," Elizabeth lied. "We were just catching up on the latest gossip. She was telling me again about the shark."

"Did you learn anything interesting?"

"No, just the same old news," Elizabeth said, twirling her necklace again.

At the touch of the gold lavaliere, Elizabeth suddenly felt afraid for her sister. There was no rational reason for her fear. But as identical twins, Elizabeth and Jessica shared a particularly close relationship. And at times one or the other had felt as if she were picking up on the other's emotions, even over a distance. Now a shiver skated down Elizabeth's spine. Wherever her sister was, Elizabeth was suddenly sure of what Jessica was feeling—*terror*.

Tears were running down Jessica's face as she huddled in the front seat of Scott's car. Scott had been gone for an awfully long time, and she was petrified that something had happened to him.

Suddenly a dark figure appeared outside the door. Jessica stifled a scream.

Then she laughed with giddy relief. She fumbled to open the door lock and Scott slid into the driver's seat, panting.

"Scott, what happened? Did you catch him? Did he hurt you? Oh, gosh! That's blood on your hand."

"I'm OK," Scott said between gasps. "My hand's fine. I guess I scraped it against some thornbushes. But I didn't catch the guy. I chased him a long way into the woods. Then I lost him in the trees."

"It was the man from the marina!" Jessica insisted.

Scott's eyes widened. "What man?"

"There's a scruffy guy who hangs around the docks a lot. Sometimes he comes into the café. He watches me." She shuddered. "I always thought he was scary."

Scott turned to her, his eyes blazing. "Are you sure it was him? Think hard, Jessica. Did you get a good look at him?"

"No. I could see through the window that he had brown eyes and needed a shave. But I'm not sure I'd recognize him again."

"You'd recognize him from the marina, wouldn't you?"

"Maybe not," Jessica admitted. "I've never gotten a good look at his face. But it has to be him, Scott! Who else could it be?"

"All I know is that the guy I was chasing was wearing a big coat. And he was holding something soft in his hand. A hat, I think."

"Yes! Yes! He always wears a hat at the marina! That's why I couldn't see his eyes—until tonight, when he took it off. Should we go to the police?"

Scott shrugged. "We can if you want to. But looking in a car window is hardly a crime. I doubt the police would take it seriously. They'd probably assume he was some thrill-seeking Peeping Tom."

Jessica sank back into the leather seat cushion with a sigh. "You're right. Besides, if my father hears about this, he'll chain me to the house until I'm twenty-five. He's incredibly paranoid lately."

Scott smiled. "It looks like tonight he might have had a reason to be. I'm sorry our date got ruined, Jess. But I think you'd better let me take you home. You look pretty rattled."

Jessica sighed. "I am rattled. But Scott, I don't want to wreck your evening too."

"It's not your fault. Besides, I was supposed to meet a guy down at the marina later tonight to give him a couple of things."

"What guy?"

"Just a guy I met last weekend. He's teaching me about the seedier side of town." Scott grinned. "Every television drama has to have its scenes of squalor, you know. I'll just drop you off at home, and then meet him a little earlier than I'd planned."

"It doesn't sound like a fun way to spend a Friday night."

"No, but it's all in the line of duty. Of course I'd rather spend the rest of the evening with you, looking at the stars. But there will be other starlit nights. And the moon is just about full now; it'll be even better in a day or two. Let's plan to do this again in a couple of days—minus the high-speed chase into the woods."

Jessica smiled. "OK. I'll take a rain check."

"I'm counting on it."

Jessica was still a little breathless with fright, but suddenly she laughed. "My dad will have a heart attack when I show up before eleven o'clock on a Friday night! He won't know whether to jump for joy or interrogate me for two hours."

"I'm sure your father will be very glad to have you at home, safe and sound."

Mr. Wakefield chewed his left thumbnail, thinking of the stolen necklace. From what Elizabeth had said, it was clear that the necklace belonged to Jessica.

Marin was close enough to Jessica to take that necklace from around her neck! Mr. Wakefield couldn't keep the thought out of his mind, even with the television blaring in front of him.

It didn't make sense. Mr. Wakefield could think of no logical reason for Marin to steal a necklace, send it to him, and then steal it back again.

Suddenly he froze. "What was that noise?"

"What noise?" Elizabeth asked.

"Outside the house!" *Did Marin have the gall to waltz in while he was at home?*

"Hello! I'm home!" Jessica called from the foyer.

Mr. Wakefield realized he hadn't exhaled in almost a minute.

"Hey, Dad!" Jessica said in a cheerful voice as she

leaned over to kiss him on the forehead. "Hi, Liz." But her grin looked forced, and her hair was disheveled.

Mr. Wakefield's eyes narrowed in concern. "Jessica? Is everything OK? Did something happen tonight?"

"Nothing out of the ordinary," she said, turning to face Elizabeth. "Except that all of this waitressing is beginning to cut into my social life. I was too tired to stay at the Beach Disco past the first set. Once everyone hears that I was home by eleven o'clock on a Friday night, my reputation will be ruined."

"Did you have a good time?" Elizabeth asked. "I mean, with Lila and Amy?"

"Yeah. But I should get to bed right now, before I die of exhaustion."

Mr. Wakefield winced at the word *die*.

Jessica had avoided facing him directly since she entered the room. But as she turned to leave, Mr. Wakefield was sure he saw tearstains on her face.

"Elizabeth—" he began after Jessica hurried upstairs.

"I'm sure it's nothing, Dad," Elizabeth said. "Probably just the usual kind of guy trouble. But I'll go talk to her."

He nodded. Elizabeth was probably right. Maybe it was another of the typical adolescent heartaches Jessica was always going through. *Maybe she had an argument with this Scott character that Battaglia mentioned.* Whatever it was, Elizabeth certainly had a much better chance of getting the truth out of her than he did.

As Jessica had done, Elizabeth kissed him lightly on the forehead. Then she climbed the stairs after her sister.

"Jessica, what is it?" Elizabeth asked as she entered her sister's room. "Don't tell me it's nothing. I *know* something happened tonight."

"Nothing happened tonight," Jessica insisted. "Lila and I went to the Beach Disco, and—"

"Save it, Jess. Lila called an hour ago, looking for you."

"Oh."

"Who are you seeing, Jess?"

"Seeing? What do you mean?"

"I mean that you've been sneaking out of work and slipping off on fictitious shopping trips all week. I know you're dating somebody."

Jessica pulled out a bottle of violet polish and began stroking it meticulously onto her fingernails. "Of course I'm dating somebody. I'm dating Ken."

"What happened to 'love the one you're with'?"

"Who is there to be *with* in Sweet Valley? You've been saying it yourself all week. All the glamorous, sophisticated people are from out of town, like the customers in the café."

"Jessica, we're twins. If there's something going on with you, I should know about it. You don't have to keep secrets from me. I promise I won't be judgmental."

"You're a good one to talk about keeping secrets," Jessica said. "I'm not the only one who's been slipping away from work with no explanation."

171

Elizabeth grimaced. She'd been afraid Jessica would bring that up. "We're not talking about me!"

"Then why don't we?"

"OK, I'll stop prying. You know I'm here for you if you decide you want to talk about it. But please, just tell me this. Did something scare you tonight?"

"What do you mean?" Jessica's eyes were wide and innocent.

"I think you know what I mean," Elizabeth said quietly. "Less than an hour ago, I felt as if you were afraid of something. And when you came in, I could tell that you'd been crying."

"It's not important."

"Jessica, if it's anything that could hurt you, then you have to tell me."

"I swear, Elizabeth. Nobody hurt me. I was scared for a few minutes, but it turned out to be nothing. It was nothing at all."

Mr. Wakefield had to keep himself from rushing upstairs and sticking his ear against the door of Jessica's bedroom. He was desperate to know if Jessica sensed danger. The phone rang, and he leaped from his chair.

"Dad! It's for you!" Elizabeth shouted from upstairs. He sprang to his den to grab the extension there. It was after eleven thirty; a phone call at this hour could only be bad news.

"Ned, it's Jim Battaglia. I've got great news!"

"Hold on a minute. . . . Elizabeth, are you off the extension? . . . All right, Jim. We're alone. What's up? Do you have a new lead?"

"Forget new leads," Battaglia said, practically singing into the phone. "The police have your man in custody!"

Mr. Wakefield laughed with relief. "You're sure? You're serious? Marin's behind bars, where he belongs?"

"Actually, the cops say Marin's been using so many aliases that it could take a day to sort them out and get a positive identification on him. Naturally, the suspect is unwilling to talk. But it's him, Ned."

Mr. Wakefield felt a wave of caution. "Tell me how you know for sure."

"My man at the marina has been posing as a customer at the café where your daughters work. Personally, I think he overdid the yachtsman routine a little; he looked like something out of a bad movie about sailing. Lots of brass buttons and epaulets. But the clothes and the mannerisms did the trick—people assumed he was a rich, eccentric type. He said he was sailing around the world from Portugal."

"Yes, I remember the girls mentioning someone like that. So what did your admiral learn?"

"He did some asking around, and several people at the café pointed out a mysterious guy who's been watching Jessica and Elizabeth constantly, from inside and outside the restaurant. People kept using the word *creepy*."

"Some creep's been watching my daughters, and the girls didn't think it was important enough to mention to me?"

"Calm down, Ned. Your daughters are attractive

girls. They might not have realized that this was different from the kind of surveillance they must be used to from men."

Mr. Wakefield sighed. "I suppose you're right."

"After your talk with Cabrini tonight, the police decided they had enough probable cause to bring the guy in for questioning."

"So Marin's only in for *questioning*?" Mr. Wakefield asked, feeling a sinking sensation in the pit of his stomach. "What do you want to bet they won't be able to charge him with the threats or the break-ins? He'll be free in an hour. All my evidence against him is circumstantial."

Battaglia chuckled. "The gold necklace they found on him sure wasn't circumstantial."

"He had Jessica's necklace on him?"

"So it was Jessica's lavaliere and not Elizabeth's?"

"Yes, I just found out."

"Well, that necklace was the key. It enabled the police to charge him with possession of stolen property. That's enough to hold him while the cops further investigate the harassment, the threats, and the breaking and entering. They think they'll be able to find enough evidence so that the district attorney can make a case for the other charges. Not to mention the fact that he's violated his parole."

Mr. Wakefield jumped up from his chair. "I can be at the police station first thing in the morning to identify the piece of scum!"

"Absolutely not! The defense attorney doesn't

want you anywhere near her client. She says you've got too much history with him."

"But I'm the one with the complaint against him!"

"No, you aren't. You could identify him only as a man who threatened you ten years ago. The police can't charge him with that. You didn't *see* Marin write the threatening notes this week. And you didn't see him break into your house. So you're not a witness to anything. In other words, it's time to sit back and relax."

"How can I relax when—"

"I'm sure you can remember relaxation if you put your mind to it. Personally, I intend to lounge around my house for the next two days, watching movies with my feet up. I suggest you do the same."

Mr. Wakefield frowned. "Are you telling me that my family is out of this from here on?"

"No. I think Cabrini will decide he can make a harassment charge stick, probably in a day or two. When he does, he may want your daughters to come down to identify the suspect as the guy who's been watching them at the marina."

"That means I'll have to tell the twins what's been going on—as soon as the police decide they can make the case. Elizabeth and Jessica will be terrified to know how close they were to this maniac."

"But you knew you couldn't keep it a secret forever. At least the girls don't have to be afraid of Marin anymore."

Chapter 13

The girls' locker room at Sweet Valley High was dark, and it smelled like coffee instead of sweat socks. Rock-and-roll music was playing. Jessica was dancing with Scott, her bare feet cold against the tile floor. Suddenly a man's face was staring at them from the high window. Jessica screamed. . . .

Scott and the locker room disappeared, and Jessica sat up in bed, panting. It was Saturday morning. Music blared from her clock radio, and the smell of coffee drifted up from the kitchen.

"Man! What a crazy dream!" Jessica gasped, not sure whether she should be frightened or amused. "I didn't even know I'd fallen asleep."

For most of the night Jessica had lain awake, remembering a pair of vacant brown eyes staring at her through the back window of Scott's car. But now it was morning, and all she could see through her bedroom window was bright yellow sunlight. Jessica stretched and tried to gather her sleepy thoughts.

She came fully awake when she caught sight of the clock. "Oh, my gosh! It's nine thirty! I'm late for work!"

She leaped out of bed and nearly tripped on a pile of purple notebooks that cascaded across the floor at the touch of her bare foot.

"Elizabeth!" she called in the direction of the bathroom that separated the twins' rooms. Of course there was no answer. Elizabeth had already been at work for an hour—collecting all the breakfast tips.

"Shoot!" she said, reaching for her rumpled khaki shorts. "The tip contest ends today, and I'm missing my last chance for breakfast tips. Why didn't Elizabeth wake me up? It's not fair!"

"It's not fair!" Elizabeth complained to Jane as they both reached for the coffeepot behind the counter at the café. "Of course you're ahead of the rest of us on tips. You've been doing this for years."

Jane grinned. "Sorry, Liz. But that's the way the Danish crumbles. This may be hard to believe, but I was a greenhorn once too. I wasn't always the fastest waitress in the West."

"Who won the tip contest your first year?"

Jane smiled. "I did."

"That's encouraging."

"Don't give up hope yet, kid. You're a quick study. You and your sister have given me some real competition this year."

"Do you think I have even a slight chance of winning?"

Jane shrugged. "Sure. A slight one. Very slight."

"That's it!" Elizabeth said. "You're sounding way too smug about this. I swear I'm going to give you a run for your money."

"You mean Mr. Jenkins's money. But before you hustle over to snag that party of six that's walking in, I think you'll want to take care of this one guy who just sat down at the counter."

"Oh, no!" Elizabeth began. "You're not going to give me one measly little customer while you grab six—"

She turned around and stopped midsentence. The single customer was Ben, with the morning sunlight pulling golden highlights from his light brown tousled hair.

"'We watched the ocean and the sky together, under the roof of blue Italian weather,'" he quoted, smiling.

Elizabeth felt the frustrations of the morning slide away, like water under the prow of a sailboat. "Shelley, right?" she asked, recognizing the poetry. "But I think you mean California weather."

"Venice, Waikiki, Sweet Valley—they all have their own unique attractions." He lifted her hand to his lips and kissed it. "I had a great time Thursday afternoon. What do you say we take the boat out again sometime?" he asked in a husky voice. "There's going to be a full moon tonight."

Elizabeth gripped the counter to keep from

swooning. "I've never been for a moonlight sail."

"Then it's about time someone took you for one. I'll meet you on the pier at nine o'clock."

She was so intent on watching Ben's broad shoulders as he walked out of the restaurant that she didn't notice the young man who squeezed by him at the door and moved purposefully toward the counter.

"Who was that?" Todd asked, turning to watch Ben disappear into a crowd of tourists out near the marina.

"No one," Elizabeth said. "Just a customer."

"What time should I pick you up tonight?"

"Pick me up for what?"

Todd grinned. "That's a surprise. But believe me, you're going to love it."

"But Todd, I have plans for tonight."

"*We* have plans for tonight."

Elizabeth's hand flew to her mouth. "Oh, Todd! You're right. I totally forgot."

"So who did you make plans with? Enid? Olivia? Jane? They'll understand. Just tell them I already had dibs on your Saturday night."

"Todd, I can't. It's, uh, my father. I told you how upset he's been. Mom and Steven are away, so I told him I'd do something with him tonight." Elizabeth felt terrible about lying to Todd, but she knew she would feel even worse if she missed a moonlight sail with Ben.

"*Your father?* You're standing me up so you can spend Saturday night with your father?"

"What's so strange about that? I didn't mind last

night when you couldn't go out because you were doing a favor for *your* father."

"That's different. I didn't break a date with you to do it."

"I'm sorry, Todd. I told you, I forgot we had plans. And I'm worried about my dad. Besides, I'm working an extra-long shift today—all the way to closing. I'll be too tired to be much fun by the time I'm out of here."

"But Liz—"

"Why don't you and I get together tomorrow instead?" Elizabeth continued. "I've got the whole day off. I know, let's go to brunch!"

Todd shot her a wounded look. "I'm not sure. I have to check my social calendar first." Then he spun around and stomped out of the restaurant.

Elizabeth watched him with a sinking heart.

"Sorry," Jane said, bustling over from the other end of the counter. "I couldn't help overhearing some of that. Are you all right, Liz?"

"I guess so. I just hate to lie to Todd." She began collecting a handful of menus for the table of six. "But I wish he wouldn't act as if I've committed some horrible crime."

"It seems to me that Todd has fallen into the habit of taking you for granted."

Elizabeth stared at her. "You're right. I hadn't thought about it before, but that's exactly what he's doing. Still, I'm not sure I'm doing the right thing."

"What does your gut tell you to do?"

"My gut wants to go sailing with Ben in the moonlight." Elizabeth laughed. "So does the rest of me. You know, Jane, it's exactly the kind of thing I promised myself I would do this summer—meet new people, experience new things, and have un-Elizabeth sorts of adventures."

"Then go for it, kid. Todd loves you. He'll get over it."

Jessica crossed her fingers and stared at Mr. Jenkins, willing him to get on with the announcement of the tip contest winner on Saturday evening.

"I've seen some excellent customer service from all of the serving staff this week," Mr. Jenkins said. He made a sweeping gesture to encompass the waitresses, who sat around him in the storage room. "You all deserve a pat on the back for a job well done."

Jessica mouthed the words with him as he began reciting his favorite speech about the importance of providing excellent customer service. Elizabeth, sitting across from her on an overturned twenty-gallon plastic drum, caught her eye and smiled. Jessica glared at her. *It's your fault if I don't win,* she thought. *You let me oversleep today.*

Elizabeth rolled her eyes and looked away.

"And now, I'd like to announce the recipient of the movie passes, dinner for two, and the fifty-dollar gift certificate," Mr. Jenkins said. He paused for effect. "The winner of this year's tip contest is Jane O'Reilly!"

Jessica kicked the edge of a metal shelving unit, stubbing her toe painfully. She gritted her teeth and tried to smile. In her mind, the beautiful red miniskirt dissolved in a puff of scarlet smoke.

"But I want to recognize two other waitresses who tied for a close second place," Mr. Jenkins said after presenting Jane with her prizes. "Jessica and Elizabeth Wakefield, congratulations on an outstanding first week."

Jessica smiled, and this time she meant it. The week had been outstanding. Work was mostly kind of fun, a lot of the customers had been cool, and it was nice to be able to see her friends at odd moments throughout the day. Of course, the most outstanding thing about the week was Scott. Through her turquoise polo shirt she fingered the beautiful necklace he'd given her.

Who needed a fifty-dollar gift certificate? If everything went according to plan, in another few weeks she'd be making a fortune for appearing on television. She'd be able to buy a different red miniskirt for every day of the week.

"Bye, Jane!" Elizabeth called that evening.

Jane turned in the doorway of the restaurant, a dark silhouette against a pink-tinged sky. "Everyone else has left. Are you sure you two are all right, locking up by yourselves? Neither of you has ever closed before."

Jessica shrugged. "Big deal. You already did the money part. I think we can handle putting away the last few things."

"The air conditioning shuts off by itself around

eight o'clock," Jane told them. "So don't panic if you hear a weird noise. Oh, and I forgot to check to see if the back door is locked—"

"Go on, Jane!" Elizabeth interrupted. "We know what to do. Now get out of here! You'll be late for your date at the Beach Disco."

"All right," Jane said. "I'm game if you are!"

"And congratulations again on winning the contest," Elizabeth said. "If it couldn't be us, I'm glad it was you."

After Jane left, Elizabeth turned to Jessica. "You're not still mad at me because *you* overslept this morning, are you?"

"You could've woken me up."

"I told you, I tried to. But you were dead to the world. Besides, I'm tired of being taken for granted," Elizabeth said, thinking of Todd more than Jessica. "You shouldn't always expect that I'll be there whenever you want me to be."

Jessica smiled. "What good is a sister who can keep track of the time if she refuses to pull an occasional shift as a human alarm clock?"

Elizabeth smiled back, relieved that Jessica's anger had subsided. "Human alarm clock, huh? I'm glad I have a second career to fall back on if restaurant work doesn't pan out," she said. "Speaking of restaurant work, we've still got to finish up here tonight. Do you want to take that stack of trays back to the storage room, or would you rather wipe the counter?"

"I'll take the trays. If I touch one more wet

sponge today, my hands will look as red and gross as Winston's sunburned nose."

"Can you go through the kitchen first and make sure the back door is locked?"

"No problem," Jessica said.

Elizabeth grabbed a sponge and watched absentmindedly as Jessica disappeared through the kitchen door. Suddenly Elizabeth felt a tingling on the back of her neck. *Was that the sound of footsteps?* No, it couldn't be. She and Jessica were the only people left in the restaurant. But Jessica was in the kitchen, and the noise seemed to be coming from the storage room.

Elizabeth decided it wasn't anything to worry about. It was probably just the air-conditioning system cutting off, as Jane had said. She began pushing the sponge around the countertop in wide circles.

Her hand stopped. "There's that sound again!" she whispered. "This time, I'm sure it's footsteps. But whose?"

Jessica balanced her stack of trays against one hip while she locked the kitchen door. Then she hurried across the room and placed her hand on the door to the storage room. She stopped suddenly, hearing something inside. She took a deep breath. It was probably the sound of the air conditioner shutting off. But when she stepped into the cluttered room, she held the door open behind her.

Jessica gazed around the storage room, clutching the round metal trays that she was gripping under her right arm. The room looked the same as ever. Metal shelving units lined the walls, holding an array of restaurant supplies and equipment. Drums of flour, crates of vegetables, and boxes of paper products were stacked in the dimly lit corners of the room. Out of the corner of her eye, she caught the movement of something large and dark. Jessica jumped, the trays clattering together under her arm. But it was only her own shadow, cast by an unshaded lightbulb.

Jessica took a deep breath, but the shadowy room suddenly seemed eerie and unsafe. Of course there was nothing to be afraid of, she told herself. But after the minutes spent alone and terrified in Scott's car the night before, she wasn't taking any chances. She wouldn't venture another step into the room without Elizabeth by her side.

She began backing out through the door when a shadow fell across her face. A man was standing only a few feet away, a dark silhouette against the hanging lightbulb.

Jessica dropped the trays with a metallic clamor as she threw her arms up in front of her face. Then she was paralyzed by the sight of the man's shadow, looming up beside her.

In his hand was a knife.

"Elizabeth!" she screamed.

The knife clattered to the floor. A rough hand shoved Jessica aside, and the man ran past her into the kitchen, heading toward the dining room. A few seconds later she heard the front door slam shut.

◦ ◦ ◦

"All right, girls," the tall, black-haired police detective said to the twins a half hour later. "I was hoping to wait until we could get hold of your father, but I can't seem to locate him. Do you want to try to pick out the man in a lineup? Or would you feel better if we waited until your father can be here with you?"

Elizabeth smiled at his concern. She turned to Jessica and saw that her sister was calmer now too, after the initial fright of seeing the man with the knife. "We're fine, Detective Cabrini," she said. "We might as well do it now and get it over with."

"Good. Here's how it works. This panel is one-way glass. You can take as long as you need to look at the suspects. But they won't be able to see you."

Elizabeth shook her head. "I'm not sure how much good this will do. He ran by me so fast, right after I heard Jessica scream. I didn't get a good look at him."

"Neither did I, tonight," Jessica admitted. "I mostly saw his shadow. But I'm sure I know who he was. There's this man who hangs out at the marina. He's been watching both of us all week."

"I've seen him too," Elizabeth confirmed. "And I'm sure Jessica's right. He was the same height and build. It had to be the same creepy guy."

The detective nodded. "All right, girls. Here come the suspects. Do you see the man here?"

"Number four," the twins said together instantly. The fourth man from the left was the scruffy, unshaven guy they'd noticed around the marina all week.

The detective seemed surprised. "Are you absolutely sure?"

"That's definitely the man who's been watching us at work," Jessica said. "I'm sure of it."

"Elizabeth?" Detective Cabrini asked.

"Yes, that's him," Elizabeth said. "And it could also be the man I saw running out of the storage room tonight."

The detective sighed, scratching his head. "No, it couldn't be," he said. "We did pick him up near the marina, but not today. That man has been in jail since last night."

Mr. Wakefield was working late at the office on Saturday. He had to make up for all the time he'd lost during the week, worrying about the girls. Now he felt as if he were the one who'd been released from prison. He was free of the fear and anxiety of knowing Marin was out there, stalking his daughters. The twins were safe. Marin was in jail.

The phone rang.

"Ned, this is Tony Cabrini at the police station," the detective began. "I'm afraid you're not going to like what I have to tell you."

A few minutes later the detective had reviewed the events of the evening. Mr. Wakefield felt a wave of panic engulfing him. "I don't understand!" he choked out. "The man you have in custody was caught with Jessica's necklace! How could it not be our guy?"

"This guy has been locked up since yesterday. So

it had to be another man who almost attacked Jessica tonight."

"But Battaglia said the man in custody matched Marin's photograph."

"I can't explain that. I can tell you that your daughters said the scruffy-looking character is definitely the guy who's been watching them all week. But we finally got a positive identification on him, and he's not Marin. He's a vagrant named Pilchard, and not very bright."

"So there's no connection to Marin at all? I don't understand. The necklace—"

"Oh, there's a connection, all right. Pilchard finally talked tonight, after the girls picked him out of the lineup. Pilchard says a man hired him to keep an eye on your daughters, and that this man gave him the gold necklace as part of his payment."

"Marin! So where is he now?"

"I don't know, and I don't think Pilchard knows either. It looks like Marin set his own man up. He had him spy on the girls openly, probably figuring that Battaglia would think Pilchard was Marin."

Mr. Wakefield nodded. "And then Marin framed Pilchard by planting Jessica's missing necklace on him," he said grimly. "So what was Marin himself doing through all this?"

"Hiding in the background, pulling everyone's strings—"

"Especially mine," Mr. Wakefield said.

"And obviously Marin was the man with the knife at the restaurant tonight."

Mr. Wakefield gulped. "Where are my daughters now?"

"They're on their way home," the detective said. "I'm arranging to have your house guarded again."

"Did you tell the girls why?"

"I didn't tell them anything about it. They think the incident at the restaurant tonight was random."

"I wish I'd been there at the police station. The twins must have been terrified."

"They're OK, Ned. They're tough kids. I tried to call you earlier, but I couldn't find you. In the end I couldn't put off the lineup any longer without explaining your involvement in this case to the girls."

"I was doing some research in our legal library," Mr. Wakefield explained. "I thought it was safe for me to work late again."

"Ned, you can't keep the truth from your daughters any longer. They have to know about Marin."

"I know. I'll tell them as soon as I get home. I'm on my way there, as soon as I make one more phone call."

Mr. Wakefield slammed down the phone. Battaglia had Marin's mug shot. But somehow, the private investigator and his hired surveillance man had been duped into identifying the wrong person as Marin. Mr. Wakefield wanted to know how. But the telephone at Jim Battaglia's house rang and rang, with no answer. Mr. Wakefield tried his office number, but the detective's answering service said he was at home. Mr. Wakefield fought down another wave of panic. Battaglia was always reachable. And he'd said he'd be home that night, watching movies.

Mr. Wakefield took a deep breath. There was probably nothing to worry about. But the private investigator's house was on his way home; it wouldn't hurt to stop by and make sure everything was all right. At least he could leave a note, asking Battaglia to call him.

Twenty minutes later Mr. Wakefield stood outside the door of Battaglia's house and raised a fist to knock. Then his mouth dropped open. The door was ajar. His scalp prickled.

"Jim?" he called, stepping inside. He raised his voice to be heard above a television set that was blaring somewhere nearby. "Is anybody home?"

Mr. Wakefield walked into the living room and stopped, shaking his head. Jim Battaglia lay on the floor, a knife handle protruding from his chest. Blood, still wet, soaked his sweatshirt and was seeping into the cream-colored carpeting beneath his body. Nearby a Bette Davis videocassette was playing on the television. Obviously he'd been killed in the last hour or two.

Mr. Wakefield noticed a slip of paper pinned to the collar of Battaglia's shirt. He leaned over to read Marin's now-familiar scrawl.

It's hard to get good help these days. Isn't it, Ned?

Chapter 14

Elizabeth ran along the dock Saturday night, late for her date with Ben. *So much for sailing into the sunset,* she thought. The sun was gone; only a few pinkish streaks remained in the midnight-blue sky. She was relieved to see the *Emily Dickinson* still bobbing in its berth.

"Hi, gorgeous!" Ben shouted. His smile was dazzling in the near dark as he extended a hand to help her aboard.

Elizabeth's foot slipped, and only Ben's steadying arm prevented her from dropping into the dark, glimmering slice of water between the dock and the boat.

"Hey, watch it!" Ben said, pulling her safely aboard. "You wouldn't want to fall in. I hear someone saw a shark yesterday."

"Thanks for the hand," Elizabeth said breathlessly. "But I doubt there really was a shark. We don't

191

get them too often around here. Anyway, I'm sorry I'm so late. You wouldn't believe the night I've had."

"Tell me about it."

Elizabeth opened her mouth to describe the events at the restaurant and the police station, but then shook her head. "No," she decided. "Not right now. I don't even want to think about it. Let's do some sailing!"

A few minutes later the lights of Sweet Valley Marina twinkled off the stern and the salt-scented breeze fanned Elizabeth's face.

"I'm surprised you managed to get out at all," Ben said as she helped him adjust a sail. "It sounds like your father's been pretty overprotective of you and your sister lately. I can't imagine he was excited to hear you were going sailing at night with some guy he's never met."

Elizabeth felt her face turn pink. She was glad it was too dark for Ben to see her blushing. "I didn't exactly tell him I was going sailing with you," she admitted. "In fact, I didn't tell him anything. Luckily Dad was working late when Jessica and I got home. If he'd heard about our evening, he never would have let me leave the house tonight."

Ben sighed. "I hate for you to sneak around behind your father's back, and your sister's. Maybe you should tell them the truth."

"Actually, I did tell Jessica. We had such an intense evening together that keeping secrets seemed—I don't know, trivial. On the way home tonight I just blabbed the whole story about how we met at the café, and about your boat and your book."

It had been a relief to tell Jessica the truth about Ben. But Elizabeth still felt a twinge of guilt for lying to Todd and her father. She shoved aside her guilt. The night was beautiful, the sails billowed like clouds as the boat glided toward the open ocean, and Ben was the most exciting, romantic guy she had ever met.

"It was a good thing I told Jessica the truth," she continued. "I needed her to cover for me tonight. When Dad gets home, she'll tell him I'm out with Todd."

"She's out with Todd," Jessica said, staring from her father to Detective Cabrini. "I don't understand, Dad. We just left the police. Why did you bring them home from work with you?"

"Where did Liz and Todd go?" her father demanded.

"I don't know. The usual places, I guess. What does it matter?"

"I'm afraid it matters a lot," the detective said. He pulled a folder from under his jacket. "A lot of things have been happening this week that you're not aware of, Jessica."

Her father led her into the living room and motioned for her to sit on the couch. "I'm afraid I've been keeping some information from you and your sister—not to mention Steven and your mother—for the past few days." He stopped, as if he wasn't sure what he wanted to say next.

Jessica put her hands on her hips. "Is somebody going to tell me what's going on? Or do we have to play Twenty Questions?"

"You know that I worked in the district attorney's office a long time ago," her father said finally. "It was when you were a little girl."

"Sure. I think I was in first or second grade when you left there. Why?"

"This is serious, Jessica," Detective Cabrini told her. "Ten years ago your father put away a very dangerous man—a kidnapper and murderer named John Marin."

"Lawyers put people in jail all the time. What's this got to do with Liz and me?"

Ned closed his eyes for a second. "When he was convicted, Marin blamed me," he said. "He threatened my family. In particular, he said he would come after you and your sister. Last week they let him out on parole."

Jessica's eyes widened. "Then that was the weird guy who's been watching us all week! He's a murderer?"

"No, he isn't," Cabrini said. "The man you identified in the lineup tonight was paid by Marin to spy on you and your sister. But he wasn't Marin." He pulled a photograph from the folder and handed it to Jessica. "This is Marin."

Jessica sighed, relieved, when she saw the wide grin and handsome features of the man in the photograph. She shook her head. "No, it isn't! That's Scott Maderlake," she said, her hand automatically reaching up to grasp her new necklace. Jessica's eyes widened when she saw the official-looking police identification label in the corner. Detective Cabrini pointed to the name: *John Marin.* Jessica took a deep breath. "Oh, my gosh!"

"You know this man?" her father asked.

"No! I mean, yes. I mean . . . There must be a mistake, Dad. That's a picture of Scott, and he's a great guy. The caption has to be wrong."

Mr. Wakefield shook his head. "I spent a week in court with that man ten years ago," he said, pointing to the photograph. "I don't care what else he's calling himself. That is John Marin."

Jessica squeezed back tears. "Dad, I've been dating him all week! He told me he was an intern for a television production company." Her voice dropped to a whisper. "I really liked him!"

Mr. Wakefield leaned forward and covered his eyes.

"*You* were dating this man?" the detective asked. "Your sister wasn't. Well, that fits, anyway. Your father said the necklace was yours."

"Necklace?" Jessica asked, confused. She hadn't shown her new necklace to anyone, not even Lila.

"Didn't you lose your lavaliere?" her father asked.

"You found my lavaliere? Scott—I mean, *Marin* had it?" Jessica looked from her father to the police detective, horrified. She remembered the touch of Marin's hand on the bare skin of her neck the night before.

Her father nodded, and Jessica gulped. Marin

could have killed her. He'd had every opportunity.

"What about Elizabeth?" the detective asked. "Did she know this Maderlake as well?"

"No," Jessica whispered. "I never told her about him."

"Then Elizabeth is probably fine, Ned," Cabrini said. "Apparently Marin decided to target Jessica first."

"Maybe, but John Marin is a slick character. We can't underestimate him."

"You said that Elizabeth and her boyfriend, Todd, are sensible kids. They're probably in a public place somewhere, having a burger."

Jessica opened her mouth to speak, but before she could say anything, the phone rang. Her father picked it up.

"Todd?" he asked, surprised. "No, Liz isn't here. I thought she was with *you*." He stared at the receiver for a moment and then placed it in the cradle.

"That was Todd, calling for Elizabeth," Mr. Wakefield told them in a quiet voice. "He hung up on me." He stared at Jessica, eyes narrowed.

Jessica grimaced. "Oops," she said. The interruption had given her a chance to catch her breath. Now she felt calmer. She had learned the truth in time; now the police could protect her. Jessica noticed her father's concerned expression and tried to make her voice sound normal. "Todd must have figured out that Elizabeth is seeing somebody else," she explained. "But don't worry, Dad. The police photo is definitely the guy who was *my* secret boyfriend. Elizabeth has a different one altogether."

Mr. Wakefield's mouth dropped open. "Elizabeth has a secret boyfriend?"

Jessica shrugged. "This sailor guy she's going out with sounds completely safe. He's a writer, for heaven's sake. What could be duller than that?"

"*Sailor?* What is your sister up to?"

"I don't see what the big deal is. That photo is not Ben what's-his-name, so Elizabeth isn't in any danger."

"Jessica, where is your sister? And who is Ben?"

Jessica sighed. "Elizabeth went sailing with this Ben guy—he has a boat docked at the marina."

"Did you meet this new boyfriend of hers? What does he look like?"

"Search me. I never saw him. All Elizabeth said was that he's a real hunk, and he likes to quote poems." Jessica rolled her eyes. "I still don't understand why you're having a conniption fit. It's *me* that Marin was after, not Elizabeth." Her voice broke on the last sentence.

Mr. Wakefield bit his lip. "Jessica, that might be true. But the situation is more serious than you think. There was another murder tonight. The victim's name was Jim Battaglia. He was a private investigator I hired to watch you girls. Marin got to him just before I did."

"A murder?" Jessica shook her head, remembering Scott's deep blue eyes and cute smile. "I can't believe that Scott—"

"Believe it," her father cut her off. "And Battaglia's murder wasn't the only one this week. Tony just informed me that a man's body was found today in the woods near Miller's Point. He was murdered last night."

Jessica gasped. "*I was at Miller's Point last night! With Scott.*"

Her father's face turned white. "Did you see anything suspicious?"

Jessica nodded as a chilly prickling sensation ran down her back. "A man was looking in the window at us. Scott chased him, but he got away in the woods. I didn't get a good look at the guy."

"*Why didn't you say anything last night?*" Mr. Wakefield would have continued, but Cabrini pulled another photograph from his folder and handed it to Jessica.

"Jessica, this is a photograph of the man who was murdered last night. We don't have an identification. Was this the man you saw looking in the car window?"

Jessica stared at the familiar face in dismay. Hot tears began sliding down her face. "*Murdered?* I don't know for sure if it was him I saw at Miller's Point," she said between sobs. "But I do know the man in the picture. I was beginning to like him."

"Who is he?" the detective asked gently.

"I don't know his name. He was in the café almost every day this week. He always orders—*ordered*—peanut-butter sandwiches."

"Do you know anything else about him?"

"He was sailing around the world, starting from Portugal. He always wore funny clothes."

Mr. Wakefield stared at her. "Brass buttons and epaulets?"

Jessica raised her eyebrows. "Yes! How did you know? Who is he?"

Her father turned to the detective. "I don't know his name. But it sounds like the man Battaglia hired to keep an eye on the girls."

The detective sighed. "I guess that's what he was trying to do at Miller's Point last night. He just might have saved Jessica's life."

Twenty minutes later Cabrini pulled his unmarked car into a parking space outside the Beach Disco. In the backseat Mr. Wakefield grasped Jessica's hand. "So you're sure that this other waitress can identify the guy Elizabeth is out with tonight?"

Jessica shook her head. Her blue eyes were wide and frightened in her pale face. "Not for sure. But Elizabeth did say she introduced Jane to Ben at the café. So she's our best bet."

"Most likely Elizabeth is fine," Tony assured them. Mr. Wakefield couldn't catch his eye in the rearview mirror. He wondered if Tony was as confident as he sounded. "Still," the detective continued, "we'll all feel better if this Jane O'Reilly can tell us more about Ben and verify that he's not in any of these photographs."

"Well, Jane said she was meeting her date here tonight," Jessica said. "But the Droids sound awfully loud, even from here. We won't be able to talk inside, and you two will stand out like, well, like a couple of cops. I'll run in and bring Jane out."

Mr. Wakefield opened his mouth to protest. He felt sick to his stomach at the thought of letting either of his daughters out of his sight, even for a minute. But at the detective's nod, he let go of Jessica's hand. He watched as she rushed into the noisy, ramshackle building, her hair flying behind her.

A few minutes later Jessica half dragged Jane from the Beach Disco.

"What is this, Jessica? What was so important that you felt compelled to haul me away from the man of my dreams?"

"More like nightmares," Jessica muttered under her breath. Jane's date had been pretty funky looking—long hair and a tattoo. Nevertheless, Jane's smile as they danced had made Jessica suddenly ache for Ken—handsome, solid, and safe. She put her boyfriend out of her mind; Elizabeth's whereabouts were more important now. "Forget it!" she said. "We need you to tell us everything you can about this Ben guy Elizabeth went sailing with tonight."

"Jessica! Your sister wanted to keep that a secret!"

"No more secrets," Detective Cabrini's voice said. A streetlight shone down on him and Ned Wakefield, who stood near Cabrini's gray Accord, their arms folded.

Jane looked from Jessica to the two men. "Jessica, is this some kind of a joke? What's going on?"

"Jane, this is my father, Ned Wakefield, and this is Detective Cabrini of the Sweet Valley police. We need your help. Elizabeth may be in a lot of danger."

"Danger? What do you mean?"

"A convicted murderer with a grudge against Ned has been stalking the twins," Cabrini explained. "He managed to deceive Jessica. We don't know if he got to Elizabeth as well." He turned suddenly to Jessica. "Jessica, do you remember anything unusual happening to you at the restaurant Wednesday morning? Anything frightening?"

Jessica shook her head. "I don't think so."

"I just remembered something Pilchard told me. He's the seedy-looking man Marin hired to watch you girls—the one you identified in the lineup tonight." Jane's eyes grew wider as the detective continued. "Pilchard says he was told to scare one of the twins in a back room of the café so that Marin could come to her rescue and gain her trust. Was that you?"

Jessica shook her head. "It must have been Liz," she whispered. "Oh, no!"

Mr. Wakefield's eyes blazed. "Jane, did you meet this guy, Ben?"

"Yes, I did. And you don't have to worry about Elizabeth. Ben's not the guy you're looking for. He's a sweet kid—clean-cut, kinda preppie, and perfectly harmless. He quotes poetry." She smiled. "He's definitely not the black-leather-and-motorcycles type."

The detective motioned her into the front seat and switched on the overhead light. "I want you to look at this photograph. Take your time, and be absolutely sure before you answer. Is this the man who took Elizabeth sailing tonight?"

Jessica saw him pass Jane the photograph of the man Jessica had known as Scott Maderlake.

Jane nodded. "That's Sailor Boy, all right! I'd recognize those baby blues anywhere!"

"His name is John Marin," Cabrini said quietly.

Jessica's heart plummeted to her feet. Elizabeth was out on the ocean, alone with a maniac.

"I can't believe how perfect this is!" Elizabeth murmured, snuggling against Ben's broad chest as they danced on the deck of the *Emily Dickinson*. "I think I've died and gone to heaven."

Soft guitar music rippled from Ben's stereo system, water lapped gently against the side of the boat, and stars twinkled overhead in a black velvet sky. Elizabeth had never spent a more romantic evening. She gazed up at Ben's handsome face and admired the way the moonlight shot streaks of gold through his light brown hair.

I really have found my soul mate, Elizabeth thought as he leaned forward. When his lips brushed hers in a soft kiss, her heart pounded in her chest. She felt as if she'd been lifted from earth and set on a cloud.

Suddenly the moon and stars were swallowed up in a flood of light that washed over the deck. Elizabeth staggered backward, almost blinded by white-hot lights from just off starboard.

"What the hell—" Ben began in a surprisingly harsh voice.

"Drop your weapon and put your hands up!" boomed a voice through a loudspeaker.

Elizabeth shook her head. "You've made a mistake!" she screamed toward the boat that had pulled alongside. She squinted into the lights. U.S. COAST GUARD was painted across the side of the boat. Ben pulled her toward him, and Elizabeth's mouth dropped open.

A knife glinted in his hand.

Elizabeth looked up into the eyes of her soul mate, and all she saw was hatred.

Chapter 15

A young officer had told Jessica and her father to stay below on the Coast Guard cutter. But through the porthole she saw Marin grab Elizabeth on the deck of the *Emily Dickinson,* anchored nearby. A knife flashed in his hand. Jessica dodged the officer and sprang onto the deck of the cutter. Her father was right behind her.

"Elizabeth!" Jessica screamed. "He wants to kill you!"

A few yards away the sailboat's deck was bathed in white light. Elizabeth and Marin's bodies cast huge, elongated shadows, giving the scene an air of unreality, like a theatrical set. But the knife flashed again, decidedly real. Elizabeth screamed.

"If anyone tries anything, Daddy's little girl is dead!" The voice sounded like Scott's, but it was transformed by evil. He held Elizabeth in front of him, using her body to shield his own. The knife gleamed like a star at Elizabeth's throat. "Ned!" Marin yelled. "I see you over there! Glad you could come watch the fun. How does it feel, Counselor? Was it worth it?"

"Let the girl go, Marin!" came Detective Cabrini's voice. "If you hurt her, you'll never get out of here alive!" Jessica jumped when she heard the click of a rifle being prepared to shoot.

Marin's laugh echoed across the water. "Jessica, it was so nice to see you in the storage room at the restaurant tonight. If you hadn't spotted me and screamed for help, I'd have finished you off right there."

"Let her go, Scott!" Jessica yelled, using the alias out of habit. She knew that everything he had told her about himself was a lie, but part of her mind still rebelled at the idea that sexy, fun Scott was a murderer. She wanted it all to be a mistake. Or a nightmare.

"Don't worry, Jessica! Your sister won't have all the fun. I've got plans for you too. You want to be a star? You'll play the starring role in my *next* murder."

Elizabeth's white slacks gleamed as she stomped, hard, on Marin's foot. Then she grabbed his arm with both hands. For what seemed like an hour they struggled for the knife. Against the network of masts and furled sails above them, their shadows struggled in a deadly dance.

• • •

Elizabeth broke free of Ben—or whoever he was—and raced toward the back of the sloop. She expected him to follow, but he headed for the port side, away from the Coast Guard cutter. She kicked off her sandals and jumped to the railing, preparing to dive from the stern. For a fraction of a second she remembered Enid's news of a shark sighting. But Ben presented a more immediate danger. As she dove over the railing, she noticed a small dinghy that hung over the port side. Ben leaped into the tiny boat.

Suddenly Elizabeth's foot caught against the brass railing, with a jerk that shuddered through her body. She tumbled, headfirst, toward the gleaming water. Then something slammed into the back of her neck, and Elizabeth blacked out.

Marin was getting away. The Coast Guard boat powered up, and only Jessica seemed to notice that Elizabeth's usually perfect dive had faltered.

"Elizabeth!" she screamed. Then she dove off the side of the boat toward her sister.

Two hours later the twins huddled together on the couch in the Wakefields' living room. Their father wrapped a blanket around their shivering shoulders.

"Dad, I can barely keep my eyes open," Elizabeth said, trying to keep her teeth from chattering. She expected she would have nightmares about Ben—about John Marin—for most of the night. But for now, a hot shower and a warm bed would feel like heaven. And first thing in the morning, she would call Todd and apologize for the way she'd treated him. Suddenly she couldn't think of anything more exciting than a solid, predictable relationship with someone she could trust.

"Sorry, Elizabeth," Detective Cabrini said. "We'll be finished questioning you girls in just a few minutes. Then you can get some sleep."

"Are you sure you're all right, Liz?" her father asked. "I know the Coast Guard doctor said it wasn't a concussion, but we can take you to the emergency room if you think—"

Elizabeth shook her head. "No. I'm fine, thanks to Jessica." She hugged her sister. "I just have a little bit of a headache."

All four of them jumped when the doorbell rang. Cabrini rose to his feet, pulling out his gun. They all knew that Marin was still out there somewhere. He had managed to escape in his motor-powered dinghy. Cabrini motioned the Wakefields to stay put. "I'll handle this."

Elizabeth sighed with relief when he returned to the room a few seconds later with a Coast Guard officer who had been on the cutter. The sparkling white of the woman's uniform reminded Elizabeth of the sails of the *Emily Dickinson*. She closed her eyes, wishing she could put the whole thing out of her mind.

"Are you feeling any better?" the young officer asked, sitting down beside the twins. She was holding something navy blue in her hand.

"I'm OK," Elizabeth said. "Just tired." She yawned, and decided that a shower could wait until morning. For now all she wanted was a warm bed with a soft pillow.

"What's that noise?" the officer asked, rising to her feet.

Cabrini waved a hand. "It's nothing to worry about. I've got a police locksmith in the back, putting a dead bolt on the kitchen door."

"In the middle of the night?"

Cabrini shrugged. "He owed me a favor."

"I should have had that lock changed a lot sooner," Mr. Wakefield admitted. "I didn't want the girls to know there was any danger. But at this point, we're not taking any more chances."

"Who cares about locks?" Jessica exclaimed, echoing Elizabeth's thoughts. *"Did you find Marin?"*

"We found pieces of his damaged dinghy," the woman said. She held up the blue bundle. "And this. Do you recognize it, Elizabeth?"

She unfolded the navy blue fabric. It was part of a man's windbreaker. And the torn edge was stained with blood.

Elizabeth nodded, her eyes wide. "Ben—I mean, *Marin* was wearing it tonight."

"Are you sure?" the police detective asked. "A lot of men wear navy windbreakers."

"I know. But that's definitely his. I recognize that little red-and-gold logo near the shoulder."

"I recognize it too," Jessica piped up. "Scott, uh,

Marin wore it the day we broke into the school."

The police detective stared at her. *"The day you did what?"*

"Uh, can I tell you about it tomorrow?"

Cabrini and her father each gave her a long, hard stare.

Luckily for Jessica, the Coast Guard officer began speaking again. "That's exactly what we thought. If you girls are sure this jacket belonged to Marin, then your problems are over. We haven't recovered the body yet. But the man who was wearing this windbreaker was apparently attacked and killed by sharks about an hour ago. We don't have a forensics match on the blood yet, but that's just a formality. John Marin is dead."

Elizabeth felt her sister shudder at Marin's gruesome ending. She squeezed Jessica's hand. "How horrible," Elizabeth whispered. "But I'm glad he's gone."

Mr. Wakefield watched the twins' backs as they plodded up the stairs, arm in arm. The Coast Guard officer had left, and Cabrini was walking through the downstairs of the house, at Mr. Wakefield's request, making sure every door and window was secure.

"We'll both be sleeping in Elizabeth's room," Jessica called down to her father, her voice unsteady. "So don't worry if you don't see me in my bed."

Mr. Wakefield nodded, wishing he could have spared his daughters so much fear. "Good night, girls. Try to get some sleep."

A few minutes later Tony Cabrini emerged from the kitchen. "Everything looks safe, Ned. The locksmith has gone. Here's the key to your new dead bolt. Every door and window is secure. But I don't know why you're still worried. Marin's dead. He can't harm your daughters anymore."

Mr. Wakefield shook his head. "I know the Coast Guard says so. But something tells me that Marin is still out there. And nearby. I can feel him, Tony."

"I think you've gotten so used to worrying about Marin that you don't know how to break the habit."

"Possibly. Just the same, I don't think I'll sleep tonight."

"Don't do that, Ned. You need your rest. Your daughters are going to need you to be there for them tomorrow, one hundred percent. Look, if it makes you feel any better, I'll hang around until daybreak and watch the place from the outside."

"What about *your* rest?"

The police detective shrugged. "I won't be able to sleep anyway. I've had enough caffeine tonight to float that sailing sloop. And I can read the Coast Guard report in my car just as easily as I can do it sitting at my desk."

Mr. Wakefield bolted the front door behind Cabrini and examined the lock to make sure it was secure. Then he walked from room to room, checking every door and window, as the police detective had done a few minutes earlier. He glanced out the window at Cabrini's Honda Accord, parked at the curb. He sighed as he let the curtain fall. Everything appeared to be secure, but he still felt uneasy. Mr. Wakefield stopped at the bottom of the stairs and listened for the girls' voices. Nothing. They were probably asleep already.

"That's strange," he suddenly said aloud, still facing the stairs. "I haven't seen Prince Albert once since we got home. Where could that dog be?"

"The mutt's in the basement, drugged," said a voice behind him in the living room. "He should wake up in another hour or so—after you and your precious little girls are dead."

Mr. Wakefield turned sharply. John Marin stood a few feet away, grinning evilly. In one hand he gripped a long wooden board, its edges jagged and splintering. "I've been in the basement myself since just before you got home tonight, Counselor," Marin said with a sneer. "Looks like you were a few hours too late in changing that lock on the kitchen door."

Mr. Wakefield clenched his fists. "You—"

Before he could say another word, Marin swung the heavy board. The harsh blow caught Mr. Wakefield across the side of the head, and his skull seemed to explode with the pain. The room spun, crimson, as he fell to the carpet. Then everything went black.

Marin chuckled at the sight of Ned Wakefield lying on his tasteful, off-white carpeting, blood trickling from his temple.

Back on the sloop, Marin had thought it was all over when the Coast Guard arrived with those bright lights. It was a good thing he'd thought to prepare the dinghy, just in case he needed a quick getaway. And the recent shark sighting had provided a perfect escape. Once he reached shore, he'd hacked a hole in the little wooden boat. Then he'd killed a stray cat he found wandering by the docks and smeared its blood on his jacket. After that, all he had to do was tear the jacket and leave the bloody piece with the broken remains of the boat so that the whole mess would look as if it had just washed ashore.

Now he dropped the wooden plank near Wakefield's lifeless body and began stalking up the staircase. As he walked, he slid his knife from its sheath. A board was the perfect weapon to use on Ned Wakefield. But it was too crude a way for such delicate beauties as Elizabeth and Jessica to die. A knife was more elegant. It had style. He eyed its lethal edge and smiled. Then he pushed open the door to Elizabeth's room.

Through the window, moonbeams shone like a spotlight, illuminating the bed where the two girls lay. It was easy to imagine the twins as six years old, as they had been when their father sent Marin to prison. Their faces looked relaxed and innocent—and touchingly young. Ten years had passed, but Elizabeth and Jessica were as vulnerable now as they had been then.

In sleep, the twins were indistinguishable. Two

heads of golden hair glittered. Two mouths breathed deeply. Soon, Marin told himself, the golden hair would be stained with blood; the breathing would be silenced. He flashed the same grin that had captivated them both when he pretended to be Scott and Ben. But this time, he didn't bother to hide the hatred in his eyes. He raised the knife and began to slice down with it, toward the bed.

Something slammed into the side of Marin's body and he flew across the room, the knife clattering on the floor. For an instant Marin caught a glimpse of Ned Wakefield standing grimly in front of his daughters' bed, a trickle of blood sliding down his left temple. Behind him, the twins' eyes were wide in the moonlight.

Then Marin crashed into the glass window on the other side of the room. Sharp, hot pain splintered his body a split second before the sound of shattering glass exploded in his ears. The cool night air seemed to rush upward around him as he fell toward a tiled patio that seemed very far away. Marin braced himself for the impact of his body against the ground, but he was unconscious before he reached it.

Jessica was trembling. She clung to Elizabeth and her father, all three of them still staring at the shattered remains of the window Marin had fallen through.

"Is he dead?" Jessica asked when Detective Cabrini appeared in the doorway of Elizabeth's room.

"No, he's not," the detective told her. "Marin is alive, and I think he'll be OK in a few days. But for now, he's hurt too badly to move."

"You left him alone down there?" Mr. Wakefield asked.

"Don't worry. I've got him handcuffed to my car, just in case. And I called for backup. We'll have an ambulance and more officers here in two minutes. I had to see if you folks needed medical help. Is anyone injured? I saw blood on the floor downstairs."

Elizabeth gasped. Jessica followed her gaze and saw that blood was dripping from their father's temple.

Mr. Wakefield touched the side of his head. "Marin was already in the house when we arrived home earlier. He must have been hiding until you left, Tony."

"Dad!" Jessica wailed. Her father hugged her close.

"It's all right, honey," he assured her. "We're all fine."

"Exactly what happened here?" the detective asked.

Mr. Wakefield took a deep breath. "After you left, Marin sneaked up on me and bashed me with a board. I guess I was out for a minute or two, but it's nothing serious." He smiled weakly at Elizabeth and Jessica. "It's a good thing I'm so hardheaded."

"What's going to happen to Scott—I mean, *Marin*?" Jessica asked.

Mr. Wakefield put his arms around both his daughters. "We don't have to be afraid anymore," he said. Jessica saw tears glistening in his eyes. "John Marin is going back to prison. And this time, he's going to stay there for the rest of his life."

A KILLER ON BOARD

SWEET VALLEY High®

A KILLER ON BOARD

Written by
Kate William

Created by
FRANCINE PASCAL

BANTAM BOOKS
NEW YORK · TORONTO · LONDON · SYDNEY · AUCKLAND

To John Stewart Carmen

Chapter 1

A hand tightened on Elizabeth Wakefield's shoulder. She gasped. The silverware she'd been holding clattered to the dining-room table. Elizabeth whirled around, expecting to see the handsome, cruel face and the glittering midnight-blue eyes that had haunted her dreams for days.

Instead she found her identical twin, Jessica, staring at her with startled blue-green eyes. "Oh, Liz," Jessica began. "I'm sorry I scared you. You must've thought . . . I mean . . ."

Elizabeth sighed, knowing her own eyes had the same unsettled look as her sister's. "It's all right, Jessica. I guess we're all jumpy after what happened Saturday night."

"Can you blame us?" Jessica asked. "That creep would've murdered us if Dad hadn't—" She swallowed. "Anyhow, sixteen is definitely too young to die."

Elizabeth shuddered. "I don't want to talk about Saturday night, or last week, or John Marin. I wish I could forget he ever existed."

"Me, too," Jessica declared. "And usually I'm so good at forgetting things!" She tossed her sister a handful of napkins.

With only a small flicker of a smile, Elizabeth caught the napkins and began folding them in triangles by the sides of the dinner plates. Under normal circumstances she would have been grateful for her sister's company. Usually nobody was better at cheering her up than Jessica. But right now even her entertaining twin couldn't take Elizabeth's mind off last Saturday night.

Elizabeth stared at a butter knife that lay on the table in front of her. She remembered the starlit sky above the Pacific Ocean, off the coast of their southern-California town. For the first hour of her date on Saturday, she'd been in heaven. It had been a breezy, romantic night, and she had danced on the deck of a sailing yacht with a young man she had found exciting and glamorous—a man whose name was supposed to be Ben.

Then the night had crashed down around her like a cold ocean wave. Elizabeth remembered the wind ripping at her long blond hair and the sailboat's deck lurching under her feet. Nearly blinded by the searing searchlights of the nearby coast-guard cutter, Elizabeth had struggled desperately with Marin as he'd tried to stab her with his gleaming knife.

The knife on the dining-room table flashed as Jessica slid it into place in front of their mother's chair. Elizabeth jumped.

"Liz?"

"Oh, I'm sorry, Jess. I guess I was spacing out."

Jessica stared at her. "I know. I've been doing the same thing all week. I'll be talking to Mom, or listening to a CD, and all of a sudden—wham!—I'm back in the storage room at the cafe, seeing John Marin's shadow on the wall as he tries to stab me." She shuddered visibly. "I think it's contagious. Mom and Dad seem spooked, too."

Elizabeth nodded her head in agreement. "It must be really hard on Mom. Can you imagine coming home from a business trip and finding out that your daughters and your husband were nearly murdered while you were gone?"

Jessica bit her lip. "I sure wish *I* had been away on a business trip Saturday night."

"I'm glad you weren't," Elizabeth told her, her voice softening. "You saved my life, Jess. If you hadn't been around to jump into the water when I hit my head—"

Jessica shook her head. "Don't, Liz. I don't want to think about it."

"Neither do I, but the images keep coming back."

Jessica sighed. "For me, too. This afternoon Prince Albert brushed up against me in the kitchen, and I actually screamed—as if Marin would come waltzing into our kitchen disguised as a golden retriever."

"I wouldn't put it past him, if he ever got paroled again," Elizabeth said. "He managed to fool both of us about his real identity for a whole week. I can't believe he had me convinced he was a novelist and a sailor."

Jessica momentarily covered her eyes with her hands. "That's nothing," she sighed. "I actually thought he worked for a television producer. I halfway believed I was falling in love with that degenerate."

"So did I," Elizabeth added softly.

Jessica took a deep breath and managed a smile. "Well, we're safe now. Marin's back in prison, waiting for his trial. At least they didn't let him out on bail."

"Not with all those parole violations," Elizabeth said. "Besides, the charges are too serious. It's two counts of murder—"

"For killing those poor men Dad hired to protect us—"

"Along with all the other charges," Elizabeth continued with a shudder, "for the things he tried to do to us."

Jessica faced her twin and her eyes flashed. "I'm sure he'll get convicted of everything. So don't be afraid, Lizzie. John Marin can't hurt us anymore."

• • •

A half hour later Jessica let her fork fall to her plate with a loud clink. "That's it, Dad!" she said in an exasperated voice. "I can't take another second of this."

Her father's brown eyes widened with a look of fake innocence. "Whatever do you mean?"

"You've been smiling like a jack-o'-lantern from the moment you walked in the front door," Jessica told her father. "What's the big secret?"

Mr. Wakefield grinned more broadly. "I was going to wait to spring it on you over dessert."

"Spill it, Dad," Jessica urged. "Secrets were meant to be blabbed."

"Spoken by one who knows," Elizabeth said with a smirk. Jessica threw her a dirty look.

"I'm with Jessica this time," Mrs. Wakefield said. "We could all use some good news, Ned."

"OK, OK! You've beaten it out of me." He sat back in his chair and smiled at his family. "How would you all like to go on a little vacation?"

"Where—" Jessica began.

"I don't know, Ned," Mrs. Wakefield said, interrupting her daughter. "I'm right in the middle of my remodeling job." The twins' mother ran a successful interior-design firm in the Wakefields' hometown of Sweet Valley, California.

"Can't you take a little time off, Alice? The mansion in Bridgewater will still be there next week," her husband said. "Let the architect handle things without you for a few days. Besides, didn't you suggest just a week ago that we get out of town for a little while?"

Jessica opened her mouth again, but her mother spoke before she had the chance to make a sound.

"Yes, I suppose I did," Mrs. Wakefield said wistfully. "And it sounds tempting. After last week, we do need to spend some time together as a family."

"Some time *where*—?" Jessica asked.

"What about Steven?" Elizabeth asked at the same time. "Will he be able to get back from Sacramento to come with us?" The twins' eighteen-year-old brother was a summer intern with his father's law firm. Mr. Wakefield had sent him to the state capital for a few weeks to help an attorney who was working with a legislative subcommittee.

"No, I already called Steven," Mr. Wakefield said. "I sent him to Sacramento to keep him safe from Marin, but he's been so much help to Amanda that I doubt she'll want to let him go."

"*Go where?*" Jessica practically screamed. "In case you hadn't noticed, I'm dying of curiosity here—"

"Oh, Ned," Mrs. Wakefield interrupted. "Surely, Amanda would—"

"Of course she would let him take a week off if I asked her to," Mr. Wakefield said. "But Steven doesn't want to leave, as long as we're all safe and sound. He says he's learned more in the last two weeks than he did in his entire first year of prelaw classes."

Jessica grabbed a bowl of salsa and stood up. "Is someone going to tell me exactly where we're going?" she demanded. "If I don't find out within the next minute, I swear I'll drink this entire bowl of extra-hot salsa right here and now—and then you'll all have to watch me writhing on the floor in agony!"

Her father laughed. "I was thinking of an island vacation—"

"Hawaii!" Jessica shrieked, almost upsetting the bowl of salsa. "We're going to Hawaii! Wait till I tell Lila!" For once she would have a vacation that could compete with her wealthy best friend Lila Fowler's exotic trips. "I'll need a new bikini, and—"

Her father took her arm and gently pulled her back into her seat. "Jessica, slow down. Hawaii isn't exactly what I had in mind. But how about a week on Catalina Island?"

"That's not as good as Hawaii," Jessica admitted. "But it's a whole lot better than a week here!"

Her mother smiled. "It sounds wonderful, honey."

"What about work?" Elizabeth asked. "Jessica and I started waitressing less than two weeks ago. I don't know if Mr. Jenkins will be able to find replacements on such short notice."

Leave it to Liz to bring up work, Jessica thought. "Don't worry about it," she told her sister. "Jane and the other waitresses are desperate for more tips. They would love the extra shifts!"

"Are you sure?" Mr. Wakefield asked. "I could call Mr. Jenkins in the morning and talk to him myself."

"Well, Mr. Jenkins has been awfully nice to us, after what happened last weekend," Elizabeth said. "He said to take off some time if we thought we needed to—although I think he meant only a day or two."

"It's not a problem," Jessica said, waving her hand. "He probably feels guilty that Marin tried to attack me in his restaurant. He'll let us take as long as we want."

"I know!" Elizabeth said, snapping her fingers. "Maria Santelli said she wanted to earn some money for her cousin's wedding present. She'd jump at the chance to take on a few shifts at the Marina Cafe."

Jessica snorted. "Especially since Winston Egbert, Mr. Geek, is working at the beach nearby. It's sickening, the way those two are all over each other."

"I think it's sweet," Elizabeth said. "They make a nice couple."

"What's Winston doing at the beach this summer?" Mr. Wakefield asked, an amused look on his face. Like the twins, Winston was a junior at Sweet Valley High, and even the adults in town knew of his reputation for being the class clown.

"Winston is in charge of beach maintenance," Jessica said. "That means he's the beach *janitor*. Can you think of anything more gross than cleaning up after people?"

"It's no worse than being a waitress," Elizabeth reminded her. "Besides, Winston says he's a 'coastal-enhancement engineer.'"

Jessica rolled her eyes. "He would."

Elizabeth sighed. "Anyway, Maria is very responsible. And she has waitressing experience. I'll call her tonight. I think Mr. Jenkins will go along with the idea."

"Whatever," Jessica said. "So when do we leave?"

"I have us penciled in for two rooms at the Hotel Orizaba, beginning Saturday night," the girls' father told them. "We'll drive down to San Pedro the day after tomorrow and take the channel boat to Catalina."

"Cool!" Jessica said. "The Orizaba is supposed to be one of the ritziest resorts on the island. That'll show Lila!"

"How in the world did you manage rooms at the Orizaba, Ned?" Mrs. Wakefield asked. "Or anywhere on Catalina? I thought every room on the island was booked solid every summer, months in advance."

Her husband shrugged. "One of the partners in my firm—you know Marianna West—was supposed to go on vacation next week. But the depositions in the West Coast Oilcam case were pushed back. I know you've all heard me talking about the Oilcam case. It's a wrongful-dismissal action—"

"This is all very exciting, Dad," Jessica interrupted, rolling her eyes. "But is there a point to this story?"

"The point is that Oilcam is Marianna's case," Mr. Wakefield explained patiently, "so she's stuck with the extra work. She'll be at the office all weekend, in fact."

"I thought you were working on that case with Marianna," Elizabeth pointed out. "Won't you be tied up all weekend, too?"

"Not anymore. We decided today that it would be good experience for Griffin Pierce to take over for me." Mr. Wakefield smiled gleefully. Jessica remembered that Griffin Pierce was a money-grubbing young associate that her father couldn't stand. "Anyway," he continued, "it means that Marianna has to give up her reservations for two rooms for all next week—"

"I always liked her!" Jessica interrupted, grinning.

"We certainly could use some relaxation," Mrs. Wakefield added. "Ever since I got back into town Sunday, I've been so skittish that I jump every time the phone rings. I don't think I slept at all last night."

Her husband put his arm around her shoulders.

"You're not the only one," he said, glancing at the twins. The whole family, Jessica realized, looked worn and haggard. Mr. Wakefield sighed. "It'll be nice to leave our troubles behind for a week of nothing but pure relaxation."

Chapter 2

Later that night Elizabeth leaned her elbow on her desk, cradling the telephone against her ear. She heard a door creak open behind her. "Get out, Jessica!" she called without turning around. Only one person ever came through the door that led to the bathroom between her room and her sister's. "Can't you see I'm on the phone?"

"I'll wait," Jessica said, punctuating her words with a snap of bubblegum. Bedsprings squeaked as she made herself comfortable.

Elizabeth whirled in her seat to glare at her twin, who was sitting cross-legged on the neatly made bed, spreading some papers in front of her on the comforter. Elizabeth turned back to the desk. Ignoring Jessica was always easier than trying to get rid of her. "I'm sorry, Todd," she said into the receiver. "It's only Jessica."

Elizabeth's longtime boyfriend, Todd Wilkins, had never been one of Jessica's biggest fans, but now he laughed. "As usual," he said. "Well, for once I'm not going to complain about Jessica popping in unexpectedly. I owe her one, since she saved your life last weekend."

"And I owe *you* one. I'm sorry I acted like such a jerk all last week," Elizabeth said softly, apologizing for the fourth time since Sunday morning. She could feel her sister's gossip radar tuned in on the conversation, and she was glad that Jessica could hear only one side of it.

"Liz, you have nothing to apologize for," Todd said. "*I* was the jerk—for not realizing how bored you were."

"No, Todd—"

"Yes, Liz. You were right. We've been in a rut. If I hadn't been so oblivious, we could have worked it out together. Then you wouldn't have thought you had to sneak around with Ben, or Marin, or whatever the guy's real name is."

Elizabeth shook her head. "But it was wrong of me to see someone else," she admitted. "I knew it, and I did it anyway."

"I won't argue with you there. And if you hadn't nearly got yourself killed, I'd probably be furious. As it is, I'm just glad you're all right." He lowered his voice, and Elizabeth sensed anger beneath his words. "But if you ever date somebody else behind my back again . . ."

"Don't worry!" she assured him. "I've learned my lesson. And I've had enough excitement these last few weeks to last for a year. As soon as I return from Catalina, I'm looking forward to going back to our happy little rut!"

"Have a great week, Liz," Todd said tenderly. "And remember that I love you."

With a pleasant warmth in her chest, Elizabeth slowly hung up the phone, thinking about Todd's deep-brown eyes and soft, wavy hair. It was hard to believe that she'd been dissatisfied with him only a week earlier.

"How's lover boy?" Jessica asked.

Elizabeth turned to see her blowing an enormous pink bubble. "Haven't you ever heard of a private conversation?"

Jessica deflated the bubble with her tongue. After she'd loudly sucked the gum back into her mouth, she said, "Private? But we're identical twins. We share everything, remember?"

"Right. The way we share *my* sweaters, *my* jeans, *my* blouses . . ."

Jessica shrugged. "That's a nice way to talk to someone who saved your life."

"I already thanked you for that!" Elizabeth objected, annoyed.

"You know, the whole coast guard may have been there Saturday night, but I was the only one who was watching you instead of Marin," Jessica reminded her.

"Don't change the subject!" Elizabeth broke in. "We were talking about your interrupting me. Todd and I were having a private conversation."

"What's the big deal? It was pretty tame, if you ask me."

"OK, OK," Elizabeth said with a sigh. Sometimes arguing with Jessica just wasn't worth the trouble. "Let's drop it. So what's up? I assume you came in here for something besides eavesdropping on my phone calls."

"What did Maria say?" Jessica asked. "I didn't start eavesdropping soon enough to hear that call."

"She said she'd love to be a waitress for a week. I'll speak to Mr. Jenkins in the morning, and she'll have an interview with him tomorrow afternoon about taking some of our shifts."

"Great!" Jessica said. "We definitely got the best of that deal. Catalina's going to be fantastic!" She waved a handful of glossy pamphlets.

"What are those?"

"Brochures about the island and the Hotel Orizaba," Jessica replied. "Dad said we should read through them and get an idea of all the fun things we want to do next week."

"I'd be happy just sitting on a nice, warm, safe beach, reading a mystery novel."

"Bor-ing!" Jessica pronounced. "Are you sure you're my sister? Sometimes I think you were abducted by aliens as an infant and replaced with an Elizabeth look-alike."

"Boring is exactly what I'm looking for," Elizabeth said. "Don't you think we've had enough adventure for one summer?"

"Nah," Jessica said. "Just the wrong kind of adventure. Sitting on the beach is OK, but reading books is definitely out. School ended two weeks ago! Beaches aren't for reading, anyway. They're for showing off in a bikini, working on your tan, and scoping out good-looking surfers."

"What about Ken?" Elizabeth asked. In the last few months Jessica had begun seriously dating Ken Matthews, the star quarterback for the Sweet Valley High Gladiators.

"If Ken were on the beach in Catalina, I'd scope him out, too," Jessica said diplomatically. "But he's still on vacation with his parents. So what's wrong with looking at other guys?"

"Isn't that what got you into trouble last week?" Elizabeth asked.

"*Looking* at cute guys never got anyone in trouble." Jessica smiled at her sister. "It's all that stuff you do *after* you look that can be a problem."

Elizabeth folded her arms. "Since when do you stop at just looking?"

"Don't worry," Jessica said. "After what happened with Scott—I mean *Marin*—I plan to restrict myself to just looking for a while."

"I'm sure that dozens of surfers on Catalina will be sorry to hear that."

"But really, Liz, we're perfectly safe now. The

odds of running into *another* super-sexy guy who's also a serial killer are practically nonexistent. There just aren't that many murderers out there, and we already found one this summer. So, statistically, there's no danger anymore."

Elizabeth laughed. "I can't argue with logic like that."

"Of course not," Jessica said. She snapped her gum. "Remember, I took statistics last year."

"And got a C-minus, I seem to recall."

"Oh, *grades* are no big deal," Jessica said, waving the whole concept away with her hand. Studying had never been high on her priority list.

"I'll keep that in mind," Elizabeth said, thinking of her own straight-A report card. "So what's in these brochures? Tips on the best beaches for watching surfers?"

"Yep. That's in this one," Jessica said, pointing to a pamphlet. On the cover a blond man and woman stood on a sandy beach, silhouetted against an orange sunset. Jessica fanned out the other brochures. "There's also stuff on shopping, snorkeling, and tennis. We're going to have the best time, Liz."

"This does look like fun," Elizabeth agreed, scanning another brochure. "Listen to this, Jess. It says here that visitors aren't allowed to drive cars on the island. Everyone gets around by walking, taking the shuttle bus, or renting golf carts."

"Lame!" Jessica announced. "It'll be difficult to look glamorous on a shuttle bus." She paged through another leaflet and then glanced up at her twin excitedly. "I've got it! We'll go horseback riding! It says here that the resort we're staying at has a ranch. We can rent horses and go on guided horseback rides."

"We haven't been horseback riding in ages," Elizabeth said.

"True," Jessica agreed, nodding her head. "But we used to be pretty good at it. And horseback riding is like riding a bicycle—you never forget. You know, I'm always amazed at just how good guys look on horseback."

"Jess, do you ever think about anything else?" Elizabeth asked.

"Not if I can help it," Jessica replied.

Elizabeth shook her head and pulled another brochure from the pile. Jessica was hopeless. "The botanical garden sounds beautiful," she tried. "And look at these pictures of the shoreline! Isn't this gorgeous?" She pointed to a photograph that showed an isolated cove surrounded by sheer bluffs.

"It says you can take a tour around the coastline of the island in a glass-bottom boat. That might be cool."

"No, thanks!" Elizabeth said. "As much as I love boats, I've had enough of them to last me a long, long time." She shuddered, her mind flashing back to her desperate struggle for Marin's knife on the deck of his sailboat. "Once we get to the island, I'm going to keep my feet on solid ground for the whole vacation!"

Chapter 3

Leighann LeShay adjusted the gun in her shoulder holster. Then she smoothed her frizzy black hair and took a deep breath. Thursday's night shift was about to start. "I hate this job," she told her reflection in the women's bathroom mirror.

"You aren't the only one, honey," said a short, round woman who emerged from a stall. "I've worked in this stinking prison for fourteen years. And believe me, those filthy-mouthed Neanderthals never let up for a minute." She pulled out a comb and ran it through her short gray-blond hair. "By the way, the name's Phyllis," she said, sticking out a hand.

"I'm Leighann. And you're right about the filthy language. In the last two weeks I've heard more four-letter words than I knew existed."

"I bet you have," the older woman said. "The

inmates must think you're real pretty. And you're young." She cocked her head. "How old are you? You don't look any more than eighteen."

Leighann stretched to her full height of five foot one. "I'm twenty-three."

Phyllis nodded. "Like I said, you're young. So these reptiles probably hassle you a heck of a lot worse than they hassle me. How long you been on the job, hon?"

"Exactly two weeks," Leighann said. "Cellblock A."

Phyllis laughed. "That says it all. Cellblock A always seems to have the worst, uh, *customers*. The cream of the scum, you know?"

"Tell me about it," Leighann said. "Is there any way to shut them up?"

"Not really," Phyllis replied. "But you've got to act like it doesn't bother you. They'll hassle you worse if they see that it's getting to you."

Leighann smoothed out the blouse of her guard's uniform. "But how can I pretend it doesn't bother me when they say nasty, disgusting things?"

"Just put on your best poker face when they start to get rowdy." Phyllis demonstrated her best uncaring expression in the mirror—her eyes closed halfway, and her mouth became a tight, hard line. "Then visualize yourself as John Wayne or Clint Eastwood. Cool and confident."

Leighann tried to copy Phyllis's expression, but she thought her eyes still looked too friendly and trusting. She grimaced. "I was always lousy at poker," she said with a sigh. Then Leighann turned away from the mirror and pushed open the bathroom door. "Well, it's time to enter the reptile house. See you around."

She moved slowly toward cellblock A, steeling herself for the catcalls and leers that always followed her as she walked the block. There were only a few female guards at the state prison, and most were much older than Leighann. When she was on duty, the prisoners vied with each other to come up with the raunchiest jeers. All except the prisoner in cell 202. He seemed to be a real gentleman.

Leighann passed through the metal detector and stopped at the steel-barred gate at the entrance to the cellblock. Again she straightened her blue-gray uniform. Then she pushed her way into cellblock A, hoping the polite, handsome young man in 202 would be awake.

Jessica sat in the driver's seat of the black Jeep the twins shared, drumming her fingers on the steering wheel. She and Elizabeth had just finished working Friday's lunch shift at the cafe, and she was eager to get home and start packing for the trip.

"Finally!" Jessica exclaimed as her twin opened the passenger-side door and climbed into the Jeep. "What took you so long? You said you were coming out right behind me."

"Sorry, Jess," Elizabeth said. "But Todd came in to say good-bye."

"We're spending a week on Catalina—not a year in Kathmandu," Jessica reminded her sister. "Can't you two get along without each other for seven measly days?"

"Of course we can," Elizabeth said with a grin. "But we haven't caught up yet from not seeing much of each other last week. Can you blame us for wanting to say good-bye?"

Jessica gunned the engine. "I swear, Liz, you were more interesting when you decided to add some excitement to your life."

"That kind of excitement I don't need," Elizabeth said. "And neither do you. Besides, don't you miss Ken at all?"

Jessica was about to open her mouth to say she didn't. But she shut it. She liked to think she was totally independent and didn't need any one guy to make her happy. But every time she thought of Ken's sun-bleached hair and broad shoulders, a wave of loneliness washed over her. "Yes," she admitted. "I guess I do miss him."

Elizabeth gave her a knowing look. "You say that as if you were confessing something awful. There's nothing wrong with liking somebody special. Ken's a great guy."

"I know. But I'm supposed to be Jessica love-'em-and-leave-'em Wakefield, the free agent. I can't believe I've actually got myself tied down."

Elizabeth stared at her curiously. "Are you saying you're not in love with Ken anymore?"

"That's just the problem," Jessica said. "I do love Ken! I'm happier when he's here. Isn't that a drag?"

"I see what you mean. Love and happiness—ugh!"

"I thought there was some hope for you last week," Jessica said. "But I was wrong. You're as boring as ever."

"Well, excuse me. I still don't see what the problem is. I think it's great that you're in love with Ken."

Jessica sighed dramatically. "Don't you understand anything? Think about it. Right now I want to be with Ken all the time. That's how it always starts. Next thing you know, we'll spend our weekends sitting around in the house in Sweet Valley High sweatshirts, watching sappy old movies on the VCR. Or worse yet, we'll go *bowling*!" She grimaced. "We'll be as boring as you and Todd."

"How would you ever live with yourself?" Elizabeth asked.

"Exactly."

"Jessica, I was joking," Elizabeth explained with a sigh.

"I hate it when you get sarcastic," Jessica complained.

"And I hate it when you criticize me and Todd."

"What's not to criticize?" Jessica shot back.

"This is getting nowhere," Elizabeth said. "Let's talk about something else."

"Fine." Jessica turned the Jeep onto Calico Drive. "Have you decided what you're packing for Catalina?"

"I plan to travel light," Elizabeth said. "Just a few tops, a couple pairs of walking shorts, and maybe a pair of khakis. Oh, and both of my bathing suits."

"Are you crazy? We're staying at a classy resort! We'll go dancing at night, eat at the best restaurants on the island, meet rich, interesting people . . . and you want to do it wearing *walking shorts?*"

"Jessica, the last time I dressed up, it was for John Marin—and look where that got me! I thought *he* was a rich, interesting person." Elizabeth rubbed the sides of her arms. "Just thinking about him now makes my skin crawl. Rich, interesting people are very low on my priority list for this vacation. All I want to do is relax."

Jessica smiled. "While Maria waits tables at the cafe instead of us."

"I'm glad Mr. Jenkins liked her so much at her interview today," Elizabeth said.

"Me, too," Jessica agreed. "Now we won't have to call in every day and pretend we're both sick."

"Jessica! We couldn't have done that!"

"Why not?" Jessica asked breezily. "People do it all the time."

"*I* don't! I'd stay home all week before I did something so dishonest."

"Well, excuse me, Miss Perfect Twin. You didn't seem to mind lying last week when you were sneaking around with Marin," Jessica reminded her sister.

"I wasn't the only one who was sneaking around last week," Elizabeth pointed out. "I seem to remember a certain person who even admitted to breaking into the school through the locker-room window, just to impress a phony television producer."

"Nobody's perfect!" Jessica said cheerfully. Actually, she was secretly glad that Elizabeth had been taken in by Marin, too—and that she also had lied about dating him. Jessica loved her sister more than anything, but at times Elizabeth's good-twin routine got tiring—especially since it implied that Jessica was the evil twin. Of course, Jessica had never wanted to see her sister in danger. She glanced at Elizabeth, and her annoyance dissolved when she remembered how close she'd come to losing her.

"Anyhow," Elizabeth said, "Mr. Jenkins seemed impressed that we took the trouble to find somebody to fill in for us. He said"—she lowered her voice into a reasonable impersonation of their boss—"'It's gratifying to see a person your age who has such a strong sense of responsibility, *Jessica*.' Yes, he called me Jessica. As usual."

Jessica laughed as she pulled the Jeep into the driveway of the Wakefield house. "What a jerk! He'll never be able to tell us apart."

"Not unless you dye your hair black again," Elizabeth said, laughing.

"No, thanks," Jessica replied, remembering a time early in the year when she had dyed her hair and changed her image, in order to show everyone that she had an identity apart from her twin. "That was a long, long time ago, when I was young and stupid. Now I know the truth: Blondes really do have more fun. And I plan to prove it this week on Catalina Island."

The twins' mother rifled through the nightgowns in her bureau drawer Friday night, searching for one to take to Santa Catalina. She was looking for something—well, a little romantic. Her husband had been so tense for the past week that he had felt like a stranger. *It's no wonder,* she thought, watching him out of the corner of her eye as he sat on the bed, sorting socks. *He spent the whole week trying to protect his family from a murderer.* She selected a long, elegant gown of aqua silk and folded it gently into her suitcase. *This vacation will do Ned a world of good,* she thought.

Then she shook her head. As concerned as she was about her husband, Mrs. Wakefield had to admit that she was angry with him as well. It was his own fault that he'd spent a week in agony, trying to cope all alone, while his family was in danger. *He should have told me*, she thought.

Suddenly a loud crash echoed through the house, and Mr. Wakefield jumped to his feet. *"What was that noise?"* he shouted, his voice trembling.

Mrs. Wakefield's annoyance abated when she saw the fear in her husband's eyes. "Calm down, Ned," she said in a soothing voice. "I'm sure it's nothing. My guess is that Jessica's trying to pack."

"Ahhh," he murmured, nodding. The chaotic state of Jessica's bedroom was legendary.

"I bet all the shoes and handbags she's got crammed onto the top shelf of her closet just took a flying leap when she pulled out her suitcase."

Mr. Wakefield laughed, but it sounded forced. She crossed the room and stood behind him. "You need to relax, honey," she said, kneading the tense muscles of his shoulders. "You've been on edge for so long."

Her husband groaned appreciatively.

"I still wish you had told me last week that Marin was out of prison and coming after the girls," she said. "We could have helped each other through it."

"Do we have to go over that again, Alice?" he asked. "I told you, I didn't want to scare you."

"Why not? It seems to me that we all had a legitimate reason to be scared. You shouldn't have taken it all on yourself. They're my daughters, too."

"But the whole thing was my responsibility," Mr. Wakefield insisted. "It was only because of me that Marin was stalking the twins."

"You can't blame yourself, Ned. You were just doing your job when you got Marin convicted. You can't honestly tell me that you regret putting him away." Mrs. Wakefield spoke forcefully, but she had repeated the same words so many times that she barely knew what she was saying anymore. Deep inside, she was wondering if an aqua silk nightgown and a week on Catalina Island would be enough to heal the hurt she felt at being excluded from protecting her children.

"No, of course I don't regret sending Marin to prison," her husband replied. "What I regret is that the parole board let him out. I wanted to tell you about it as soon as I read in the newspaper that he was free. But I knew how afraid you'd feel."

"How I would *feel*, Ned?" Mrs. Wakefield asked, her voice rising. "Think about how I felt Sunday morning! I thought I was going to have a heart attack when I pulled into the driveway. Arriving to find four police cars in our driveway, a broken window, and blood on the carpet is not my idea of a pleasant homecoming." She saw his face cloud over and instantly regretted her words. The last thing her husband needed to be reminded of was blood on the carpet. She forced a grin. "And then there was poor Prince Albert, floating around like a helium balloon."

Her husband chuckled, genuinely this time.

The dog had still been feeling the effects of the drugs Marin had given him the night before, to put him to sleep so he wouldn't bark.

She sighed. "I've never been so happy to see you and the girls safe as I was that morning."

"And we were never so happy to be safe. That was some wild night."

"I should have been with you through it," she said, unable to keep the anger from creeping back into her voice. "I'll never understand why you let me go off to Oakland when you knew the girls were in danger."

Mr. Wakefield turned to his wife and put his hands on her shoulders. "I thought you might be in danger, too," he said softly.

Mrs. Wakefield turned away from him and began to fold clothing into her suitcase. "In case you hadn't noticed, Ned," she told her husband, "I'm not a teenager. I have as much right to defend this family as you do. You should have trusted me enough to tell me the truth."

"It's not a question of trust, Alice," Mr. Wakefield said. "We're talking about your safety. Marin said he'd come after the girls *first*. But he threatened you, too."

"Then I have the right to defend myself!" Mrs. Wakefield spoke bravely, but she sat down heavily on the edge of the bed and shuddered. She knew she and her daughters were safe now, but she suddenly felt violently, inexplicably afraid.

○   ○   ○

Jessica stood firm beneath the avalanche of shoes and handbags that tumbled down from her closet. She and Elizabeth, standing side by side, had just jerked out her old powder-blue suitcase. Jessica laughed as a black silk scarf drifted downward and draped itself over her sister's face.

Elizabeth swiped the scarf aside. "Honestly, Jessica, I don't know how you can ever find anything in this mess."

"It's easy," Jessica replied. "Everything I own is in plain sight. All I have to do is look around the room, and I can see whatever it is I want." She tossed the suitcase onto her unmade bed. "*I* don't know how *you* can find anything in that echo chamber you call a bedroom."

"I know what you're going to say next," Elizabeth began. She raised her voice to mimic Jessica's more dramatic style of speaking. "*We have nothing at all in common. If we didn't look exactly alike, you'd swear we weren't even rela—*"

"Actually, we have one very big thing in common," Jessica interrupted, suddenly thoughtful. "We both fell for Marin."

"Yes," Elizabeth said in a quiet voice. "We did."

"What was the first thing that attracted you to him?" Jessica asked.

Elizabeth turned toward the window and

shook her head vehemently. "I don't want to think about it."

"But you should," Jessica urged. "You're *supposed* to talk about traumatic things like unhappy love affairs; it helps you analyze what went wrong so you don't fall into the same kind of dysfunctional-relationship pattern again."

Elizabeth spun to stare at her. "Where did you hear that?"

"I read it in *Ingenue* magazine," Jessica answered.

"This is a little more than an unhappy love affair, Jess. This creep tried to murder us! And Dad." She wrapped her arms around herself, as if for warmth.

"Exactly! That's why you have to talk about it." Jessica shoved a huge pile of clothes across the bed to clear a space. Then she flopped down onto the bed, motioning for Elizabeth to take the desk chair.

"Hey!" Elizabeth exclaimed, lifting something blue and wrinkled from the seat. "This is my favorite blouse!"

Jessica shrugged. "Oh, I forgot to tell you—I borrowed your blouse."

"Thanks a lot. I just ironed this!"

Jessica smiled at her sister. "Well, it doesn't look like you did a very good job."

Elizabeth glared at her.

"OK, OK! I'm sorry. I'll iron it for you tonight so you can pack it," Jessica offered.

"No, thanks," Elizabeth said. "Scorch marks aren't in style this season. I'll do it myself."

Jessica grinned. There were advantages to having no domestic skills. She picked through the clothes on the bed until she found the shortest pair of cutoffs she owned and tossed them into the suitcase. "You never answered my question," she persisted. "What was it that attracted you to John Marin?"

Elizabeth took a deep breath. "The first time I saw him, I was with Todd at the Dairi Burger. Todd was getting on my nerves—"

"That's not surprising," Jessica said, arching an eyebrow.

Elizabeth ignored her. "—and I was wondering if Todd and I were really all that compatible. I wished I could find a guy who was my true soul mate." She paused, her eyes glassy.

"And then?"

"And then I looked up, and this amazing-looking guy was sitting by himself in a corner booth, writing in a notebook," Elizabeth continued, staring at her hands. "He had broad shoulders and tousled light-brown hair. He looked up. And our eyes locked, just like in the movies." She turned to her sister, but her voice was so low that Jessica could hardly hear it. "Even from that far away, I could see that his eyes were deep, dark blue."

Jessica shuddered. "They certainly were."

Elizabeth felt a shiver run through her. "Then I had this sudden rock-solid conviction that he was my soul mate—that we were meant to be together."

"If I didn't know you're talking about Marin, I would think that was a terribly romantic story," Jessica said.

"How could he do something like that to me?" Elizabeth asked, tears sprouting in her eyes. "Now just thinking about him makes me want to throw up!"

"Me, too," Jessica said. She rooted through a tangle of panty hose, searching for a pair with no runs. "The first time I saw Marin was at the Marina Cafe," she remembered. "I was mad at you because our shift was over and you were going home."

"Oh, good reason to be mad at me," Elizabeth complained sarcastically.

"I had every right to be mad! You were leaving, but I had to stick around at work, dead on my feet and smelling like french fries. I had this dorky customer who was taking six years to drink one cup of coffee."

Elizabeth rolled her eyes. "And naturally that was my fault."

"OK, maybe that part wasn't your fault," Jessica conceded.

"I wasn't getting along with Todd at all last week, so you probably got the better end of that deal," Elizabeth reminded her.

"Well, you and Todd at least *looked* happy together. I guess I was missing Ken. Then I saw this really hot car pull up outside—a fire-engine-red Mazda Miata."

"Oh, gosh!" Elizabeth exclaimed. "I remember that car! We were pulling out of the parking lot, and Todd went wild over this great sports car that zoomed past us. But we didn't notice the driver."

"That was Marin. Or Scott Maderlake, as he was calling himself." She closed her eyes, remembering the instant attraction she'd felt when he'd walked through the door of the restaurant. Now the thought of him made her skin crawl. "Do you have any panty hose that aren't torn to shreds?" she asked, suddenly desperate to change the subject. "I need to borrow two or three pairs."

"If you planned ahead, you wouldn't be stuck without them at the last minute."

"If I planned ahead, nobody would be able to tell us apart," Jessica replied. "Everybody would call me Elizabeth, like Mr. Jenkins does."

"I give up!" Elizabeth exclaimed. "You can have *one* pair of panty hose—but that's all. I'll get them for you later. But you were telling me about Marin. I suppose you practically threw yourself at him."

"No way!" Jessica objected. "Besides, I didn't have to. He asked me if I could answer some questions about Sweet Valley. It wouldn't have been very friendly of me to refuse, would it?"

"So that's when you started seeing him?"

"We made a date for me to show him around town the next day," Jessica said. "And the rest was history." She held up a strapless red tube dress. "Do you think Dad would have a heart attack if he saw me wear this in public?"

"What is it, a sock with sequins?"

"Very funny," Jessica said with a snort. "It's a dress, dummy. If you had any fashion sense—"

"And if you had any *common* sense—"

Jessica held up her hand. "OK, so I'll take along a jacket to wear over it." She smiled. "Until I'm out of Mom and Dad's sight, that is."

Mrs. Wakefield's golden hair shimmered softly in the darkness. From her slow, regular breathing, her husband knew she was finally asleep. *This past week has been terrible for her*, he thought sadly. *And so much of that is my fault*. At least she was safe now; Marin hadn't touched her. But he sensed a new distance between himself and his wife—a gap he couldn't seem to bridge. *I should have told her about Marin*, he thought. He vowed to make it up to her. It would do them good to spend some time together, with no worries and no responsibilities.

But he couldn't stop horrifying images from flashing through his head: Jessica's eyes widening with fear when she recognized John Marin's photograph as her new boyfriend . . . Elizabeth's scream as she fought for Marin's knife on the deck of the sailing yacht . . . the searing pain that exploded in his temples as Marin bashed him with a board . . . and the glint of Marin's knife as the killer stood over the twins, who had slept together that night in Elizabeth's room.

"I'm never going to fall asleep tonight," he whispered, swinging his legs over the edge of the bed. His wife murmured something and turned on her side. He slipped out of bed and into the hallway.

The house was utterly silent—as silent as it had seemed at midnight, six days before. That night the peacefulness had been a cruel facade. Deep down, he doubted that he would ever again trust the silence of night.

Elizabeth's door was ajar. Her father stood outside it, listening to her deep, soft breathing. She was asleep. No doubt Jessica was sleeping, too, behind her own door—with Prince Albert stretched across the foot of her rumpled bed. Marin was in prison. Certainly the twins were as safe now as they'd ever been.

Their father's thoughts returned to a time ten years years ago, when he had stood behind the prosecutor's table in the courtroom where Marin had just been sentenced to prison. Handcuffs clinked as the police led the murderer away.

"I won't forget you, Wakefield!" Marin shouted

over his shoulder. *"You or your whole family. Your precious little girls will never be safe again!"*

Mr. Wakefield closed his eyes and leaned against the wall outside Elizabeth's room, the plaster cold and smooth against the tense muscles of his back. Following the memory of Marin's threat, a wave of anger, fear, and hatred overwhelmed him—as it had on Saturday night, when he'd stepped through the door and seen the killer leaning over his sleeping daughters. In their sleep the girls had seemed nearly as young as the pretty six-year-olds they'd been when Marin had first threatened them. And just as fragile.

The scene in Elizabeth's bedroom replayed itself in his mind, in slow motion. *Adrenaline rushed through his limbs as he hurled his body into Marin's. And the murderer flew through the window in an explosion of glass.*

"It's over," he had whispered when he'd spotted Marin's crumpled form on the ground below, illuminated by the headlights of police cars.

But now he wondered if it ever really would be.

Chapter 4

"Hey, sugar!" called the brutish inmate in cell 206.

Leighann scowled at him, trying to look taller than she was. Jerry "Pit Bull" Pitts had a face like Frankenstein's and a physique to match. Even behind bars, he could intimidate her. But she was a prison guard. She would not allow the inmates to see that she was afraid.

"Shut up, Pitts!" she demanded in her toughest voice. It was well before dawn on Saturday morning, but Pitts seemed wide-awake and ready for action. Leighann, on the other hand, was only halfway through the night shift, and she was dead tired. She straightened her back and tried to visualize herself as alert and confident—like Clint Eastwood.

"When you gonna come visit me, baby?" Pitts asked. He licked his lips suggestively. "I'd sure make it worth your while."

"Bug off, creep!" Leighann shot back.

"Ooh, listen to her talk tough!" Pitts called, his voice echoing through the cellblock. "It makes me crazy when you do that, honey."

Leighann narrowed her eyes and tried to look menacing. "Go ahead—make my day!" she challenged. "I'll put you on report if you say another word."

"Man, I'm scared now! That would make—what, four times this month?"

"That's it, Pitts. You're going on report!"

"Why don't you come a little closer, baby? I'll give you something to report!"

Leighann felt so frustrated she wanted to scream.

"Leave her alone, Pit Bull!" commanded a deep voice from two cells down. John Marin's voice sounded angry but controlled. "If I hear you giving her a hard time again, I swear I'll make you sorry."

Leighann saw genuine fear in Pit Bull's eyes as he backed away from the bars. "That's right," she told Pit Bull. "You'd better listen to John." She took a deep breath and smoothed the soft wings of frizzy hair that always insisted on breaking free of her guard's hat. Then she walked to Marin's cell.

"Thanks for your help, John," she said softly. "I'll never understand how a guy your size manages to intimidate a goon like Pitts."

"What do you mean, a guy my size?" Marin demanded. He pretended to be insulted, but a grin broke through, making his chiseled features even more handsome. "I'm not exactly a ninety-eight-pound weakling," he reminded her, brushing a lock of light-brown hair from his startlingly dark-blue eyes.

"No, you're certainly not," Leighann said. She glanced over his body admiringly. Marin wasn't nearly as big as Pitts. But he was over six feet tall, and powerfully built. Even the shapeless slate-gray prison uniform couldn't mask his broad shoulders and narrow hips.

Steady, girl, she told herself. *This man may be innocent, but he's still an inmate here.* Leighann was new enough on the job to remember the exact words in the employee manual: *"Fraternizing between inmates and guards is strictly prohibited."*

"So how do you get a guy like Pit Bull to back down?" she asked.

John leaned his head close to the bars, as if he were about to impart a great secret. "Psychology," he said, tapping his temple with his finger. "If you pay attention and learn enough about people, you can figure out what makes them tick and know exactly what to say to have them eating out of your hand."

"I'll have to try it sometime," Leighann said. Suddenly she noticed that Marin had one arm curled protectively around his abdomen. "John, is something the matter? Are you sick?"

John shook his head. "It's nothing. Just some indigestion from last night's dinner. You know—prison food!"

"Don't I know it! We eat the same stuff in the employee cafeteria," Leighann said. "Is that why you're awake so early?"

"Yeah, I guess so," John said. "I've been tossing and turning all night. What was in those sloppy joes? It feels like I've swallowed a handful of rocks."

Leighann peered worriedly into John's cell. "Can I bring you an antacid from the infirmary?" she asked.

"Thanks for being concerned. But don't go to any trouble. I'm sure it'll go away on its own." He smiled so warmly at Leighann that she had to forbid herself to blush. "Seeing you is the best medicine, anyway," he continued. "It doesn't hurt nearly as much as it did before you stopped by."

"Are you sure you don't want me to get you something?"

"I'm sure," he answered. "Besides, I want to talk to you. I made you something in wood shop yesterday."

"That was sweet of you," Leighann said, a little nervously. "But I'm not allowed to accept gifts from inmates."

"I know," he said with a shrug. "But I couldn't

help myself. You've been so kind to me."

She frowned. "Why shouldn't I be? You're the only guy in this whole rotten cellblock who isn't a degenerate."

"And you're the only person in this whole rotten prison who believes in me," he said. "The rest of them think I'm guilty of killing those two men."

"Well, they're wrong," Leighann said staunchly. "My supervisor and the warden keep telling me you're evil. But I know it's not true. You're not a killer, like that worm Pit Bull. Anyone can tell you're innocent just by talking to you."

John shook his head. "Nobody else seems to think so."

"Don't worry," Leighann told him. "It'll all come out at the trial. Once you tell the judge how you were framed, you'll be home free."

John hesitated. "And then," he said, suddenly shy, "I mean, if you want to, the two of us can spend some time together—without bars separating us."

Leighann searched his face for any hint that he might be joking, or just leading her on. She had felt an almost irresistible attraction to John Marin right from the moment she first saw him. But she knew that a lot of good-looking guys were completely insincere; they flirted almost as a matter of habit. *And he's a prison inmate, of all things!* she warned herself. Still, the look in John's eyes was honest, open, and full of affection.

"Do you mean that, John?" she asked suspiciously.

"Of course I do," he said, his stunning blue eyes staring directly into hers. "I know it's corny. I've only known you a few days, but being locked up in this place gives a guy a lot of time to think. And all I can think about is you."

Leighann felt a fluttering in her chest, like butterflies. It was the first time John had come close to admitting that he shared the same strong emotions that she felt for him.

From the day they'd met, Leighann had been blown away by John's looks. As she got to know him, she'd decided that his appeal was more than physical—he was a truly nice person, and he always treated her with respect. At first she worried that she was too old for him. After all, Leighann was twenty-three; John didn't look older than twenty. That wasn't an enormous difference, but some guys had a problem with dating older women. Then Leighann had done some checking, and she had learned that he was actually twenty-eight.

Now, with him gazing at her with his mysterious dark-blue eyes, Leighann knew she would fall for him no matter how old he was. "I seem to be thinking about you a lot lately, too," she admitted.

"Does that mean you'll accept the present I made you?" he asked, smiling shyly at her.

Leighann looked down cellblock A to see if

Manuel Ramos, the shift supervisor, was nearby. Manuel wasn't in sight—he was probably doing his rounds of the prisoners on the upper level. "I don't know, John. I've only been in this crummy job two weeks. I can't afford to get in trouble. What if somebody notices me carrying a present from you out of here?"

John smiled. "I already thought of that," he said, pulling a small bundle from beneath his pillow. "This is so tiny, it will fit in your pocket. No one will notice a thing." He stuck it through the bars.

Leighann turned the paper-wrapped package in her hands. "John, you really didn't have to go through the trouble of making me a present. Especially since I don't have anything for you."

"You can owe me one," he said, smiling impishly. "Don't worry—I won't forget to collect."

His gaze made Leighann feel warm all over. Embarrassed, she turned her attention to the bundle in her hands and was surprised to find her fingers trembling as she unwrapped it. She hadn't felt this way about a guy in ages.

"Oh, John!" she breathed. "You *made* this? It's absolutely gorgeous."

In her palm was a perfect, tiny replica of a sailboat. Its miniature sails were so realistic, they seemed to billow in the breeze. "Oh, John," Leighann sighed. "It's lovely."

"To me a sailboat means freedom," John said

quietly. "If I ever get out of this place, I'm going to buy a sailboat and travel anywhere I want to go."

Leighann stared at the beautiful little boat. In her mind it grew to full size. John Marin stood on the deck, his hair tousled from the ocean breeze and his eyes squinting against the sun-gilded waves. "I bet you will, too," she said, unable to keep the wistfulness from creeping into her voice.

"Leighann," John asked, his expression solemn, "if I do get out of here, will you go sailing with me?"

"I would like that," Leighann murmured, deeply moved. She heard a noise at the far end of the cellblock and whirled to see Manuel descending the open spiral staircase from the upper level. "I'll treasure the boat always, John. But I've got to finish my rounds. I'll stop by to see you again before my shift ends, to see how you're feeling."

"Until then I'll think about the two of us together on the ocean, free," he said in a low, sexy tone that left her breathless. "Have you ever been on a moonlight sail, Leighann?"

"I've never even been on a boat," she admitted.

"You'll love it, Leighann," he assured her. "Trust me."

Through the window of her father's rust-brown Ford LTD, Elizabeth watched the safe and sleepy ranch-style houses of Calico Drive glide by in the early-morning sunlight. The neighborhood looked as cheerful and orderly as it always did, but Elizabeth couldn't help feeling that something lurked beneath Sweet Valley's peaceful appearance on that cheerful Saturday morning. Something dangerous.

She shook her head as if to clear the thought from her mind. *Don't be so melodramatic*, she told herself. *Marin is in prison. We don't have to be afraid anymore.*

Her father sighed from the front seat. "It's good to finally be on the road," he said quietly. "It will be a relief to get away from here."

"Oh, my gosh!" Jessica exclaimed suddenly. Her eyes were wide with fear.

Elizabeth saw her father's fingers tense on the steering wheel. "What's the matter?" he asked in a choked voice.

"I forgot to turn on the answering machine!"

Elizabeth laughed. To Jessica, a missed phone call was a major catastrophe. "Oh, no!" she commiserated. "And I thought you were worried about something minor—like a natural disaster."

"This *is* a disaster! What if Ken calls?"

"It's all right, Jess," her mother said, smiling. "*I* turned on the answering machine. But what about Prince Albert? Did you girls find someone to look after him while we're away?"

"It's all taken care of," Elizabeth assured her. "Maria said she and Winston would stop by on their way to the marina every day."

"Winston?" Jessica asked. "Talk about disasters! By the end of the week, Prince Albert will be reeling off one-liners and terrible puns."

"I asked Maria and Winston to take in the mail, too," Elizabeth added. "She has the spare key."

"Thanks, Liz," her mother said. "I completely forgot about the mail. I guess I've been preoccupied."

Elizabeth caught a glimpse of her mother's face in the rearview mirror. Her forehead was wrinkled with tension, as it had been all week.

"*You* shouldn't have had to think about the mail!" Mr. Wakefield snapped. "*I'm* the one who sprang this trip on everyone at the last minute. I should have made all the arrangements. How could I have been so thoughtless?"

Jessica glanced at her twin, and Elizabeth knew that the surprised, worried expression on Jessica's face identically matched her own. Their father was showing the strain of the last week more than anyone. Again Elizabeth noticed the dark circles under his eyes and the tension in his face as he clenched his jaw. "Dad, it's not a big deal," Elizabeth said. "We've taken care of everything."

"*I'm* the one who should be taking care of everything!" Mr. Wakefield exclaimed.

Elizabeth watched her parents from the backseat. Mrs. Wakefield pursed her lips and stared at her husband helplessly, but his gaze was fixed on the road ahead. Elizabeth shifted uncomfortably on the warm vinyl. In front of her, her father was gripping the steering wheel as if he wanted to break it in half.

Suddenly Jessica bounced on the seat like a small child. Her eyes twinkled and a grin lit her face. "I've got it!" she cried. "Let's sing!"

Elizabeth raised an eyebrow. "Sing?"

"You know—traveling songs!"

"But nobody in this family can carry a tune," Elizabeth objected. "Especially you."

"Good!" Jessica said. "Since we're all tone-deaf, we won't be able to tell how off-key we are."

"Jessica, I don't think—" her mother began.

"Come on, everybody—sing along!" Jessica interrupted. She raised her hands and began waving them as if she were conducting an invisible band. "*Cat-a-lin-a, here I come, right back where I started from. . . .*"

Elizabeth smiled and then began to giggle. Nobody could resist Jessica's good humor for long. She opened her mouth and joined in, singing as enthusiastically and as tunelessly as her sister.

Leighann yawned as she checked her watch. "Eight o'clock in the morning," she mumbled sleepily to herself. *Less than an hour until I can go home and finally get some shut-eye.* She simply had to find a way to get transferred to the day shift.

Well, there is one advantage to working nights,

she thought, casting a cold glare at an inmate who whistled as she walked by. *At least this place is as quiet as a tomb for most of my shift. Too bad the prisoners wake up before I leave.*

She smiled as she caught sight of another advantage to her job. John Marin was sitting on his bed in cell 202. She turned to see if her supervisor was nearby; she didn't want Manuel to know how close she was getting to the handsome young prisoner. She was in luck. The supervisor was nowhere to be seen.

"Hi, John!" she said cheerfully. "How're you feeling? Any better?"

John didn't answer. He was leaning over awkwardly, as if trying to tie his shoelaces.

"John?" Leighann asked. "Are you all right? *John?*"

With agonizing slowness, John turned his head to look at her. His face was twisted in pain. "Just . . . indigestion," he whispered, clutching his stomach. "I'll be OK in a minute."

"It doesn't look like indigestion to me," Leighann protested. "And you're *not* OK!" She pulled the cellular intercom from her belt. "I'd better buzz the infirmary and have them send a doctor up right away."

"No!" John croaked. "I'm fine . . . really." Then his body rolled to one side, and John Marin collapsed onto the floor.

* * *

"Oh, give me a home where the buffalo roam," Jessica sang as the Wakefields' car cruised down the freeway, "where the water-skiers and the Windsurfers play. Where seldom is heard a discouraging word, and the guys flex their muscles all day!"

"Very inspiring," Elizabeth said in what Jessica thought of as her superior-twin voice. "I'm glad you appreciate the natural wonders of the channel islands."

Jessica sighed. "You don't have to sound so sarcastic. You say that you only have eyes for Todd. But I've seen you scoping out the guys on the beach at home."

Mrs. Wakefield grinned from the front seat, and Jessica noticed that the tension was finally smoothing away from her mother's face. "You can't expect your sister to sit on the beach with her eyes closed," Mrs. Wakefield pointed out.

"Exactly," Jessica said. "She just doesn't like to admit it."

"OK, OK. So I sneak a peek now and then," Elizabeth said. "Sue me."

Mrs. Wakefield glanced mischievously at her husband. "Personally, I plan to keep my eyes wide-open on Catalina this week."

"Oooh, Dad!" Jessica called. "I hope you brought your new swim trunks!"

"What was that?" the twins' father asked, still sounding distracted. At least, Jessica thought, he was no longer clenching the steering wheel as if it were Marin's neck.

"Never mind," Mrs. Wakefield said, watching him. "Here's San Pedro. This is where we catch the boat."

"How long is the boat trip?" Elizabeth asked, her voice suddenly lowered almost to a whisper.

"Only about an hour," Mrs. Wakefield replied. Jessica saw her mother's worried eyes watching Elizabeth in the rearview mirror.

Elizabeth sank back in the seat and turned to stare out the window. Jessica looked at her curiously. For the first time in a week, the twins and their mother had seemed relaxed. Mr. Wakefield still looked tense, but even he was beginning to loosen up. Now, all of a sudden, Elizabeth looked scared again. Jessica followed her sister's stare and finally understood. Elizabeth's eyes were fixed on the sleek white lines of the channel boat as the Wakefields drove closer to the dock. She was afraid of the boat. In Elizabeth's mind, Jessica realized, she was back on the deck of that other boat, fighting for her life.

This won't do, Jessica thought. She had to find a way to cheer up her sister and get her mind off the evening on Marin's yacht. Jessica pointed to the harbor. "There's the channel boat! Awesome! Can we sit on the front part, near the railing?" she asked in a bubbly voice. "I want the guys on the beach at Catalina to see me coming."

Elizabeth laughed. "Honestly, Jessica, you've got such a one-track mind!"

"Oh, well," Jessica said with a smile. "At least my one track has got some great scenery along it!"

Leighann frantically fumbled with her keys. She knew there was a correct procedure for dealing with inmates who needed medical attention, but she had no time to worry about procedures. This was a life-or-death situation.

"John?" she called as she tried the wrong key in the lock. "Talk to me, John!"

The prisoner's body lay still on the floor of the cell. Leighann couldn't tell if he was breathing.

Finally the lock clicked. Leighann shoved the door open and knelt beside the prostrate form. "Oh, John! Please don't be dead, John! Please don't be dead!"

She heard a few voices from the cells around her—some concerned, others mocking—but she had no time for the other prisoners. She suddenly realized that she was completely in love with John Marin. And now he might be dead, or dying. She leaned close, holding her hand near his mouth to check for breathing, while she took Marin's wrist in her other hand to see if he had a pulse.

Suddenly his wrist sprang to life and flicked around to grab her hand.

"Thank heaven!" she began with a sigh. "I thought—"

"Shut up," he hissed into her ear. She felt him whisk her gun out of its shoulder holster.

"John, what is this? If this is some kind of a joke—"

"It's no joke, darling," he whispered, expertly tying her hands together to the bedpost with a rope that Leighann guessed he'd made from his sheet. He yanked the cell phone from her belt. "Call that supervisor of yours," he ordered. "Tell him to come here now, alone."

"John! I don't understand."

He shoved the gun painfully into her chest. "If you try anything funny, I'll kill you."

Leighann nodded, her eyes wide. She could barely catch her breath. Through her uniform shirt, the barrel of the gun was cold and hard against her chest—almost as cold and hard as John's eyes.

"Uh, Manuel," she said into the receiver, wondering if the supervisor could hear her heart pounding through the receiver. "I need you down here for a moment. Can you meet me at number two-oh-two?"

"What's the problem this time, LeShay?" Manuel asked, an edge of annoyance in his voice.

"I'm, um, not quite sure," Leighann stammered. "I think Marin's sick, but I can't tell if it's serious enough to call the infirmary."

"I'm a prison guard, not a doctor," he said. "Let the professionals decide."

The gun barrel pressed harder against her breastbone, and Leighann gasped. "Please, Manuel! I'd feel a lot better if you'd come take a look." She was so surprised that John was treating her roughly that she barely knew what she was saying on the phone. The man she thought she loved was actually *hurting* her.

"I get it," Manuel said. "Another crisis like last week, when the guy in cell three-oh-nine had athlete's foot."

Leighann desperately tried to focus and think up an argument that might convince her boss to come to Marin's cell. "If you call the doctor and there's nothing really wrong with Marin," she pointed out, "then we're both going to look pretty silly, aren't we?" She felt close to tears with pain and disappointment, but she knew her voice sounded relatively normal.

Manuel sighed. "All right, Leighann. I'm on my way."

Mr. Wakefield breathed deeply and gazed over the ship's prow. The salt-tinged air felt fresh in his lungs, and the warm breeze that swept over his face was pure and cleansing. For the first time in two weeks, he felt free.

His wife held on to his arm and snuggled against him, strands of her golden hair blowing across his neck and chest. She smiled up at him. "This was a great idea," she said. "We're not even on the island yet, and already I feel a hundred percent better."

"Me, too," he replied. "For the first time all week, I don't feel as if I should be looking over my shoulder—not to mention keeping an eye on the girls twenty-four hours a day."

Jessica and Elizabeth were standing a few yards to his left. Over the buffeting of the wind, their father could hear only occasional snatches of the twins' conversation. It sounded as if Jessica was entertaining her sister with a lively patter about the shopping, the sights, and the boys of Catalina. Elizabeth was giggling so hard she had to lean on the ship's railing for support.

Then Mr. Wakefield noticed the way that Jessica was protectively holding on to her sister's arm, much the same way that his wife held his own. Suddenly he realized what Jessica was doing. Elizabeth hadn't said anything to her parents, but her father knew she'd been afraid of being on a boat again. Now her fear seemed forgotten as she laughed at her sister's silly commentary.

As usual, his wife knew exactly what he was thinking. "I see that Jessica is determined to keep Elizabeth's mind off last weekend," Mrs. Wakefield murmured into his ear. "And it seems to be working. I haven't seen Elizabeth laugh like that all week."

"She's lucky to have somebody nearby who cares that much about her," the twins' father said, looking into his wife's beautiful blue eyes. "I know from personal experience how much of a difference that can make."

"How are you feeling?"

He brushed a strand of hair from his wife's eyes. Then he leaned down and kissed her gently on the lips. "Much, much better," he said. "You know, I really believe we're going to be able to put this all behind us."

Marin lay tense on his cot, peering out from under the thin prison-issue blanket. Outside the cell, he could hear approaching footsteps echoing down the corridor.

"Remember, darling," he whispered to Leighann, "I've got your piece right here in my hand." From below, he poked the barrel of the nine-millimeter handgun against the blanket. "If you say anything wrong when your friend Manuel gets here, I'll blow away your pretty little head."

Through a wrinkle in the blanket, he caught a glimpse of Leighann's wide-eyed nod. He felt a rush of gratitude toward the young prison guard, mixed with contempt. She had certainly made his work easier by falling in love with him. And her looks didn't hurt, either. He studied her from his woolen cavern. Leighann's eyes were large and dark, and her clear skin was the color of hot chocolate. Her black hair was frizzy and untamed, making her features appear even sweeter and more innocent in contrast.

Now she crouched by the side of the cot, as if leaning over Marin to check on his condition. Marin had draped the blanket so that one corner fell over her wrists; from the cell's entrance, Manuel wouldn't be able to see that her hands were tied. Of course, her gun was missing from her shoulder holster. But with luck Manuel wouldn't notice that until it was too late.

The footsteps came closer and then stopped. Marin sensed that the supervisor was standing directly outside the cell.

"Dammit, LeShay," came Manuel's deep, weary voice. "You know the rules. What are you doing in a prisoner's cell? And with the door unlocked!"

"Forget the rules!" Leighann answered, her voice quavering. "This is a life-or-death matter."

Marin held his breath, out of anxiety as much as anything. Would Manuel take the bait?

Manuel's voice seemed uncertain. "I swear, LeShay, you exaggerate more than anyone I've ever met. It's probably nothing. I'll call the infirmary."

"No!" Leighann cried. "There's no time! I can't tell if he's breathing!"

"OK, let me see what we've got."

Manuel leaned over the bed and pulled the blanket from Marin's face. As he did, Marin leaped from the cot and caught him in a stranglehold.

"Drop your gun and your intercom on the cot," Marin ordered. He jabbed Manuel's spine with Leighann's weapon. "Now!"

The supervisor began to shudder in the stranglehold. Manuel's eyes grew round and filled with a sick sense of realization as he stared into Marin's face.

"And if you make a sound," Marin continued, "you and the little lady here are both dead."

Manuel's fingers were trembling as he pulled the intercom from his belt and tossed it onto the bed. Marin nodded toward the gun. The only sound in the cell was metal sliding against leather as Manuel slipped the weapon from its holster. His eyes were riveted to Marin's face, as if hoping to catch the inmate in a moment's distraction. Marin sneered, and Manuel lowered his gaze. With a last, wistful glance at his weapon, Manuel dropped it onto the cot.

Then Marin swung an arm around to bash Manuel in the side of the head with Leighann's gun. Leighann stifled a scream as her boss dropped to the floor, scarlet streaming down the side of his face.

Marin knelt beside Manuel and felt his pulse. Then he began unbuttoning the man's guard uniform.

"Is he dead?" Leighann whimpered.

"He's dead," Marin said flatly, yanking Manuel's arms from his uniform jacket.

"What are you doing to him?" Leighann choked out.

"Shut your mouth," Marin barked. "Unless you want to end up like your boss."

Marin quickly pulled on Manuel's uniform jacket. His own prison pants were a close enough color to pass for a guard's pants. Then he untied Leighann's bonds. "Get up and do exactly as I say," he ordered, smiling coldly. "Darling, it's time for our moonlight sail."

Chapter 5

The door to her office opened, and Marianna West looked up from the conference table. Her mouth puckered in distaste when she saw who was entering. "Hello, Griffin," she said in a controlled voice. She pointed to the clock on the wall. "I was expecting you nearly two hours ago. It's almost eleven."

Griffin Pierce wiped his high, shiny forehead. He was only thirty years old, but his receding hairline made him look closer to fifty. "Lighten up, Marianna. It's Saturday morning! And I don't appreciate having this case dumped on me at the last minute, just so Ned could go on vacation."

"You don't have to appreciate it," she said sweetly. "You're an associate, Griffin. Ned's a partner. And so, I might mention, am *I*," she added pointedly. "Besides, you know what Ned's been through in the last week. His family needs to get away." At that moment Marianna wished she, too, could get away—from Griffin.

"So what do you need me to work on?" he asked with a resigned sigh.

She held out a folder. "I need six copies of these records," she said. At least if Griffin was photocopying papers, he would be out of her office.

"*Copies?*" Griffin asked, in shock. "You want *me* to photocopy files? Man, am I glad I went to law school to prepare for this."

Marianna glared at him, and Griffin's mouth snapped shut. He snatched the papers from her and stalked out of the room. Marianna sighed happily after he had gone. Without Griffin in it, the office seemed extraordinarily peaceful.

"Oh, we'll all have chicken and dumplings when she comes!" Harry Emerson sang as he drove the family car through the desert late Saturday morning. It wasn't quite lunchtime, but he was feeling awfully hungry. Chicken and dumplings would pretty much hit the spot.

Unfortunately, he realized, he and his family were in California now—the land of bean sprouts and pita bread. There probably wasn't a single dumpling between there and home, American Fork, Utah.

"Daddy! You stopped singing in the middle!" complained five-year-old Margie from the flat, decklike part of the station wagon, the section the kids called "the way back."

"Lucky for us," said Harry, Jr., staring glumly out the window. At eleven years old, Harry, Jr., was just too cool for family vacations—and easily embarrassed by fathers who sang in public. Even if the public, in this case, was only his family.

Harry, Sr., patted his potbelly. "How about stopping for lunch soon?" he asked. "I'm getting pretty darn hungry."

"Dear, it's only eleven o'clock," replied his wife, Beatrice. "I thought we were going to wait until Los Angeles to eat lunch. If we stop now, we'll upset our whole schedule."

Harry sighed. Beatrice didn't like doing anything unexpected. Usually Harry went along with her. But today he was feeling rebellious. "Is that such a terrible thing?" he asked hesitantly. "I mean, does it really matter if we eat at eleven instead of twelve thirty?"

"Of course it matters! Margie is only five. Children's systems are very sensitive to changes in routine."

"Yes, I guess you're right," he said meekly. "What was I thinking?"

From the corner of his eyes, Harry watched his wife, who was sitting smugly on the seat beside him. As always, Beatrice had been confident that he would do exactly as she wanted. He gripped the steering wheel tighter. He was tired of living by her rules. Right then and there, he made a decision. Sometime on this vacation, he vowed, he would do something completely unexpected—something that would drive Bea crazy.

Leighann lay on the floor of her Geo Metro, wincing as Marin tied her wrists together.

"Hey!" she yelled. "You're cutting off my circulation!"

"Sorry, darling," Marin said with a smile, loosening the bonds a little. "I didn't mean to hurt you." Leighann noticed that he had reverted back to his polite, gentlemanlike self, now that they were away from the prison and he was free. *If the words "polite" and "gentlemanlike" can be used to describe a guy who would make you fall in love with him, and then murder your boss, kidnap you, and force you to drive him into the desert,* she thought grimly.

"What's going to happen now?" Leighann asked.

"Well," John began, "now that the car is hidden in this canyon, far off the road, I plan to leave you here in it—and then to be on my way. So don't trouble your mind about me anymore, darling."

"I'm not your darling!" Leighann yelled. She could hardly believe what was happening to her. Just twelve hours earlier she'd been dreaming of having a real relationship with this creep. Now she wished she'd never met him. She still couldn't believe she'd been so blind to his true character.

"Don't be mad, baby," Marin said in a soothing voice. He reached down to stroke her face.

Leighann caught sight of her own gun sticking out of his belt. Once again her mind replayed the image of the blood on Manuel's face as he lay on the floor of cell 202, his skin as pale as bone. She shuddered and twisted her face away from Marin's touch. The warden and poor Manuel had been right. Marin was evil. And she had been taken in by him. She had even believed he could fall in love with her. *How could I have been such an idiot?* she chided herself. "Don't you dare touch me!" she ordered bravely, fighting back her tears.

"I'm sorry, Leighann," Marin said simply. "You don't have to be afraid of me. I won't hurt you." The desert sun, almost directly overhead, plucked golden highlights from his hair as he stood in the car doorway, but his face was in shadow.

"Why should I believe you, after what you did to Manuel?" she demanded.

He began tying her ankles. "I needed Manuel dead. He would have sounded the alarm."

"I wish I had," she said, glowering at him.

Marin went on as if she hadn't spoken. "I needed you to get me through the prison security system. Also, I knew you had a car—transportation away from that rat hole. Of course, I can't risk going any farther in your car now. They'll be searching all the roads for it. So I'll have to locate some alternate transportation."

"So you don't need me anymore. Does that mean you're going to kill me?" Leighann was surprised at how flat and matter-of-fact her voice sounded.

Marin shrugged. "Killing you would serve no purpose. You don't know where I'm heading, so you can't talk. By the time anyone finds you in this desert, my trail will be cold."

"I get it," Leighann said bitterly. "You don't pull the trigger, so you think my death won't be on your conscience. But I'll still die out here in the middle of nowhere. You know it as well as I do."

Marin shook his head. "No, you won't, sweetheart. We're only a few miles from the prison. Somebody will find you."

"Right. After it's too late."

"I'll give you a hint," Marin said. "Keep working at the ropes. You'll be able to loosen them by tonight—probably enough to get your hands free."

Leighann grimaced. "This is the desert! It'll be a hundred thirty degrees in this car by afternoon. If it takes me too long to die of thirst, I'll fry to death first."

"No, you won't, sugar," Marin told her with an amused grin. "This canyon's in shade almost all day long. Trust me, darling. I wouldn't let anything bad happen to you."

"Right," Leighann fumed. "You're a real

humanitarian. I trusted you before—and look where it got me!"

"Once you're free, forget about driving straight to the authorities," Marin continued. "I've slashed all your tires. And by the time you walk to the main road, I'll be far away from here."

Suddenly Leighann's anger fell away like a mask. She felt more depressed than she'd ever been in her life. Everything was clear now. From the moment they'd met, every word out of Marin's mouth had been an act. He'd planned his whole escape around her. He'd manipulated her into falling in love with him, to make her want to rush into his cell when she thought he was dying. He'd used her—not only to escape, but also to kill Manuel. And she'd helped him all the way.

"I thought you liked me," she said as tears began streaming down her face.

"I do like you. And I'm grateful for your help in busting out of that place. That's why I'm going to give you a little career advice: Don't get too close to the prisoners." He winked. "They're scum."

"My career as a prison guard is over!" Leighann screamed. "I'm quitting my job the second I get back to that rat hole—right before the warden opens his mouth to fire me."

"I'm really sorry about this next part," Marin said, leaning toward her. He held a satin scarf that he must have found in the trunk of her car. The long scarf was stretched out in Marin's hands, and

Leighann's eyes widened as she realized the truth. He was going to strangle her with it. Marin had lied about letting her live, just as he had lied about everything else. Leighann's entire body went numb with horror.

Her scream was sliced short as Marin stuffed the scarf into her mouth.

"I hate to have to gag you," he said. "But it's a necessary precaution. I can't have you screaming for help, can I?"

"Mmmpphh!"

Marin smiled as if he were dropping her off for tea at the Ritz-Carlton Hotel. "I have to say goodbye, sweetheart. You'll be a lot more comfortable if you don't panic too much." He blew her a kiss. *"Arrivederci!"*

The car door slammed shut, and Marin sauntered away, the sound of his jaunty whistling fading into the hot, dry breeze. Leighann was alone. In fact, in her whole life she had never felt so lonely. Or so betrayed.

Tears started rolling down her cheeks, and that made her angry again. She was angry at Marin for betraying her, but she was even more angry at herself. She couldn't believe she'd been so stupid and so trusting—and that she had liked him enough to feel so hurt, even now.

In defiance of Marin's last suggestion, Leighann shifted awkwardly in the cramped space. Something small and hard in her pocket jabbed into her hip.

She tried to change her position, but she couldn't seem to move away from the object.

Then she remembered what was in her pocket—a perfect miniature replica of a sailboat, carved in wood. To Marin it had meant freedom. To Leighann it brought only pain.

"Awesome!" Jessica cried, surveying the central courtyard of the Hotel Orizaba as the Wakefields searched for their rooms.

Sparkling adobe walls stretched around three sides of the piazza, rising two and three stories above the ground. Within those walls, pillared colonnades held private balconies that overlooked a swimming pool. Above it all, a peaked roofline of red tile shone in the midday sun.

"It's wonderful, Ned," the twins' mother murmured, leaning close to her husband.

Even Mr. Wakefield's nervous tension had finally lifted. "Yes, it is," he agreed, giving her a peck on the cheek. "And we're going to have a wonderful time here."

Jessica caught sight of a tall, bronzed body in swim trunks diving into the pool. "I think I'm going to have a great time here, too," she said with a smile.

On the far end of the pool, four teenagers played badminton. At tables scattered throughout the courtyard, relaxed-looking people with great tans sipped colorful drinks, as if posing for a cranberry-juice-cocktail commercial.

Jessica bounced on her toes. "What do we do first?"

Elizabeth cocked her head. "Unpack?"

Jessica's mouth dropped open. "Of all the boring—" she began. Then she saw that her sister was laughing.

"It's eleven thirty," Elizabeth said, checking her watch. "How about a swim in the pool first, and then a late lunch?"

"Now you're talking!" Jessica said. "And there's our room, right here on the first floor—number one-fourteen. Come on! I'll race you into our bathing suits!"

"Girls, we're next door in room one-twelve," the twins' father said, sliding the electronic key into the slot beside the door. "Knock when you're ready, and I'll come down to the pool with you."

Jessica sighed. The anxious look on her father's face did not bode well for her social life. He was likely to spend the whole week hovering over her and Elizabeth, scaring away all the great-looking guys.

Her mother obviously had a similar thought. She gently placed a hand on her husband's shoulder. "Ned, the girls don't need a bodyguard," she said softly. "Marin is locked up, and we can all finally relax."

Harry Emerson scratched his head and stared down the empty desert road. The last few puffs of dust vanished in the distance, beneath heat waves that rippled in the air like snakes.

"That was awesome!" Harry, Jr., declared. "That hitchhiker had a real gun! How totally cool!"

Harry, Sr., shook his head. "Son, this isn't the time—"

"Daddy!" Margie cried, tugging on his pant leg. One thumb was in her mouth. "Why did that man take our car?"

"You had to be the big risk taker!" Beatrice yelled, pointing a finger at Harry. "You had to do an idiotic thing like pick up a hitchhiker. You said it would be an adventure. Well, it's an adventure all right! It could be hours before another car comes along."

"Wow, this is so cool!" Harry, Jr., exclaimed. "Does that mean we get to walk through the desert, all the way to Los Angeles? Wait until the kids at school hear about this!"

Harry gazed at the horizon, half expecting the clean-cut young hitchhiker to make a U-turn in their wood-paneled station wagon and race back to the Emersons. The hitchhiker's eyes would crinkle with laughter as he explained that he'd only been joking.

But the horizon was clear. The hitchhiker was gone, along with the Emersons' car, their cash, and much of their luggage. Harry sighed, trying to tune out his wife's litany of charges. *Risk taking*, he decided, *isn't all it's cracked up to be.* On their next vacation, he'd carry traveler's checks.

Griffin was driving Marianna crazy.

"This case shouldn't be going to court at all," he argued, sitting with her in her office at the law firm early Saturday afternoon. "The client ought to settle."

Marianna heard her own voice rising. "He doesn't want to settle! He's more interested in justice than in money."

"Great," Griffin said sarcastically. "And our percentage of his justice comes to how much?"

"Excuse me?" questioned a new voice from the doorway. A clean-cut young man with light-brown hair stood at the threshold, carrying a metal toolbox. "Is this Ned Wakefield's office?"

"Right firm, wrong office," Marianna said, grateful for the distraction. "Ned's on vacation. Can I help you?"

"I'm sorry to bother you on a Saturday," the man said with an apologetic grin. "But I'm with your voice-mail company." He consulted a notebook. "I got a call late yesterday from a Trudy Roman, your office manager. She said Mr. Wakefield was having trouble with his voice mail."

"I didn't know the voice-mail people worked on weekends," Marianna said.

"It must be in your service contract," the man said. "Has anyone else experienced voice-mail problems?"

"Not that I know of," Marianna said. "Well, Mr.

Pierce will show you to Mr. Wakefield's telephone," she offered. She raised her eyebrows at the associate. "Griffin, remember the policy on weekend visitors in the offices."

Unauthorized personnel weren't allowed in the office during off-hours, unless accompanied by an employee. Griffin would have to wait in Wakefield's office—no doubt bored out of his mind—while the phone man fixed the voice mail. Marianna felt a perverse sense of satisfaction from the look of annoyance in Griffin's eyes.

John Marin pretended to be placing a test call from Mr. Wakefield's office. In reality he was watching out of the corner of his eye the obnoxiously preppy attorney who had escorted him there and who now leaned against the doorjamb. Griffin Pierce, the tall, attractive woman had called him. Even his name sounded stuffy.

"This may take a few minutes," Marin said, disguising his contempt with a cheerful voice.

"Oh, there's no rush," Griffin responded with a sneer. "I'm only an associate. I've got nothing better to do. Not like those busy, important partners."

Marin sized the man up instantly. He cocked his head in the direction of the woman's office. "She sure gets up a full head of steam," he remarked conspiratorially.

"That's an understatement," Griffin replied. "I sweat through years of law school, and the Ice

75

Queen expects me to do her photocopying!"

"Women bosses are the pits!" Marin sympathized. "Hey, I know how boring this must be for you, standing around watching me push buttons. If you want to sneak out for a cup of coffee or something—"

Griffin slumped against the door frame. "I can't," he said glumly. "Company policy."

Marin grinned. "I won't say anything to you-know-who."

Griffin peeked down the hallway through the open door, then gave Marin a thumbs-up signal. "I'll be back in ten minutes," he said.

As soon as Griffin had gone, closing the door behind him, Marin tapped into voice mail. There wasn't a thing wrong with Mr. Wakefield's telephone. Yet.

"Please enter your security code," ordered a mechanical-sounding female voice over the phone line.

"Dammit!" Marin whispered, staring at the closed door. "What would Wakefield use as his security code?" He thought back to conversations he'd had with white-collar criminals in the state prison. Most people used four to ten characters for passwords, spelling out something they knew they'd remember. He punched in the letters A-L-I-C-E.

"That is not a valid security code," chastised the recorded voice on the line.

"Come on, Ned," Marin said aloud to a framed family photograph on Wakefield's desk. "What's your security code? I know—you live on Calico Drive. How about C-A-L-I-C-O?" He jabbed at the letters.

"That is not a valid security code."

"Talk to me, Ned!" he ordered the photograph. Then he batted it aside. "If I were Ned Wakefield, what word would I choose? He tried S-T-E-V-E-N, the names of both girls, and then, thinking of the Wakefield family dog, even A-L-B-E-R-T. No luck. And he didn't have much time. That windbag Griffin Pierce would be back soon.

Suddenly Marin smiled at the receiver. "I've got you now, Wakefield!" His fingers skipped over the keys as he typed in T-W-I-N-S.

"Your voice mail is on," the computerized voice said. *"You have one message. Dial five to listen to your message."*

"Yes!" Marin cried in a stage whisper.

The message was from Detective Cabrini, the police officer who had arrested him at the Wakefield house the night he'd crashed through Elizabeth's window.

"Ned, I know you're vacationing on Santa Catalina, but I don't know which hotel," Cabrini said in a frantic voice. "I hope you'll phone in to the office for your messages. I've got urgent news, and it's not good."

Marin smiled. *Not good? That all depends on*

your perspective, Detective, he thought.

"Marin is out!" Cabrini continued. "He escaped from prison this morning. The warden still doesn't know how that lunatic managed it, but he left one guard dead—bashed the man's head in."

"No big loss," Marin said, narrowing his eyes to slits. Manuel had been one of those domineering, by-the-book guards that Marin hated.

"He kidnapped another guard," Cabrini said. "She's a twenty-three-year-old woman who had only been on the job for two weeks. As far as we know, Marin left with her, in her car. He's probably headed into the desert. The warden called in an all-points bulletin. And the police and the FBI are scouring the place now, for some sign of Marin or the car—" He paused. "Or the guard's body."

Marin grinned. "Now, would I do a rotten thing like that to a harmless little twit like LeShay?" he asked, as if he expected an answer from the detective's recorded voice.

"Call me as soon as you receive this message," Cabrini ended. "If Marin's smart, he's already hundreds of miles away from here. But he still might come after your daughters again. Call me from Catalina, and we'll work out a plan to keep them safe."

"Catalina Island?" Marin said thoughtfully.

He keyed a code into the voice-mail system to erase Cabrini's message. Then he punched in another code to have any future calls forwarded to a phony number. The next time Cabrini called, his message would be sent harmlessly into cyberspace. The Wakefields would continue to believe that Marin was tucked away safely in his prison cell. *Until it's too late*, he thought, chuckling to himself.

Marin rifled through the papers on Mr. Wakefield's desk until he found one with the name of a hotel on Catalina Island.

"The Hotel Orizaba," he murmured. "Not bad! I've got to hand it to you, Counselor, you sure know how to show the ladies a good time. You know, a week in prison has absolutely ruined my tan. Maybe an island vacation is just what I need."

Chapter 6

Mr. Wakefield smiled and stretched out on a chaise lounge next to his wife's. He shaded his eyes from the bright afternoon sun as he turned to look at her. For the first time in a week, she seemed truly relaxed and happy. The dark circles were fading from beneath her eyes, and her forehead had lost the pinched look it had worn since the morning she'd returned from Oakland to find her household in an uproar.

"Hi!" said a perky voice. A shadow fell across Mr. Wakefield's legs, and a bouncy college-age woman with straight black hair and almond-shaped eyes smiled down at him. "I'm Debbie Clayton, and I'm your poolside hostess this afternoon! Can I get either of you anything to drink? Seltzer? Iced tea? A wine spritzer?"

"Iced tea would be lovely," Mrs. Wakefield said.

The twinkle in her eyes told her husband that she found the girl's enthusiasm as amusing as he did.

"I'll have the same," Mr. Wakefield said.

Debbie bounced away, and the Wakefields cracked up.

"Were we ever that young?" Mrs. Wakefield asked after they'd caught their breath.

"I never was," her husband said, turning on his side to get a better view of his wife. "But you look as if you still could be." He could have sworn that his wife had hardly aged at all in twenty years of marriage. Her golden hair, so much like her daughters', was untouched by gray. Her eyes were as blue as the cool water of the hotel swimming pool. And her figure, in her modest but flattering aqua swimsuit, was still slender.

She pointed to the pool. "The twins sure seem to be settling into things here."

Her husband followed her gaze. Jessica was wading into the shallow end of the pool, wearing a blue-and-white bikini so skimpy he would have outlawed it if he'd seen it earlier. She nonchalantly wandered into a raucous game that seemed to have no rules or boundaries, except that it involved a beach ball and two handsome teenage boys. Mr. Wakefield shook his head. Even after a week of dating a murderer, Jessica had the guts—or was it recklessness?—to seek out strange guys.

Elizabeth, as industrious as always, executed a perfect dive from the low board and began swimming laps on the other end of the pool. Her racing-style swimsuit, in green-and-blue plaid, was stylish but practical.

Suddenly the twins' father jumped to his feet. A young man with light-brown hair was wading quickly toward Elizabeth, churning up ripples in his wake. His height and muscular build seemed familiar—*like John Marin's.*

"Elizabeth!" her father yelled, knocking over a plastic table as he leaped toward the pool.

Elizabeth and Jessica both stopped in the water and turned toward him, mortified. Meanwhile, the man with light-brown hair jumped out of the water to catch a Frisbee that was spinning above Elizabeth's head.

Elizabeth looked from Mr. Wakefield to the Frisbee player and shook her head slightly at her father. Jessica was more blatant. She threw her father a dirty look as the two handsome boys with the beach ball eyed him warily.

"Oh, Ned," came his wife's sad voice from behind him.

Mr. Wakefield slumped back to his chair. "I thought I was finally relaxed," he began. "I thought I was over last week. But when I saw that guy running toward Elizabeth, I thought—"

"I know what you thought," Mrs. Wakefield said. "But I will not put up with this kind of behavior all week, Ned. I'm putting my foot down. No watching the twins like a hawk!"

"I know they deserve to have some fun after last weekend," he conceded. "But I've got this feeling—"

"The girls are perfectly safe!" Alice objected.

Mr. Wakefield sighed. "I know, I know. And you're absolutely right. I need to chill out, as Jess would say. I have to let them enjoy their freedom. But it's not going to be easy."

John Marin sat in the stern of the channel boat, watching San Pedro recede over the water as the boat headed to Catalina Island. The salt smell of the ocean and the cries of gulls reminded him of the rented sailing yacht he'd docked at Sweet Valley Marina.

His moonlight sail with Elizabeth had been only one week earlier, but it seemed like a long, long time ago. Something about being in prison made time stretch out endlessly, so that a week might as well be a year. At twenty-eight, Marin knew he had a lot of time ahead of him, but he seethed about every day he'd wasted sitting in a nine-by-nine cell. It was all Ned Wakefield's fault—all those wasted days and wasted nights.

A few weeks earlier, after ten long years of prison, Marin had finally been paroled. He should have had enough time to accomplish his goal, but he had failed. Elizabeth and Jessica Wakefield were alive and well. Their father still had his happiness and peace of mind. *Not for long*, Marin promised himself. Soon that peace of mind would be shattered. The Wakefields' happy life would be nothing more than a gut-wrenching memory.

The day was warm, but the sea breeze was cool as it buffeted the open deck. Marin untied Harry Emerson's new Death Valley sweatshirt from around his waist and pulled it on over the blue-and-white-plaid shirt he was wearing. He'd found both in the suitcase Emerson had left in that godawful wood-paneled station wagon. Plaid wasn't Marin's style, but it was a lot less conspicuous than a prison guard's uniform.

He decided he would buy some clothes on the island. He'd pick up a pair of jeans, at least, as soon as he arrived. His gray prison-issue pants were nondescript. But now that he was out, he'd prefer to savor his freedom in civilian clothes. For all their shortcomings, the Emersons at least had traveled with plenty of cash—enough cash to keep Marin in style on Catalina Island for a few days.

"And a few days is all I'll need," he vowed, "to make sure this is the last vacation the Wakefield twins ever take."

"I'm so hungry I could eat a buffalo," Jessica said, sitting with her sister at the cafe near the pool for a late lunch. "How long ago did we order? An hour?"

"Only eight minutes," Elizabeth said, checking her watch. *If Jessica would wear a watch herself,* she thought, *she wouldn't have to ask everybody all the time*. "But I doubt this place serves buffalo. I'm sure they're a protected species on the island."

"Ha. Ha. I think we should have gone somewhere fancier for lunch. Dad said this whole trip is on him. I guess he feels guilty about Marin; we might as well take advantage of that while we can!"

Elizabeth gave her a disapproving glare but decided to let the remark slide. "You chose the restaurant," she reminded her sister. "You couldn't wait another minute for lunch, and this place was closest. But don't worry. We've got a whole week on the island to try other places to eat."

"We might be sitting here for the whole week!" Jessica complained. "Why are our salads taking so long? I bet Dad and Mom are eating somewhere chic and expensive after they finish their"—she laughed derisively—"*golf-cart tour!*"

Elizabeth took a sip of iced tea. "I think it's sweet that they wanted to take their own private tour."

"But by golf cart? That's totally tacky."

"You know that cars aren't allowed on the island," Elizabeth said. "How else would they get around?"

"Motorcycle?" Jessica suggested.

Elizabeth laughed. "Can't you just see Mom and Dad on a motorcycle?"

"In black leather, with studs," Jessica added archly. "Seriously, though, I was starting to worry about the old parental units. They hardly talked to each other all last week! It was like living in an ice box with them around."

"I know," Elizabeth said thoughtfully. "I kept thinking about that time last year when they separated and thought about getting divorced. I've been so worried! All week it seemed like they haven't really been able to connect."

"I think Mom was mad that Dad didn't tell her about Marin," Jessica said.

"I can understand why she'd feel that way," Elizabeth said. "On the other hand, I guess Dad didn't want to scare her."

Jessica shrugged; other people's problems never concerned her for long. "It doesn't matter now," she said. "They seem OK together today."

"Yeah, they do. Did you notice them over by the pool? They looked happier together than they have in a long time. Younger, too. I'm glad they're going to spend some time alone together this week."

"Me, too!" Jessica declared. "Because if they're alone with each other, then they'll leave us alone. So we can do whatever we want!"

Elizabeth shook her head. "Your selflessness is inspiring," she said. "Anyhow, I think a private tour around the island could turn into a romantic afternoon for Mom and Dad, even on a golf cart. I hope when I've been married for twenty years, I'll still want to do romantic things alone with T—" She stopped herself, embarrassed, before the word "Todd" slipped out. "With my husband."

Jessica laughed. "You're so transparent, Liz. You almost said 'Todd,' didn't you?"

"No!" Elizabeth protested, feeling her face redden. She knew she was too young even to think about marriage to any one guy in particular, but sometimes it was tempting to imagine herself in her mother's wedding gown, floating down the aisle with flowers in her hair and Todd waiting for her at the front of a candlelit church, looking totally sexy in a tuxedo. *No,* she thought, *make that black tie and tails.*

Jessica grimaced. "You and Todd are so boring that it already seems like you've been married for thirty years."

A tall, skinny waitress appeared, with "Jill" on her name badge and unnatural red highlights in her hair. She set two salads down in front of the twins, and Jessica immediately dug into hers.

"After last week boring sounds pretty good to me," Elizabeth said, reaching for the oil and vinegar. "I let you talk me into looking for adventure then. Now I've learned my lesson. Get used to having plain old boring Liz back."

"Never!" Jessica said. "I'll just have to keep working at spicing up your life for you, since you're obviously incapable of doing it for yourself."

Elizabeth glared witheringly at her twin. "Gee, thanks," she said.

"You know what else is getting boring?" Jessica asked. "Dad's basket-case act. I can't put up with him spazzing out all week long, like he did at the pool a little while ago. I wanted to drown myself. Or him."

"I guess he's still uptight about Marin," Elizabeth said with a shrug.

"Did you see the way those two gorgeous hunks backed away from me when they saw that my father was an overprotective lunatic? This could be disastrous for my social life." Jessica shoved a huge leaf of lettuce into her mouth.

"Don't worry," Elizabeth told her sister. "I'm sure he'll relax in a day or two. And Mom said she'd keep him under control until then."

Jessica held out her glass for the skinny waitress to refill. "Let's do something awesome with the rest of the day, Liz. What do you think? Windsurfing? Parasailing?"

"Not me," Elizabeth said. "I don't want to expend that much energy. Besides, as I keep telling you, I'm not here for the excitement. I'm here to sightsee and relax."

"Horseback riding!" Jessica cried suddenly. "It's perfect! You can sit in the saddle and let the horse do all the work, while I watch for good-looking guys in tight jeans and boots. The best of both worlds!"

Elizabeth grinned over a forkful of tomato. "Actually, horseback riding sounds like fun," she said. "Let's run back to our room as soon as we've finished here and change out of our bathing suits."

Debbie Clayton leaned against the registration counter of the Hotel Orizaba. She was glad to be back at her usual spot at the front desk. Debbie had served drinks at the pool that afternoon only because she'd been filling in for another employee. It had meant a long day. But it was all part of being helpful to absolutely everyone, to convince management to choose her for employee of the month. That would look awesome on her application to hotel-management school.

And the hundred-dollar bonus she'd get as employee of the month would buy the new dress she'd been eyeing in the resort's boutique. It was sparkling white, with sequins around the low-cut neckline, and a short, swingy skirt that would twirl around her when she danced. She imagined the look on her fiancé's face when he saw her in it.

Debbie was saving up for school—and planning a wedding. Her mother's houseboat-rental service paid the bills and kept Debbie and her younger sisters fed and clothed, but it left no money for extras, including college.

In other words, every cent she made at the hotel was spent before she earned it. The only way she could afford a new dress was to be named employee of the month. And the only way she would win that honor was to be perky and upbeat and to give the customers everything they asked for.

As soon as she thought of customers, one appeared at the door, as if her musings had reeled him in. And what a customer! He was young, about twenty, with thick light-brown hair. He wore an oversize, tacky sweatshirt, with "Death Valley" printed across the front. But it couldn't hide his perfect, muscular body. His eyes were a deep, hypnotic blue.

"I need a room for the next few nights," the man said, flashing her a dazzling smile.

"Do you have a reservation?" she asked. "We're completely booked for this week."

He placed his elbows on the counter and gazed into her eyes. "No," he said, "I don't have a reservation. But you look as if you're a real expert at this job. You can figure out a way to help me, can't you?"

Debbie hesitated. The Avalon Suite had been left unreserved in case any VIPs showed up. But this guy didn't look like anyone important. He hadn't even brought any luggage with him.

"I don't want to get you in trouble or anything," the customer continued. "But it would sure make my day if you could find a room for me. Maybe a last-minute cancellation?"

Debbie turned to look behind her. Her manager was nowhere in sight. She punched a few keys on the computer. The Avalon Suite was still vacant.

"Well—" she began.

He smiled. "I could tell from the moment I saw you that you're the kind of employee who will do anything to serve a customer. I'll be sure to let the management know that you've been a great help."

The white sequined dress danced before Debbie's eyes. She glanced from the computer screen to the customer's handsome, friendly face. Then she smiled and whisked out one of the hotel's electronic door keys.

"As a matter of fact, we do have a cancellation," she said. "It's one of our nicest suites, though, so I'm afraid it's a little expensive—"

He pulled out a fat billfold. "Money's no object, but I have to pay you in cash. The airline lost my luggage, and I'm afraid all my credit cards were in my bag."

"What name is this under?" Debbie asked.

"LeShay. Leon LeShay."

"All right, Mr. LeShay, if you'll just sign here, I'll have you registered in a jiffy. We'll ring you if the airline comes by with your luggage. In the meantime you might need to buy a few items. The gift shop is just over there, to your left." She pointed. "And there's a boutique and a Western-wear shop on the other side of the courtyard, past the pool."

"Thanks so much," he said. "Somehow I knew you'd be a big help."

Debbie gave him her perkiest smile. "Is there anything else I can do for you, Mr. LeShay?"

The man smiled, and Debbie couldn't help noticing his amazingly white teeth. "Actually, there is," he said. "I'm here to see my friend Ned Wakefield. Could you tell me which room he's in?"

"I'm sorry," Debbie replied, "but I'm not allowed to give out that information. If you'd like, I can leave a message for him, saying that you're here."

"Oh, no!" the man said quickly. "I mean, I wouldn't want you to go through any trouble. But I'd sure like to know which room he's staying in. Of course, you've already been so helpful that I hate to ask for another favor—"

Debbie hesitated. Employees of the month did not ignore hotel policy. On the other hand, they didn't refuse customers a simple favor, either.

"Well, I guess that will be OK," she decided. "It's not as though you're an ax murderer or anything." She consulted her computer screen. "Mr. and Mrs. Wakefield are in room one-fourteen. Oh, no. That's wrong. That's their daughters' room. Ned and Alice are next door, in one-twelve."

"Thanks, Debbie," he said, reading her name badge. "You've been very helpful."

"My pleasure, sir," she answered. "And would you mind filling out this customer-comment card? There's a space on here for evaluating staff members who've given you especially good service."

He winked. "I'd love to."

● ● ●

93

Jessica loved being high off the ground on horseback, with a glossy mare named Black Beauty moving beneath her in response to the slightest pull on the reins. Even more than that, she loved watching Brad, the cute red-haired leader of the trip. He was riding a few feet ahead of her as he led a group of riders, mostly children, down a trail through the woods. *Some guys are built to wear jeans,* she decided.

Jessica had been disappointed to find that the guided horseback ride leaving at three o'clock consisted mostly of children, but having a good-looking guide made it all worthwhile. And being the only rider old enough to be interested in Brad—except Elizabeth, of course—meant that she had no competition for his attention.

She was glad she'd chosen to dress this way, she thought, glancing down at the teeny blue-and-white-striped bikini top and her ultrashort cutoffs. Of course, Elizabeth had tried to talk her into wearing jeans, saying her outfit wasn't practical for horseback riding. Not practical? That showed how much Elizabeth knew about it. It was totally practical for getting cute trail guides like Brad to notice her. She'd finally appeased her sister by taking a sweater, but she wore it tied around her waist, where it felt uncomfortably warm dangling over her hips.

"So, Brad, what does a guy like you do for fun around here?" she called up to him. "I mean, when you're not guiding kids through the woods on horses. There must be some really hot night spots on the island."

"Oh, there are a few," Brad said. "At night the cafe at the pool turns into a disco. We get pretty funky bands here. And there's a nightclub in Avalon—"

"I was thinking of places that are a little more private," Jessica interrupted, giving him a knowing glance. Out of the corner of her eye, she noticed Elizabeth pulling up beside her on a small but sturdy roan, shaking her head slightly. Jessica ignored her. It was just like Elizabeth to want to spoil her fun.

"Oh, I can think of a few spots," Brad said, watching her with budding interest. "The beach is beautiful at night. I know a secluded little cove that you would love."

"Hmmm. That does sound nice," Jessica murmured.

Suddenly Brad reined his horse and turned around. "Hey!" he called. At his sudden yell Jessica felt Black Beauty's powerful body jerk. She patted the mare's neck to steady her. Brad was pointing at the rear of the column of riders. Two of the riders, both about nine years old, were coaxing their ponies off the trail, into the woods.

"Excuse me, Jessica," Brad said with an apologetic tip of his cowboy hat. "Duty calls." He raised his voice again. "Billy and Tiffany, I told you to stay on the trail!" He rode back along the line of riders, calling, "All riders must remain on the trail at all times!"

As soon as he was gone, Elizabeth reined her roan up close to Jessica's mare. Jessica looked down at her from her larger horse.

Unlike her sister, Elizabeth had changed out of her bathing suit. She was wearing a striped orange-and-white top and a pair of loose khaki walking shorts. Her outfit reminded Jessica of one of those orange Creamsicles from the elementary-school cafeterias. *Leave it to Liz to dress like something so . . . juvenile,* she thought. To Jessica's disgust Elizabeth had wanted to wear long pants for horseback riding, but Jessica had convinced her that the day was too hot.

"What do you think you're doing?" Elizabeth asked, tugging at the neckline of her top as if trying to fan some air against her skin. The air had grown oppressively warm as they'd traveled deeper into the woods, and Elizabeth was sweating.

Jessica shrugged. "I'm sitting on a horse, waiting for our guide to come back, same as you."

"You're flirting with a guy who's a complete stranger!"

"So?" Jessica asked. "What's the big deal?"

"I can't see why you'd want to get involved with a strange man," Elizabeth said. "After what happened last week."

"Who said I was getting involved?" Jessica

protested. "We're only talking—not eloping!"

Elizabeth shook her head again. "Sometimes I just don't understand you."

"Why are you in such a crummy mood?" her twin asked. "Aren't you having a good time?"

"No," Elizabeth answered. "I wish we had waited to go horseback riding tomorrow. These kids are so slow!"

"I thought you liked kids!"

"I do, but I'm sick of walking my horse; I want to canter. Look up ahead on the trail." Elizabeth pointed to a spot in the distance. "See that place in the distance, where the big tree branch reaches across? I'll race you to it."

Jessica shook her head. "I don't think so. Brad said we were supposed to stay together."

"I know," Elizabeth admitted. "But it's hot and stuffy here. I want to feel the wind blowing by me. Brad won't mind, as long as we stay in sight. The trail's perfectly straight. He'll be able to see us the whole way. We can wait for him and the others up ahead."

Jessica was tempted to go with her. The slow pace made the riding less exciting than she had hoped. Still, Brad looked awfully exciting in those blue jeans of his.

"You go ahead," she decided. "I'll wait for the others."

Elizabeth felt wings of hair breaking free from her ponytail as the wind rushed by. Her whole body jolted violently as she bounced on top of her reddish horse, named, inexplicably, Fred. Then the jolting stopped as Fred's trot smoothed into a gallop. The trees along the trail blended together, like a watercolor painting in browns and greens. And Elizabeth sailed along, no longer feeling the horse's feet as they hit the ground.

"This is exactly what I needed," she called into the wind. The conversation with Jessica had made her think again of how foolish she had been to fall for John Marin. It was dangerous to let her heart go like that. From now on, she decided, she would lead with her head—beginning as soon as she finished her horseback ride.

For now, it was the horse's head that was leading. And Elizabeth's troubles seemed to fly away behind her as she galloped down the quiet trail alone.

Jill Reese lay on a lounge chair by the pool, wondering if her bathing suit made her look as flat-chested as she thought it did. Occasionally a guy flirted with her while she was waiting tables—while she was dressed in real clothes. But as soon as she got off waitress duty and into her swimsuit, they stayed away as if she were poison. *What good are free pool passes for employees*, Jill wondered, *if they're the only kind of passes I ever get?*

She looked around at all the women and teenage girls with beautiful, curvy figures. She wasn't asking to be transformed into Dolly Parton. A nice, slender figure like the ones on those pretty blond twins at the cafe this afternoon—now, that would be a definite improvement. They were probably about a size six, like her. But not so tall and gangly. And unlike her, they were perfectly proportioned—even on top.

Suddenly she saw a man walking toward her. She pulled off her sunglasses. This couldn't be happening. He was the best-looking guy she'd seen all day—about twenty years old, with light-brown hair and a great body. And he really was walking directly toward her. She couldn't believe it. Her luck was finally turning.

"Hi!" he called, pulling up a chair next to hers.

Jill thought she might faint.

"You work here, don't you?" he asked.

"Does it show?"

He laughed, and she saw that he had the brightest, straightest, most beautiful teeth she had ever seen. "I saw you waiting tables a little while ago."

"That was me, all right," Jill said. "It's not glamorous, but it pays my tuition."

"I thought maybe you could help me with something," he said. "I noticed two girls eating a late lunch at the cafe this afternoon. I think you waited on them."

Jill sighed. She seemed destined to be the girl every guy talked to for advice about how to get the girl he really wanted. "I doubt I can help you," she admitted. "I waited on dozens of customers this afternoon. I'm sure I wouldn't remember who you mean."

"Oh, I think you'd remember these two," he said. "They're about sixteen years old, blond, and absolutely identical. They look like they stepped out of a Doublemint-gum commercial."

"Oh, sure," Jill said. "The Doublemint twins. I remember them. One grilled-tuna salad, one avocado-and-citrus."

"That's them," he said. "Did they say where they were heading this afternoon? It's important that I talk to them."

Jill considered telling him she had no idea where the twins were, but that he could stick around and talk to her for as long as he wanted. But she was an employee. And employees were supposed to think of the hotel guests first.

"Actually, I did hear them make plans for the afternoon," she told him reluctantly. "They said they were going horseback riding."

"You were right," Jessica said glumly as she joined Elizabeth at the place where the tree branch hung over the trail. She had followed her sister only a few minutes later. "It is dangerous to flirt with strange men."

Elizabeth's eyes widened. "What happened? Are you all right?"

"Brad is *married!*" Jessica exclaimed. "Can you believe it? And the jerk was coming on to me."

Elizabeth looked relieved. "From my viewpoint it looked like it was you who was doing most of the coming on."

"Well, he wasn't exactly discouraging it," Jessica shot back. "If that whiny pipsqueak Tiffany hadn't let it slip about meeting his wife at the stable yesterday—"

"It's a good thing she did let it slip," Elizabeth said.

Brad and the other riders caught up to them, and the twins fell in line in the middle of the group.

"I can see why you wanted to go faster," Jessica said. "The slow pace is getting to me, too. And all these little brats are bringing back horrible memories of my spring break as a camp counselor. Let's leave Brad and his kiddies behind and set off to do some exploring for ourselves."

"You know we can't do that," Elizabeth said.

"Why not?" Jessica asked. "You did it yourself, just a little while ago."

"That was different. I stayed where Brad could see me. You're talking about going off on our own for the rest of the trip."

"I don't see what difference it makes," Jessica said.

"The rules say we have to stay on the trail with the group," Elizabeth lectured.

"So?" Jessica shrugged. "Rules were meant to be broken."

"That's what people always say when they want to do things they shouldn't do."

"Liz, what would the world be like if we all did what we were supposed to do?" She searched her brain for some names that would impress her intellectual sister. "Galileo broke the rules. So did Marie Curie and, uh . . . Susan B. Anthony."

"It's not the same thing," Elizabeth said uncertainly.

"Sure it is. Besides, you said you were fed up with going so slow. Let's ask Brad," Jessica suggested, suddenly inspired. "He's in charge here. If he says we can, then we're not doing anything that's against the rules. OK?"

Elizabeth smiled. "I guess it's worth a try."

They caught up with Brad at the head of the line and made their proposal.

"I don't know, girls," he said. "It's against the rules to go off trail."

Elizabeth shot Jessica an I-told-you-so glance.

"Come on, Brad," Jessica pleaded. "You know we're good riders. Besides, we won't just plow into the woods with no direction. I see a side trail up ahead, to the right. Let us turn onto that one and do some exploring on our own."

"I don't like the idea," Brad said. "We're about to get into some rocky, hilly country. The trails twist around a lot, and some of the minor ones are overgrown. It can be hard to find your way. What if you get lost?"

"All these trails lead back to the stables eventually, don't they?" Jessica asked.

"Well, yes, they do," Brad admitted.

"So as long as we stick to a trail—any trail—we'll get back," Jessica said.

"I'm still not crazy about the idea of you kids riding around in the woods by yourself. It's almost quarter to five already. I don't want to have to come back tonight to lead the search party if you get lost."

Jessica injected just the right amount of ice into her tone. "I can see why you wouldn't want to do that," she said slowly. "After all, your *wife* would probably be waiting for you at home."

Brad gulped, and Jessica knew she had scored.

"All right!" Brad said finally. "Go ahead. But if anyone asks, you slipped away without telling me."

Mr. Wakefield let go of his wife's hand as they entered the hotel lobby at five o'clock Saturday afternoon. "There's the gift shop," he said, pointing. "I'm sure you can buy your postcards in there."

Mrs. Wakefield kissed him on the cheek. "Today has been wonderful," she said. "I never thought a golf cart could go that fast!"

He laughed. "Only if you don't mind breaking the laws of physics!"

"Next time," she promised, "we'll rent two golf carts, and I'll race you."

"You're on! But we'd better make sure the girls have enough cash to bail us out of jail for traffic violations."

"I'm not worried," Mrs. Wakefield said, grabbing on to her husband's arm. "I know a great attorney."

Mrs. Wakefield began pulling him toward the gift shop, but he pointed to the registration desk. "I left the room key with the front-desk clerk," he said. "I'll go get it and check our messages, and then I'll meet you in the shop in a few minutes."

His wife kissed him lightly on the lips as they parted.

Mr. Wakefield sauntered over to the front counter, chuckling at the memory of his wife's face as he'd floored the accelerator on the golf cart. He was sure he'd been smiling nonstop for two hours. Finally he was at peace. The afternoon had been fun and carefree, and he was more in love with his wife than ever before. The horror of the last two weeks no longer lurked around every corner of his mind, waiting to jump out and grab him off guard.

He waved at the front-desk clerk, whose name badge said "Debbie." "You certainly get around," he said in a jovial tone. "Didn't you serve us drinks at the pool today?"

"I sure did, Mr. Wakefield," she said in the bouncy, perky way of young service workers trying too hard to make a good impression. "I was filling in for a friend. This is my real job."

"I need to pick up my room key," Mr. Wakefield told her. "Are there any messages? It's room one-twelve."

Debbie checked the box. "Yep, here's one. It's from your daughters."

He unfolded the slip of paper she handed him. "Mom and Dad," began Elizabeth's precise script. "We hope you're having a good day. We're going horseback riding this afternoon. We'll see you at dinner. Love, Liz and Jess."

"Thanks," he said to Debbie. He turned around to go meet Alice in the gift shop, but Debbie stopped him.

"Actually," she said, "you did have another message. Well, sort of. He didn't leave anything written, but a friend of yours came by this afternoon. He said you didn't know he was staying here."

Mr. Wakefield heard a rushing sound in his ears. "A friend?"

"That's right," Debbie continued, oblivious to his distress. "He had light-brown hair and dark-blue eyes. About your height, but with really broad shoulders."

With every word Mr. Wakefield felt his face draining of blood. The description fit John Marin. "But that's impossible!" he blurted out.

Debbie looked at him curiously. "Excuse me? Is something wrong, Mr. Wakefield?"

He turned to her, his eyes blazing. "Did my, uh, *friend* leave a name?"

Debbie keyed a few characters into her computer. "Yes, sir. His name is Leon LeShay." Suddenly she looked frightened. "You do know him, don't you?"

"Yes, I know him, all right," he said, troubled. The description sounded like Marin, but the alias didn't seem like something Marin would use. Mr. Wakefield took a deep breath. Then he turned and stalked out of the lobby, forgetting until he reached room 112 that he was supposed to meet his wife.

"Tony?" he yelled into the phone a few minutes later, after Detective Cabrini picked up the line at the Sweet Valley police station. "It's Ned Wakefield." He crossed his fingers tightly.

"Ned!" Cabrini's voice sounded frantic. "Thank goodness you got my messages. I'm glad you're safe."

"Messages? What messages? What's happened?"

"You don't know?" Tony asked, sounding worried.

A horrible premonition came over Mr. Wakefield. *No!* he told himself. *It can't be.* He raised his voice without realizing it. "*What* don't I know?"

Cabrini took a deep breath. "John Marin is free. He escaped from prison this morning."

"*What do you mean, he escaped from prison?*" the attorney yelled into the receiver as his world crashed into splinters around him—like the window of Elizabeth's bedroom the night Marin had smashed through it.

"Marin killed one prison guard," Cabrini said. "He kidnapped another guard, and she still hasn't been found. The warden's afraid she could be dead, too."

"Do you have any leads?" Mr. Wakefield asked flatly.

"Sort of," Cabrini said. "We think Marin carjacked a station wagon in the desert, from a family of tourists from Utah. He must be heading south—probably to the border."

"The border? Yeah, right," Mr. Wakefield said, not believing it for an instant. "Dammit, Tony! You know as well as I do where he's headed. Marin's obsessed with my family. I know how this guy thinks. And I know he'd make a beeline straight for my daughters."

"Ned, don't jump to conclusions—"

"Tony, he might be here already!" Mr. Wakefield startled himself with the shrill edge of panic in his own voice.

"I doubt that," Cabrini said, trying to be reasonable. "He only just broke out of prison today. Even if he is coming after your family, it would take him a few days to track you down. He has no way of knowing where you are."

"Then why did a man who fits Marin's description tell the front-desk clerk that he's my friend?" Mr. Wakefield asked.

"Calm down, Ned," Cabrini told him. "A lot of people fit Marin's description."

"A lot of people didn't try to murder my daughters!"

"Try to stay calm," the detective urged. "I'll alert the police force there on the island. And I'll get the coast guard involved too, to catch him as he crosses the channel. Damn! I wish we could locate that missing prison guard. If LeShay is still alive, she could probably tell us a lot."

Mr. Wakefield froze. "Who?"

"Leighann LeShay. She's the prison guard Marin kidnapped."

Leighann LeShay? The "friend" at the front desk had given his name as *Leon* LeShay. Mr. Wakefield gasped, feeling as if he were drowning in a nightmare. None of this was real. It couldn't be.

"Ned? Ned!" came Cabrini's voice through the phone. "Are you still there? What's wrong?"

Mr. Wakefield shook his head, his eyes closed. "Forget about contacting the coast guard," he choked out. "It's too late for that. Marin is already on the island."

Chapter 7

Behind the stable, Joe Garcia leaned his chair back against the wall and lit up a Lucky Strike. He'd promised his fiancée, Debbie, that he would quit smoking, and he had almost managed it—he was down to only one cigarette a day. But that one cigarette was proving to be the hardest one to give up. Joe's five o'clock smoke was more than a cigarette. It was a ritual.

He gazed into the peaceful forest, where smoky shadows were beginning to gather beneath the trees. Almost everybody thought the view from the front of the stable was more spectacular—with the red-tile roof of the hotel glinting in the sun, and a trace of ocean visible in the distance. But to Joe's mind it was a tourist's view. Out here, behind the stable, was a Catalina most tourists never saw. No hype. No picture-postcard views. Just hills and trees and pure serenity.

Five o'clock was Joe's favorite time of day in the summer. His afternoon chores were finished, and he had a good twenty minutes before any of the groups who were out horseback riding started trickling back. He'd have plenty of work to do then, until six, when the three o'clock group was due to return. But for now Joe was alone, with some time to think.

Today he had to think about Debbie's twenty-second birthday. She'd been dying to buy a party dress she'd seen in the resort's boutique. Joe didn't know much about women's clothes, but he thought the white flowing dress would look really sexy with Debbie's dark hair and ruby lipstick. He'd like nothing more than to buy Debbie that dress and celebrate her birthday by taking her to Villa Portofino for dinner and then over to the Avalon Casino for some hot dancing.

Joe sighed. The front legs of his chair landed in the dirt with a soft thump, and he poked at his glasses to push them back into place. This view of the forest always worked miracles for his mood. But it couldn't work miracles for his wallet. He couldn't afford to buy Debbie that dress, or to take her out for a special evening. They would have to settle for blue jeans and Mexican food, like last year.

A horse whinnied. Joe jumped up, surprised to hear footsteps on the wooden-plank sidewalk. It was too early for one of the guided tours to be returning. He crushed the rest of his Lucky Strike into the dirt and sauntered around the building to see who was interrupting his daily meditations.

"Howdy!" called a well-built man with sandy-brown hair and a big grin. "My name's Leon. What does a guy have to do to rent a horse around here?"

Joe smiled apologetically. "I'm sorry, but you'll have to come back tomorrow. Our last guided horseback ride of the day left at three o'clock."

"That's OK," the man said. "I'm an experienced rider, and I know the island. I don't need a guide."

"Sorry," Joe repeated, trying to keep his tone friendly and polite—since, after all, this was a hotel guest. "But I'm not allowed to go against hotel policy. I can't let you take out a horse without a guide, no matter how qualified a rider you are."

Leon pulled a billfold from his jeans and began unfolding twenty-dollar bills. "I sure would like to take out a horse this afternoon," he said quietly. "Would a hundred dollars cover your trouble?"

Joe gulped. A hundred dollars would buy that white dress Debbie was in love with. He glanced at the sky. There were still several hours of sunlight left. But what if Leon wasn't as good a rider as he claimed? What if there was an accident? Or what if Joe's boss showed up and asked about the missing horse?

Joe peered into the stable, thinking fast. His boss almost never came by this late in the day. And if he chose the oldest, safest horse in the stable, surely Leon wouldn't get into any trouble. There was Old Lacey in her stall, watching them calmly from her big brown eyes. She'd be perfect.

"OK, sir," Joe said finally. "You've got a deal. You can take out Old Lacey; she's as gentle as a kitten. Just have her in by dark—and remember that the sun goes down behind the mountains early on this part of the island, even in June. And it may storm tonight, so it could get dark sooner than usual. Don't stay out late."

"Don't worry," Leon said, smiling. "This shouldn't take too long."

Mrs. Wakefield pushed open the door to room 112.

"Ned?" she asked as her eyes adjusted to the dimness. Outside, the late-afternoon sun had been bright. But inside the room the shades were drawn, and her husband hadn't bothered to turn on a light. "I thought you were going to meet me in the gift shop. The clerk at the front desk told me the girls went horseback riding."

Mr. Wakefield sat on the bed, with his back to his wife and his posture rigid. "All right," he said. "You call the police, and I'll find the girls."

"What in the world are you talking about?" Mrs. Wakefield asked. Then she noticed that he had spoken into the telephone receiver in his hand. "Ned? *What's wrong?*"

"Yes," said her husband. "I'll call if I get any leads. And call me the minute you know anything. If you can't find me, leave a message at the desk."

Mrs. Wakefield heard something crackle under her foot. A folded sheet of paper was on the floor. Obviously it had been slipped under the door. "What's this?" she asked absentmindedly. She picked up the sheet of paper just as her husband slammed the telephone receiver into its cradle.

He whirled to face her, his expression grim. "John Marin escaped from prison this morning," he said. "And he's here on Catalina."

His wife sat down limply on the bed. "Are you sure?" she whispered. She nervously tore off a corner of the paper in her hand.

He nodded, his eyes full of fear.

Mrs. Wakefield's gaze dropped to her lap, and she suddenly caught sight of the words scrawled in large, angular letters on the sheet of Hotel Orizaba stationery. "Oh, Ned!" she cried. "Look at this!"

She handed him the sheet of paper and saw her own horror reflected in his eyes. *"Horseback riding can be dangerous, Counselor,"* the note said. It was signed *"JM."*

Elizabeth coaxed her horse alongside her sister's. High up on Black Beauty, Jessica stared around her as if perplexed. Wooded hills had given way to a rocky, rugged landscape. The trees were spaced farther apart now, and interspersed with exotic, glossy-leaved vegetation and tall, stubby, cactuslike plants that left long shadows in the light of late afternoon. Elizabeth followed her sister's gaze to the unmarked ground in front of them, where patches of pine needles lay undisturbed in the sand.

Elizabeth felt her annoyance rising. "What happened to the trail you were supposed to be following?" she asked sharply.

"I have no idea," Jessica said. "It just sort of disappeared a while back."

"Then why didn't you turn around?" Elizabeth asked. "You were in the lead. It was your turn to navigate!"

"I kept thinking we were on a part of the trail that's gotten overgrown," Jessica explained. "I figured we'd hit a real trail again soon."

Elizabeth sighed. "Now we don't even have any idea what direction we came from," she said. "We've probably been traveling in circles. I can't believe I let you get us lost!"

"We're not really lost," Jessica insisted brightly. "We know we're in the woods. And we know we're still on Catalina Island—"

"Do you rehearse your lame comments ahead of time," Elizabeth asked, "or do you improvise on the spot?"

Jessica glared at her twin. "Why do you always

have to get sarcastic when we run into a little bitty problem?" Her voice rose to a high pitch, and Black Beauty, who'd seemed skittish all afternoon, did a nervous dance until Jessica reined her in. "I hate it when you get sarcastic!" she concluded.

"And I hate it when you get us into trouble!" Elizabeth responded. "Leaving the group was your idea, remember?"

"Nobody twisted your arm to follow me!"

Elizabeth sighed. "Well," she said, "somebody had to look after you, since you're obviously incapable of looking after yourself."

"Right. And I can see what a good job you've done of it!" Jessica said, gesturing toward their rugged, unfamiliar surroundings. "Thanks for looking out for me, *big* sister. What would I ever do without you? I swear, Liz, you have no right to act like you're the boss, just because you're four minutes older than me—"

"This has nothing to do with age," Elizabeth argued. "It has to do with common sense!"

Jessica put her hands on her hips, and her eyes blazed. "If you have so much common sense," she said icily, "then why are you lost in the middle of the woods, screaming your lungs out, sitting on a horse with an idiotic name like Fred?"

Elizabeth was too frustrated to answer and instead let out an exasperated groan. Besides, Jessica had a point. Deep down, Elizabeth knew she had to take her share of the blame for getting lost.

Anyhow, arguing was accomplishing nothing. "Leave Fred out of this," she said. "It's not his fault." She nudged Fred in the flanks with her left sneaker, to turn him away from Jessica and Black Beauty.

Peering into the trees, Elizabeth didn't understand how it could be growing so dark so quickly. She checked her watch. It wasn't even five thirty. But birdsong had been replaced by the repetitive chirp of crickets, and the temperature was dropping rapidly, though it had seemed hot just a half hour earlier. Elizabeth was wearing only a short-sleeved top, and goose pimples were already poking out on her bare arms. Of course, Jessica was wearing a bikini top that was much skimpier. But at least Jessica had a sweater tied around her waist.

"Gee, it's getting dark," Jessica said suddenly. "How did it get so late, so fast?"

"I don't know," Elizabeth said, double-checking her watch. "It's not late enough to be so dark, in June."

"Maybe it's an eclipse," Jessica suggested.

"Maybe your brain is eclipsed," Elizabeth responded distractedly.

Suddenly Elizabeth knew one reason why night seemed to be falling so early. The twins had been traveling around the outskirts of one of the island's rocky peaks, which now jutted up sharply between them and the afternoon sun. On top of the summit, a few trees waved wildly in the gathering wind.

"Do you recognize that peak?" Elizabeth asked. "If we can remember seeing it from the hotel, we might be able to get an idea of where we are."

Jessica shook her head. "Nope. It looks like a mound of rocks and trees to me, like all the other mounds of rocks and trees."

"I don't recognize it either." Elizabeth sighed, feeling helpless. In another couple hours it would be completely dark. And they had no idea which direction led to the hotel and their parents.

"Well, we can't be *that* lost," Jessica offered. "It's not that big an island."

Elizabeth scowled. Jessica was legendary for having no sense of direction. *Unless I figure a way out of this,* Elizabeth thought, *we'll be lost in the wilderness at night, alone.*

Brad sighed, glad that he was finally heading back to the stables with this last riding group of the day. Groups made up of mostly kids were always the hardest ones to lead. "Get down, Billy!" he yelled to a towheaded nine-year-old on a coal-black pony in the middle of the line. "We don't try to stand up when we're on a pony's back."

"I want to be in the circus!" Billy announced.

"Can I be in the circus, too?" asked Tiffany, whose pony plodded along right behind Brad's horse.

"You already *are* in the circus," Brad said. "This whole trip is a circus!" He shook his head. These little kids were driving him crazy. The only riders in this group who were over the age of twelve had been those pretty teenage twins—the ones who had stupidly insisted on going off on their own. He never should have given in and let them go. But when Jessica had brought up his wife like that—well, it had caught him off guard.

He hoped the twins hadn't got into any trouble. Sure, both girls were decent riders. But they didn't know the landscape. If they got lost or hurt, Brad knew that he'd probably lose his job at the resort.

"Who's that man?" Tiffany asked, pointing at the trail up ahead as they rounded a bend.

About ten yards away a tall, well-built man who looked a little younger than Brad sat astride Old Lacey. The man was digging his heels impatiently into the mare's dirty white flanks. "Come on, you lazy nag!" the man urged. Old Lacey, engrossed in munching vegetation by the side of the trail, calmly ignored him.

Brad frowned. "I don't know who he is," he said in a low voice. "I've never seen him before. But nobody is supposed to take out a horse without a guide. I wonder what he's up to." Then he realized he was talking to a nine-year-old. "He's just a man who's trying to get the horse to go," Brad told her. "Lacey can be pretty stubborn."

Tiffany appraised the stranger. "He's cuter than you," she told Brad.

Brad rolled his eyes. "Excuse me, sir," he

called. He tried to keep his voice polite, in case the man was a hotel guest. "Can I help you with something?"

The stranger looked up quickly. His dark-blue eyes widened with surprise, and he visibly struggled to control his frustration. When he spoke, his voice was calm and friendly. "I'm just having a heck of a time getting this old mare to move into those trees."

"There's a good reason for that," Brad said, dismounting. "Lacey is one of our oldest trail horses. And trail horses are trained to stay on the trail."

"Those two teenagers were on trail horses, and they didn't stay on the trail," Tiffany said.

"Well, some trail horses are more obedient than others," Brad said, wishing he were at home in his reclining chair, watching a baseball game on television. "And the twins did stay on the trail—they just took a different route." Brad turned to face the rest of the group. "You kids stop right where you are and wait for me!" he called.

"What twins?" the stranger asked. For an instant something about his face frightened Brad. The man's wide, easy smile seemed amused, but his eyes were glittering coldly. Brad blinked his own eyes, and the man's face returned to normal. *It must have been the late-afternoon sun in the trees*, he decided.

"There were two bee-yoo-ti-ful teenagers with long yellow hair," Tiffany explained. "But they were mean. They said we were too slow, but we weren't! They went away, over that way," she added, pointing.

"Two gorgeous blondes, huh?" the stranger asked Brad with a companionable wink. "And you let them get away?"

"I didn't have any choice," Brad replied, thinking ruefully of Jessica's low-cut bathing-suit top and long legs. "They found out about my wife."

Tiffany giggled.

"Tiffany, you go back to the other kids," Brad said. "I mean now!" He was annoyed with the little brat, but he was also feeling nervous around the good-looking young man who hadn't offered his name. The stranger seemed harmless enough, for a greenhorn without a lot of horse sense. Still, Brad was responsible for the children's safety; he wasn't supposed to let them talk to strangers while on these trips.

Tiffany didn't move. "Can I get off my horsey, too?"

"No, you can't," he told the little girl. "Go back to the other kids, like I said. And be quiet! This will only take me a minute. Now go!"

Pouting, Tiffany turned her pony around and walked it back to the other children.

"Are you one of the Orizaba's trail guides?" the stranger asked. His voice was casual, but his eyes were intense.

"Yes, sir," Brad answered.

"Then maybe you can tell me what I'm doing wrong." The man gestured helplessly at Old Lacey. "How do I get this nag to gallop?"

"Gallop?" Brad asked. "You've got a better chance of getting a wooden carousel horse to gallop. Old Lacey is the slowest, steadiest horse on this island."

"At this point I'd settle for walking," the young man said ruefully.

"Walking, she'll do," Brad said. "But not in that direction. I told you, Lacey won't go off the trail. Not for you. Not for me. Not for anyone."

"Are all the horses around here like that?" the man asked.

Brad laughed. "Most are, but not all." He patted his own mahogany-colored mount. "For instance, Big Red here is the best off-trail horse around."

"I'm sorry, sir," Joe told the frantic middle-aged man. "But hotel guests aren't allowed to take a horse out without a guide."

"So get me a guide!" the dark-haired man insisted.

"There aren't any," Joe told him. "Only one guide is still on duty this late, and he's out with a group of riders."

"Then let me go by myself!" The man's hands trembled as he pleaded with Joe. "I only need a couple of hours. It's a matter of life and death!"

121

Joe chuckled inwardly. Guests of the resort were a pampered, self-centered bunch. Rich guys like this one considered pretty much everything to be a matter of life and death—from a stock-market slump to a shortage of airplane seats in first class. "I'd like to help you, sir, but the rules—"

"I'll pay you!" the man practically screamed. He yanked his wallet from his pocket and thumbed through it. He shoved a bill at Joe.

"Fifty dollars?" Joe asked, incredulous. He wondered if there was a full moon that night—*something* was making the guests freak out. Only a lunatic would pay fifty dollars to borrow a broken-down old trail horse for two hours. And the last crazy guest, Leon, had given him twice that. Leon's hundred dollars would be enough to buy Debbie's dress. This fifty dollars would go a long way toward a nice dinner.

"I'll pay you a hundred dollars!" the guest cried, pulling out another bill. "It's all I have with me."

"One hundred dollars?" Joe repeated. *Dinner, drinks, and dancing,* he thought happily. *Plus a corsage.*

Joe accepted the money. "All right, mister, you've got yourself a horse. But be sure to have her back by sunset."

Mr. Wakefield shifted from one foot to the other as the young stable hand took his time saddling up a horse. The horse was large, a gray gelding with white speckles. The stable guy had called it Satchmo. The twins' father didn't care what color the horse was or what its name was, and he didn't want to hear Joe's mindless patter about why Western saddles were better than English ones. He just wanted to get onto the horse and go out after his daughters.

His wife had begged him to wait in the hotel room until the authorities arrived, but every minute counted. Elizabeth and Jessica were out in those woods, and John Marin was on the loose. When Mrs. Wakefield had seen that his mind was made up, she had wanted to come, too. He had asked her to stay behind and start throwing together their belongings, so the family could leave the island as soon as he returned with the twins. Besides, somebody would have to talk to the police when they arrived.

"This is beginning to feel like déjà vu all over again, if you know what I mean," the stable hand commented as he handed Mr. Wakefield the reins. "I guess it's just my lucky day."

The counselor whirled around to glare at the stable hand. "What do you mean?"

"It's the darnedest thing," the younger man explained. "But can you believe that you're the second hotel guest in here this afternoon desperate to rent a horse at any price?"

"Who else was here?" Mr. Wakefield demanded. "Tell me!"

The man's eyes widened. "I know it was against the rules, but he offered me a hundred dollars, just like you did, and—"

"*Who was he?*" Mr. Wakefield thundered.

"His name was Leon something-or-other," the stable hand said, surprised at Mr. Wakefield's intensity. "He was about your height, with light-brown hair."

John Marin.

Icy fear gripped Mr. Wakefield's heart. He swung his body onto the horse's back and cantered away from the astonished stable hand, racing headlong toward the gloom beneath the trees.

Brad sighed gratefully as the trail rounded a bend near a huge old pine tree. The stable was only a few minutes away. This terrible last ride of the day would soon be over. He plodded along on Old Lacey, longing for his usual mount's sprightly step and quick reflexes.

"I liked your reddish-brownish horse better," Tiffany said, riding up alongside him.

Brad narrowed his eyes. He liked Big Red better, too. But he wasn't about to admit that to a nine-year-old. "Get back in line!" he ordered.

"Why did you and that cute guy trade horses?" the girl asked.

"None of your business!" Brad snapped.

But the question was a valid one. Brad couldn't believe he'd let the guy talk him into trading horses. One minute they'd been standing there chatting about the stubbornness of trail horses. The next minute the man with the dark-blue eyes was swinging his lean, muscular body into Big Red's saddle, while Brad mounted tired Old Lacey.

He wished he had the stranger's persuasive powers. They might have worked wonders with pretty, blond Jessica of the low-cut bikini top and long legs.

Jessica swatted a mosquito, but not until after it had raised a red welt on her thigh. She wished she hadn't insisted on wearing shorts. At least the wind was picking up. It felt cold against her bare legs, but it might help blow the mosquitoes away. "Whose idea was horseback riding, anyway?" she asked.

Elizabeth glowered at her. "Yours."

"Oh." They plodded on in silence for a few minutes, and Jessica noticed how dark it was getting. As usual, she wasn't wearing a watch, but she guessed that she and her sister had been lost for a good two hours. "I guess we never should have left the group."

"That's a blinding flash of the obvious," Elizabeth replied evenly.

Something loomed up ahead of them. *"Liz! What's that?"* Jessica shouted.

"It's only one of those cactuslike things," Elizabeth said. Her face was calm, but Jessica heard a tremor in her voice. "They're all over the place."

For the first time Jessica noticed that they really weren't riding through woods anymore. "You're right. Those cactus things are everywhere. And the ground is almost all rock. We seem to be going up. Are we climbing a mountain?"

"I don't think so," Elizabeth said in an impatient voice. "I think we're close to the shoreline."

"How can we be close to the shoreline?" Jessica asked. "It doesn't look like any beach *I've* ever seen. I bet the shore is miles from here. Admit it, Liz. You don't have any idea where we are."

"Fine," Elizabeth said. "If you know this island so well, then *you* figure out which way to go—the same way you figured out how to get us lost!"

Jessica pouted. "You're impossible!"

"Then it must run in the family," Elizabeth shot back.

Jessica suddenly reined in Black Beauty and stiffened, listening. "What's that noise?" she asked.

Elizabeth smiled triumphantly. "It sounds like the ocean to me. But I guess it couldn't be. Remember, the shore is miles from here."

Jessica glared at her twin and started Black Beauty into motion. "You think you're so smart," she muttered dangerously.

"I never said that," her sister protested. "All I said was—"

Suddenly the horses stepped out onto a flat

rock ledge. For a moment Jessica felt as if she were on top of the Empire State Building. Her horse shied. "Whoa, Black Beauty!" she called.

The twins reeled at the unexpected vista that stretched out in front of and below them. Their long, misshapen shadows fell over the edge of the high cliff. Far below, the pounding waves of the Pacific Ocean threatened to engulf a narrow strip of creamy beach and jagged gray rocks. The water was a deep midnight-blue under an overcast sky. The only signs of life were a few ash-colored seagulls wheeling overhead.

Jessica sighed miserably. They were close to the beach, all right. But it was a totally undeveloped, uninhabited beach. And it was a good eighty feet below them, at the bottom of the cliff.

"What do we now?" Jessica asked in a small voice. She was still mad at Elizabeth. But almost instinctively, she trusted her twin to solve their problems.

Elizabeth's face looked pale, and Jessica realized that her sister was very tired. "I think I have some idea where we are now," Elizabeth said in a resigned voice. She gestured toward the sweep of coastline to the north. "If we continue along the coast in that direction, we'll get to a campground I saw on the map, right off the beach. There's a road leading from that campground to our hotel."

"So all we have to do is follow the beach, and we'll get back to civilization?" Jessica asked.

"I think so," Elizabeth replied.

"But we're way up here on a cliff!" Jessica said worriedly. "How do we get down to the beach?"

"This is the highest point," Elizabeth said. "The cliffs start sloping downward as soon as we start going north. If we follow the path along the rim of the cliffs, it should bring us down to the level of the beach. Eventually."

Jessica peered around from the top of Black Beauty. "I don't see any path!" she cried.

"It's right there," Elizabeth said, pointing to a narrow track off to one side.

Jessica's eyes widened. Now she could see the stony path leading down from the outcropping they were on. But it was overgrown and littered with rocks that had fallen from higher elevations. Even worse, the path was only a couple feet wide at some points, and it fell off sharply on the left side, revealing a straight drop down to jagged rocks peppered by ocean spray.

Jessica took a deep breath. She had got them into this. She would get them out. "I'll lead the way," she said. "Follow me."

Mr. Wakefield squinted to make out the dial of his watch. It was only seven thirty—the sun couldn't have set yet. But shadows clustered thickly under the trees, distorting the shapes and colors of everything around him. And he still had found no sign of the twins.

"Elizabeth!" he called. "Jessica!"

The only response was the faint echo of his own voice, bouncing off some distant rocky hillside.

He gripped the gray gelding's flanks tightly with his calves. "Come on, Satchmo," he whispered, feeling very small in the rugged, unfamiliar landscape. Danger seemed to lurk behind every tree, and he expected to see John Marin riding out of the shadows at any moment.

He shuddered at the thought of Marin's cold, vengeance-filled eyes. But he wished that the murderer would appear before him. If Marin was here, with him, then at least Mr. Wakefield could be sure the killer wasn't tracking down Jessica and Elizabeth, sneaking up on them in the deserted woods, and thrusting forward with that long, gleaming knife—

The twins' father pounded his fist against his forehead. *I've got to find my daughters before Marin gets to them,* he thought. *I've just got to.*

The sky was deepening to a dark, purplish blue. The ocean mirrored its color, with white strips of foam gleaming along the crests of waves. A flash of silent lightning streaked the horizon. Elizabeth realized that a storm was brewing. She was surprised not to have noticed it before.

If she hadn't felt so nervous and alone, Elizabeth would have liked to write a poem about the dramatic view of dusk from the narrow path she and Fred the Horse were negotiating. She could barely make out Jessica in front of her, on Black Beauty, whose nervous hooves sent occasional showers of rock skittering over the cliff.

Suddenly another pattering of falling rocks made Elizabeth whirl in her saddle. The noise had come from behind her. *That's stupid,* she scolded herself in a low voice. *The only other person around is Jessica, and she's in front of me. I must've heard an echo.*

She shivered. Elizabeth's short-sleeved T-shirt and walking shorts did almost nothing to ward off the worsening chill in the air. And as much as she tried to push the thoughts away, the sight of the wind-tossed Pacific Ocean at night brought back a rush of memories of being in danger and full of fear on the deck of Marin's sailboat.

Elizabeth nudged Fred into a slightly faster walk, to catch up with Jessica and Black Beauty. But the path was too dangerous to allow the horses to move with any real speed. And the quickly falling darkness didn't help.

A lumpy, vertical shape seemed to jump suddenly from a pile of rocks. Elizabeth gasped. She reined her horse so quickly that he almost sat down on his hind legs.

"Liz!" Jessica's voice came back down the path to her. "What's wrong?" Her twin appeared suddenly out of the gloom.

Elizabeth tried to catch her breath. "It's nothing," she assured her. "One of those funny tall cactus plants startled me, that's all."

"I know what you mean," Jessica said. "I keep having the same problem." She began describing her own encounters with plant life. She spoke bravely, but to Elizabeth her voice sounded more subdued than usual—as if she were afraid that speaking too loudly would awaken whatever unknown terrors were hidden in the darkness.

Elizabeth shook her head. She had to stop thinking like a character in an Edgar Allan Poe poem. Instead she latched on to her sister's voice and urged Fred to follow it, grateful for its utter normality.

Suddenly she heard a clattering sound, coming from close behind her. *"Who's there?"* Elizabeth called.

"What's wrong?" Jessica asked nervously.

"I don't know," Elizabeth whispered. "I could've sworn I heard something behind us—like another horse."

"It's that writer's brain of yours, working overtime," Jessica said bravely. "I bet it was just an echo."

"I'm sure that's it," Elizabeth said, hoping it was true. "Our voices must be bouncing off these cliffs."

"Or maybe it was a seagull," Jessica suggested.

Elizabeth nodded. "Maybe." A clatter in front of her interrupted her thoughts. "Jessica? Are you all right?" Her sister didn't answer immediately. "Jessica!"

"It's OK, Liz," Jessica called, sounding out of breath. "The trail is narrower and rockier here. Black Beauty stumbled. Don't look off the edge to your left. It'll make you dizzy."

Elizabeth nodded and turned Fred's head to the other side. He had no objections to keeping as close as possible to the rock wall that rose to their right. "Mom and Dad must be worried sick about us," Elizabeth said. "The horseback ride was supposed to be over by six o'clock. That was two hours ago."

She whirled in her saddle again, sure she had heard a noise off to one side. But she could make out only the dim shapes of lurking rocks behind her.

"So much for getting Dad to chill out about us being safe," Jessica said. "Once we get back to the hotel tonight, he won't let us out of his sight for the rest of the week."

"I just hope we *reach* the hotel tonight," Elizabeth replied. "If we do, I don't care if Dad watches us all week like Chrome Dome Cooper himself!"

Jessica giggled nervously at the mention of Sweet Valley High's hawk-eyed principal. Then Elizabeth heard another clatter from up ahead.

"Be real careful here, Liz," Jessica warned a moment later in a breathless voice. She had just

132

rounded a bend and was no longer visible from Elizabeth's position. "There's been a rock slide, I guess, and the path turns in really sharply. Black Beauty almost stepped over the edge."

"Are you OK?" Elizabeth asked quickly, alarmed.

"I'm OK, Liz," Jessica called back to assure her in a shaky voice. "So's Black Beauty. It's just that—" Her voice was cut short in a rattle of rock fall.

"Jessica!" Elizabeth spurred her horse closer. She gasped as she rounded the bend.

Black Beauty had dropped to one knee on the very edge of the precipice. Now the mare struggled to regain her footing, whinnying in terror at the sharp drop-off just below her nose. Jessica lay on the horse's back, flung forward against her neck, clinging frantically to the black mane. The saddle had come loose and was hanging uselessly around the mare's heaving flanks. The girl and the horse were silhouetted against a sky full of swirling purple clouds.

"Don't come any closer!" Jessica ordered in a tense whisper.

Elizabeth reined Fred in tightly. If Jessica or the mare made a single wrong move, both would go plummeting over the cliff.

"Well, well, well," said a mocking voice behind her. The voice sent terrible shivers up Elizabeth's spine. For a horrible moment she thought she was going to faint. She slowly turned around to see

Brad's huge reddish horse carefully making its way around the bend. But on its back sat John Marin, his perfect teeth flashing like stars through the murky evening.

"Marin!" Elizabeth whispered.

Jessica screamed, and the black mare pitched forward.

"Jessica!" yelled Elizabeth.

Chapter 8

Elizabeth froze. On the edge of the cliff, Black Beauty neighed helplessly. Jessica clung desperately to the horse's back.

As Elizabeth held her breath, the mare scrambled and managed to check her slide down the slope, but Jessica and Black Beauty were still in grave danger. The horse's mouth foamed like the waves that crashed against the sharp rocks eighty feet below. And every time the mare tried to stand up, the rocks under her shod feet slid her farther forward, over the cliff. Jessica's slightest movement threw her even more off balance. And John Marin watched the scene with a calm, amused expression on his face.

"Run, Liz!" Jessica yelled. "Don't wait for me!"

Elizabeth nudged Fred closer to the fallen mare. "Slide backward down the horse's back, Jess, and then jump off!" Elizabeth urged her sister. She stopped and looked over her shoulder. Marin, on Big Red, was swaying toward them. "You can do it, Jessica!" Elizabeth cried. "Hurry!"

Marin reined his horse in the middle of the path and sat grinning at them, two horse lengths away. "You've got yourself in quite a pickle, Jessica," he called. "Some girls just don't know how to stay out of trouble."

"Ignore him, Jessica," Elizabeth commanded. "Do as I said. Slide back slowly—don't scare the horse!"

"I can't, Liz," Jessica called. "The slope's too unstable. I'll fall! You go. Get away from Marin now! You've still got a chance."

Marin laughed but made no move to come closer. "Isn't this a touching scene?"

Elizabeth's mind raced. *Jessica can make it,* she thought, *if she takes her time and doesn't panic. I have to keep Marin away from her. It's her only chance.* She caught her sister's eye for a moment and saw Jessica's almost imperceptible nod.

Elizabeth turned to the grinning horseman, subtly maneuvering the frightened Fred as she spoke, so that he stood between Big Red and Black Beauty. "What's your problem, Marin?" she asked in her toughest voice. "A little identity crisis, maybe? Are you having trouble deciding who to be today?"

"An intriguing opening, Elizabeth," Marin said

with a chuckle. "It sounds like the kind of metaphysical ranting you and Ben Morgan were so fond of."

At the mention of Marin's alias—the one Elizabeth had fallen for—she clenched her teeth, determined not to lose her temper or her nerve. "If you were Ben right now, you'd be rushing forward to help us," she told him. "If you were John Marin the maniac, you'd probably be spooking Jessica's horse to send them both over the edge. Who are you now? It's not like you to sit back and watch."

Marin laughed. "It's a shame to kill two girls as amusing as you two. Why should I be doing anything besides sitting back to watch? You'll both die soon enough, whether it's from plummeting over the cliff or bleeding to death when I stab your warm, supple bodies." He wiped his mouth with the back of his hand. "Why shouldn't I get some entertainment first?"

Good job, Liz, Jessica thought. *Keep Marin talking. Keep him distracted while I find a way out of this.*

Her twin had been right—Jessica could slide off the horse to safety—but only if Black Beauty stayed still and didn't panic. How in the world could Jessica keep the skittish mare calm? Black Beauty couldn't regain her footing on the broken rocks; for all Jessica knew, the mare might actually be injured. Even if she wasn't injured, it would be nearly impossible for the horse to rise to her feet and move away from the edge—while carrying Jessica on her back. And one slip could send them both over the cliff.

The sight of the churning ocean below made Jessica's stomach churn, too. She turned her head. *This is just like climbing a rope in gym class*, she told herself. *If you get scared, you keep your eyes glued to the rope. Don't look down, no matter what happens.*

That's it! Jessica realized. She had to keep Black Beauty from looking down. She remembered hearing about a farmer who threw gunnysacks over horses' heads to keep them calm as they were led from a burning barn. It was worth a try. She had to cover Black Beauty's eyes so that the horse wouldn't panic until they were both away from the ledge.

"Where's a gunnysack when you need one?" Jessica muttered under her breath.

"How did you find us here?" Elizabeth asked Marin.

Good going, Liz, Jessica thought. *Keep stalling him. I just need a little more time.*

"Why, darling, you know I'd follow you and your sister to the ends of the earth," Marin replied. "I promised your daddy I'd be back for you. And I never forget a promise."

Jessica stopped listening. She frantically untied

the blue cotton sweater from around her waist. Then she threw it over the horse's bucking head. A shudder ran through the mare's body, jarring Jessica's already jangled nerves. Then Black Beauty quieted, as if by magic. Jessica began to slide slowly backward down the horse's broad, long back. Just a few inches more, and she'd be able to jump to stable ground.

"And then that redheaded waitress told me you'd gone horseback riding," Marin said, his smug voice penetrating Jessica's frantic thoughts. She realized that Marin was almost finished telling Elizabeth how he'd tracked down the twins. Her time was running out.

Suddenly a flash of lightning seared across the sky, followed by a boom of thunder that echoed against the cliffs. Black Beauty tossed her huge head, terrified. The cotton sweater dropped away and disappeared over the edge of the cliff. The horse screamed, a loud, terrifying sound like nothing Jessica had ever heard before.

She leaped backward off Black Beauty's heaving sides and landed near Elizabeth and Fred. Marin's mouth formed a grim line, and his eyes shone in the strange purplish-green glow of the sky at twilight before a storm.

"Jessica! Jump!" Elizabeth screamed, reaching a hand down as Fred began to bound away from Marin.

The twins' great-great-grandmother, Jessamyn,

had been a bareback rider in the circus. Jessica felt her ancestor's blood coursing through her own veins as she leaped toward her sister's hand. In an eye blink she was astride Fred, behind Elizabeth. She entwined her arms around her sister and helped kick the horse into a gallop along the rocky, narrow trail. "Giddyap, Fred!" Jessica yelled.

From the corner of her eye, she saw Black Beauty, now unburdened, struggling to her feet. But the image vanished as Fred picked up speed.

Behind Jessica, hooves pounded on the hard path as the first spatters of rain began to hit her face. Marin was chasing them. And he obviously had the faster horse.

Mrs. Wakefield held up a red tube of fabric, puzzled as to what its purpose might be. Then she realized it was a dress, and she grinned wryly. Like everything else she'd found in Elizabeth and Jessica's hotel room, the dress left no question as to which twin owned it.

She folded the skimpy dress into Jessica's light-blue suitcase. It was the last personal belonging to be packed. She shook her head at the thought of her own daughter wearing such a thing. But she never would have dreamed of forbidding her. In eighteen years of motherhood, Mrs. Wakefield had learned to choose her battles. It was all a matter of perspective. Some parents flew off the handle over clothes and haircuts. But such trappings were trivial. Other issues concerning her daughters were much more important. Some meant life or death.

Death, Mrs. Wakefield thought numbly. Only a week earlier John Marin had tried to kill her girls. *And now he might be trying again, at this very moment.*

She blinked back tears. She had to stay in control; she'd be no good to anyone if she fell to pieces. The Catalina police had already taken her statement about Marin. Now the police were out searching for the girls. So was her husband. Even the hotel stable had sent out some riders. But the police had instructed Mrs. Wakefield to stay behind, near the telephone. Everyone else was trying to save her daughters' lives, while all she could do was sit in a luxury hotel and wait. Her only contribution was to pack her family's bags for a hurried trip off the island. She felt utterly helpless.

Mrs. Wakefield realized with a start that she was pacing. She stopped herself, sat on the bed, and checked her watch. It was almost eight thirty. Her husband had been gone for three hours. She had heard nothing from him or the girls. A new fear gripped her heart. John Marin hated her husband with all his sick, twisted heart. What if Marin found Mr. Wakefield before Mr. Wakefield found the twins?

I don't care what the police said, she thought grimly. *I'm not waiting here all night, not knowing what's happening. I'll give them another hour. If I don't hear anything by then, I'm joining the search.*

The horse's hooves pounded beneath her, jarring Elizabeth's entire body. She wasn't sure how long they had been galloping along the narrow ledge. Jessica's mad leap onto Fred's back seemed long ago. Elizabeth felt as if she had done nothing all her life but bounce up and down in a saddle as purple clouds and rocky outcrops tilted by. Straight ahead, the half-moon was a pale, silvery lavender behind a layer of clouds. It gave little light. Elizabeth hoped Fred could see the treacherous path better than she could.

To her left, she sensed rather than saw a void where the path dropped off sharply above the pounding surf. The path had been sloping downward for some time; surely they were much closer to the beach than they'd been on the eighty-foot headland. Still, they had a long way to go before they reached solid ground. Until then a single stumble or misstep would send Fred over the edge, with Jessica and Elizabeth on his back.

"Good boy, Fred!" she encouraged the horse, patting his cold, sweaty neck. "Keep it up!" She bent low over him to reduce the wind resistance. Behind her, she felt Jessica doing the same.

Suddenly, chilly particles began stinging her face and arms; it took Elizabeth a minute to understand that it was raining. Her heart sank. Very soon

Fred would find the footing even more precarious.

"Faster, Liz!" Jessica screamed. Elizabeth could feel her sister's breath against her ear, but she could barely make out the words above the chilling wind. "I can see Marin behind us, Liz. He's getting closer!"

Elizabeth hated to cause pain to any animal, but she had no choice. She dug the heels of her sneakers into Fred's sides, and he responded with a short burst of speed.

"We can't get away!" Elizabeth called back to Jessica. "Fred can't keep this up much longer. He's too tired!"

"He has to!" Jessica shouted.

"I know," Elizabeth said. "But the path is awful, and Marin's horse is faster. We'll never make it!"

Jessica shifted on the horse. "We have to do something!"

Elizabeth saw a dark flash of movement from the corner of her eye. Marin's horse was coming up alongside Fred. *It's over,* she realized. The path was narrower just ahead. If she didn't rein in her horse, Marin would force them off the side of the cliff.

Elizabeth took a deep breath, preparing to give up and pull to a halt.

"Liz!" Jessica screamed, terrified. Her arms tightened around her sister's waist. Elizabeth could hardly breathe. She turned to see Marin reaching out for Jessica, trying to pull her off the horse.

"You can't get away from me!" he called with a burst of smug laughter.

The sound of his mocking laughter caused something to snap inside Elizabeth. Her fear was replaced by a burning, steaming rage. She refused to let Marin beat them. She wondered how high the cliff was at this point; then she realized that it didn't matter. Eight feet or eighty was all the same. Either way, she was going to do it. The crashing of the sea sounded louder than before, but the roaring in her ears and the howling wind made it impossible to tell how far below the waves might be. Lightning slashed across the sky, and the drizzle of rain grew to a real downpour.

"Hang on, Jessica!" she called, spurring the horse farther. "We're going over the side!"

At the edge of the rocky cliff, Elizabeth hesitated for only an instant. Then she jumped the horse out into the dark emptiness, feeling as if she were flying against the storm-ravaged sky and the silvery moon.

Mr. Wakefield reluctantly slowed his horse to a trot. Raindrops were splattering down through the trees, and the riding trail had become muddy and hard to follow. He hated to lose time, but he couldn't risk a fall. If Satchmo got injured, Mr. Wakefield would be stuck alone in the woods, with no way of reaching his daughters.

"Jessica!" he called into the darkened forest. "Elizabeth!"

"Hello!" called a voice from up ahead.

For one joyful instant Mr. Wakefield's heart leaped to his throat. Immediately his relief dissipated. The voice belonged to a man. Then three horses appeared on the trail in front of him. Two men in yellow rain slickers rode the first two. A large black mare was tied behind them and appeared to be limping. The black mare had no rider.

"Who are you?" one of the men demanded, shining a flashlight in Mr. Wakefield's face.

"Mr. Wakefield!" the other man called, holding up a lantern. He pulled off his glasses to wipe raindrops from the lenses. The twins' father recognized him as the stable hand who had rented Satchmo to him. "It's me, Joe!" he said. "And this is Brad, the trail guide who was leading your daughters' trip this afternoon."

"Is there any news of my girls?" Mr. Wakefield choked out.

Joe and Brad exchanged a glance that filled the twins' father with dread. Then Joe stared at him for a long, agonizing moment. In the glow of the lantern, Mr. Wakefield could see that the young man's eyes were full of pain.

"Nothing definite," Joe said, shaking his head. "But we found Jessica's horse." He gestured toward the limping mare.

Mr. Wakefield took a deep breath. "Where? What happened?"

"We found Black Beauty on the edge of a cliff overlooking the beach," Brad said. "Her knee is scratched up, but she's not hurt badly."

"So where's Jessica?" Mr. Wakefield asked. He couldn't stop his hands from trembling.

"We don't know," Joe said, his voice apologetic. "We found what looked like tracks from both girls' horses, leading out to the headland. At the edge of the cliff, the ground was scuffed up, as if a horse had lost its footing there."

"Our guess is that Black Beauty stumbled at the rim of the cliff," Brad said bluntly. "Jessica probably pitched right over the mare's head."

Mr. Wakefield felt his body go numb. "How high is that cliff?" he said, his voice almost a whisper.

Joe couldn't meet his gaze. "About eighty feet."

"Oh, no!" Mr. Wakefield gasped, a terrible shiver running through his whole body. He shook his head, refusing to believe the news.

"Sir, we really don't know for sure what happened," Joe said quickly. "We looked over the edge, but we couldn't see her at the bottom of the cliff. Maybe she never fell at all. Maybe she wasn't even on the horse when it stumbled."

Mr. Wakefield nodded, hoping the raindrops on his face would hide his tears. "Or maybe it was too dark for you to see her down there," he said. He gulped, struggling to keep his grief and horror under control. "What about Elizabeth?"

Brad shook his head. "There's no telling," he said. "We saw hoofprints from Liz's horse leading toward the ledge, but not coming back."

"Of course, that doesn't mean anything," Joe added. "The ground around there is mostly rock. She could have walked the horse away from the cliff without leaving a trace."

"We should all be getting back to the stable, Mr. Wakefield," Brad said. "Black Beauty's leg will need tending to, and we'll have to show the police what we found—"

His words were cut short by a warning look from Joe. Mr. Wakefield searched both men's faces. "What is it?" he asked. "What are you hiding from me?"

Joe sighed. "This," he said, pulling up a piece of bluish fabric from his saddlebag. "I'm sorry, Mr. Wakefield. I didn't want to worry you any further, since we're not completely sure of the situation."

The twins' father stared at what seemed to be a scrap torn from a cotton sweater. He forced himself to breathe. "What do you *think* it is?" he asked finally, taking the scrap from Joe.

Brad shrugged. "It looks a lot like a piece of the sweater Jessica had tied around her waist."

Mr. Wakefield felt as if he had been punched in the stomach. "Where did you find it?" he asked, dreading the answer.

Joe's eyes locked on to his face. "It was caught on a sharp rock, a few feet down the side of the cliff," he said in a shaky voice. "It was just below the place where Black Beauty stumbled."

The twins' father felt dizzy. He grabbed his saddle horn to keep from falling off the gelding.

"I'm afraid it gets worse," Brad said after a moment. "We found the tracks of a third horse, also heading out toward the edge of that cliff. I believe it was the horse that John Marin was riding."

Mr. Wakefield fought back panic. He closed his eyes tightly and took a deep breath, but he still almost felt like fainting.

"I am so sorry for all of this, sir," Joe repeated, his voice full of pain. "It's all my fault. If I hadn't gone against policy and rented that maniac a horse—"

The twins' father shook his head. "It's nobody's fault but John Marin's," he choked out. A moment later he added in a low whisper, "And my own."

Brad's voice was overly hearty. "I think the best thing for all of us right now is to get back to the stables," he said. "We'll get something hot to drink and wait for word from the police. Who knows? Maybe they've already found your daughters, safe and sound—"

"No!" Mr. Wakefield interrupted. "I'm not going back until I know for sure. I want to see the place where Jessica might have gone over the edge."

"You won't find anything on that cliff," Brad objected. "We already checked the area. And by now the rain will have turned the prints into mud puddles."

"I'm going to the bottom of the cliff," Mr. Wakefield insisted. "If Jessica fell, she may be on the beach injured."

"As the crow flies, that strip of beach is just through the woods, that way," Joe told him, pointing. "But you'll never make it on horseback. There used to be a trail that leads along the rim of the cliffs, but it's impassable now."

"There has to be a way," Mr. Wakefield said, his voice grim.

"The only way to scale the cliffs is by leaving your horse behind and rappelling down the side," Brad said. "And even an experienced climber couldn't do it in this rain."

"Why don't you let us take you back to the stable?" Joe offered. "The police—"

"Forget the police!" Mr. Wakefield cried. "I have to see for myself! What if Jessica is down there, hurt? It could take hours to get help to her if we have to run back for the authorities first."

"All right," Joe agreed. "There's a road to the north of here that leads from the hotel to a campground that's just off the beach. Look, why don't I come with you? I know the way—"

"I think you two have done enough," the girls' father said darkly. He closed his eyes for a moment, trying to calm himself. "You two go back for the police," he said in a voice that dared them to object. "Just tell me which way to go."

Joe nodded slowly. "Take the road to the coastline and then ride south along the beach. You can't miss the headland where we found Jessica's horse; it's the highest cliff overlooking the coast."

Without another word, Ned turned away from the other men and urged his horse northward, through the dripping trees. He had to know the truth, no matter how painful it might be.

As Fred leaped from the cliff, Jessica felt queasy—as if she were riding a roller coaster in a horror movie. She forced her eyes open and hung on to Elizabeth's waist. The night was gloomy. But far beneath the horse's body, the sandy beach glowed in the eerie light that reflected off the water.

The water, Jessica thought, focusing on the violent surf. The twins and the brave little horse were going to die. They were about to plunge into the ocean.

The ground tilted crazily below her, and a rocky ledge rushed toward the little horse. This was it. They would never even reach the water. They would crash into the granite ledge and die right there, on the rocks.

The pounding of ocean waves grew louder, until it filled Jessica's head. She heard herself screaming.

Then Fred's hooves met stone and the impact

slammed through Jessica's body. For an instant she felt as if all her bones were being crushed together. Then the horse bounded into the air.

Jessica realized, amazed, that she was alive. It didn't seem possible, but Fred was still flying down the side of the bluff, in a series of running leaps. Jessica closed her eyes and tried not to throw up.

Finally the motion stopped. Fred stood quietly on the beach, his sides slick with rain and sweat. And Jessica sensed solid ground beneath his hooves. She could hardly catch her breath. "We're alive!" she marveled, opening her eyes. She was still holding tightly to her sister's waist; she could feel Elizabeth panting.

Jessica stared in horror at the thirty-foot bluff that towered overhead. "I can't believe we jumped from up there."

Elizabeth shook her head, but it was a moment before she could speak. "We didn't do anything," she corrected her. "It was all Fred."

"Man, was it ever!" Jessica patted the horse's quivering flank. "Look at that cliff he came down. I'd have bet anything that it couldn't be done."

The bluff wasn't nearly as steep as the eighty-foot one that Black Beauty had nearly stumbled over. The higher cliff was now hidden around a bend. But the cliff they'd jumped from was clearly visible. It wasn't one sheer, vertical drop, as it had seemed from midair, but a series of steep walls and flat ledges—like a huge staircase with impossibly high steps. Fred had made the descent in a series of graceful bounds.

"What do they call that horse with wings?" Jessica asked. "The one from the mythology unit in English class? That's our Fred!"

"Pegasus," Elizabeth answered in a tense, faraway voice. Jessica followed her gaze and gasped.

The top of the bluff was black against the purplish sky. On its crest, in silhouette, a man sat on a large, powerful horse. His hair and the horse's mane streamed out in the wind like flags. Except for that, John Marin was perfectly still. But he stared down at the twins with a malevolence that was tangible, even from thirty feet below.

"Let's get out of here," Jessica whispered into her sister's ear, as if she were afraid Marin would overhear. "You said there was a campground up the beach, with a road that leads to the hotel. Which way is it?"

Wordlessly, Elizabeth turned the horse's head to the north, and they cantered along the beach. To their left, waves crashed against rocky outcroppings, inky black in the night. The salt spray spattered Jessica's bare arms and legs, slightly warmer than the fat, slimy raindrops that raised goose bumps on her skin.

For now she and Elizabeth were safe. But Marin would surely follow them. And he wouldn't give up until he had accomplished what he'd set out to do.

Chapter 9

Despite the rain, Satchmo kept up a brisk canter along the paved road. Mr. Wakefield's clothes stuck to him, cold and sopping wet. But his mind wasn't on the discomfort of riding in the storm. He had to get to the beach. He had to see for himself the place where Jessica might have fallen.

It was after nine o'clock, and the twins' father was making good time along the paved road. The campground and the beach should be no more than a half mile in front of him.

Suddenly he heard hoofbeats ahead on the dark road. A single horse was cantering in his direction. Was it Marin? He pulled Satchmo to a halt, drew him to the shadows at the edge of the road, and waited. A short, sturdy horse emerged from the gloom, its pace slow but determined. Mr. Wakefield squinted into the darkness. The horse had not one, but two riders. And their identical heads shone gold in the night, though both were soaked from the storm.

"Jessica! Elizabeth!" he cried as they passed.

At Elizabeth's sudden pull on the reins, the reddish horse spun so quickly that both twins nearly fell off. Elizabeth found her voice first. "Dad!" she cried. She directed the small, sturdy horse over to her father's side.

"Oh, Dad, you wouldn't believe who we saw!" Jessica cried, near hysteria. "John Marin is on the island!"

"I know, honey. I know," the twins' father said, reaching out to squeeze her shoulder. "I thought you were . . ." He broke off as he realized that he was crying, his tears mingling with the raindrops on his face. He swallowed, hard. "Are you both all right?"

Elizabeth nodded. "We're fine, Dad," she said, sounding close to exhaustion. "Just tired and wet."

"Me, too," he replied with a nod. "Come back to the hotel now. Your mother's waiting for us."

"What are we going to do?" Elizabeth asked.

"We're getting off the island tonight," Mr. Wakefield said.

"What about Marin?" Jessica's voice was barely audible over the wind and rain.

"The police are combing the interior for him now," her father said, trying to sound confident. "I'm sure they'll find him by daybreak." He said a silent prayer of thanksgiving as Elizabeth's horse fell into step beside his.

The wind nearly tore the umbrella out of Mrs. Wakefield's hand as she hurried down the path to the stables. Not that it made much difference. The rain was blowing onto her from all sides. The twins' mother wasn't paying much attention to the weather, even though her white blouse and khaki slacks were decidedly damp. It was close to ten o'clock, and she hadn't yet heard a single word about her daughters' whereabouts.

She had to know where the twins were. She had tried to follow the police's instructions to remain near the phone. But by nine thirty she couldn't stand waiting anymore; she had to act. Mrs. Wakefield had asked the front desk to take any calls and to notify the authorities if new information came in. Then she'd headed for the stables.

"I'm Alice Wakefield," she told the young stable hand who was shaking out a yellow rain slicker inside the warm, dry stable. His glasses were foggy. Obviously, the man had just returned from being out in the storm, probably as part of a search party. "Are you Joe? Do you have any word of my daughters or husband? Did you find anything in the woods?"

The young man looked down, as if he couldn't bear to meet her eyes.

"What is it?" Mrs. Wakefield begged Joe. "Tell me, please!"

"We're . . . we're just not sure," the man stammered. "It might not mean anything at all."

Mrs. Wakefield's mouth went dry. "What?"

"I just got back and alerted the police," he said. "I tried to call you, but the front desk said you were joining the search."

"Tried to call me about what?" she asked.

"Please take off your raincoat and have a seat, ma'am," Joe said kindly. "The trail guide, Brad, is in the office, putting water on the stove for tea."

Mrs. Wakefield's voice dropped to a near whisper, but her words were desperate and hard-edged. *"Would you please tell me what's going on? What did you find?"*

"We found Jessica's horse," Joe replied, "injured, but not badly." He gestured toward a nearby stall, where a glossy black mare ate hungrily from a leather pouch. "Her knee is scraped up, as if she fell on it."

"I don't understand what that means!" Mrs. Wakefield cried. "Where did you find the horse? Where are my daughters?"

"The mare was on an eighty-foot cliff, overlooking the ocean. From the marks in the dirt, I'd say she stumbled on the very edge." He shut his eyes for a moment. "If that's what . . . happened," he continued, haltingly, "the rider could have been pitched over Beauty's head—and over the cliff."

The twins' mother sat down hard on a wooden folding chair. "You don't mean . . ." Her voice trailed off.

Joe knelt in front of her and took her hand in his. "I'm not sure what I mean, ma'am. There are probably a dozen other explanations." He paused to wipe his eyes with the back of his hand. "I am so sorry about all of this. I never should have let that man rent a horse. . . ."

"I can't just sit here!" Alice cried. "I have to *do* something!"

"Your husband and the police are searching now to learn what really happened," Joe said. He hesitated. "But Jessica's sweater—"

"*Jessica's sweater?* You found my daughter's sweater?" Tears started streaming down Mrs. Wakefield's face. "Does that mean . . ." She couldn't finish the thought.

Joe ducked his head. "We're not sure it means anything yet. We found a piece of fabric caught on a spear of rock, just over the edge of the cliff. It may have been torn from the blue sweater your daughter had with her."

Mrs. Wakefield buried her face in her hands. "What about Elizabeth?" she whispered.

"We've found no sign of her or her horse."

The twins' mother glanced up at Joe, her eyes suddenly fierce and protective. "And Marin?" she asked.

Joe gulped. "We found tracks from three horses

near the site where Black Beauty stumbled. Two were traveling together—we assume they're Jessica's and Elizabeth's. The other horse was coming from a different direction. It may have been the one Marin was riding; the tracks were about the right size." He sighed deeply. "I'm sorry, Mrs. Wakefield. This is all my fault."

She rose to her feet, full of determination. "Do you know where the place is—where you found Jessica's horse? Could you direct me there?"

"Well, sure I could," said the stable hand. "But that wouldn't make much sense, ma'am. I mean, it's pouring outside, and it's black as pitch. The trails will be slippery and dangerous. Why don't we have some tea? I'll wait with you until the police or your husband returns with news. If they come back with nothing, I'll lead the next search party myself—and I'll stay out there until I find your girls."

"I don't want to have some tea!" Mrs. Wakefield insisted. "I'm taking a horse, and I'm going to look for my daughters—now!"

"Mrs. Wakefield, I don't think that would be a good idea. The police should be back soon. If you just wait—"

"I've waited long enough! I'm going to look for my girls," Mrs. Wakefield repeated obstinately. "If they're out in those woods, I intend to—"

She stopped, certain that she'd heard a sound outside.

Joe rose to his feet. "That must be the police," he said. "Maybe they have more information."

The wooden door swung open, and Mrs. Wakefield felt giddy with a sudden release of tension. Her husband stood in the doorway, soaking wet, with an arm around each of the twins. Their hair was plastered to their faces, and they were pale and shivering. But they were alive. Water streamed from their clothing and hair, forming a shining pool on the wooden floor.

"Mom!" Elizabeth cried, throwing herself into her mother's arms. A minute later the Wakefields were engulfed in a four-way hug. Mrs. Wakefield never wanted to let go of her daughters again.

"Our two horses are outside," her husband said to Joe and Brad, who had just joined them from the other room. "Fred there deserves an extra ration of oats tonight."

"Oh, really?" Brad asked.

"Fred saved our lives," Elizabeth said, admiration glowing in her eyes. "He was the real hero tonight."

"He's Pegasus!" Jessica piped in.

"He'll get extra oats, and a special rubbing down," Joe promised her. Alice noticed that his glasses had fogged up again as soon as the stable door opened. "Brad, you'd better bring the horses in," Joe continued. "They're only getting wetter, standing in the rain."

Brad opened his mouth as if to complain, but a

glance from Joe changed his mind. He trudged out the door and returned a moment later, leading a large gray horse with white speckles.

"I'd better notify the police that you're all OK," Joe said to the Wakefields. "Would you rather wait for the authorities here, or in your rooms at the hotel?"

Mr. Wakefield shook his head. "We're not waiting anywhere. As far as we know, John Marin is still on this island, so we're getting off it. Now."

"I know you're pretty upset," Brad said as he led the horse into a stall. "But you really should wait for the police. They'll want to speak with your daughters about what happened tonight with that maniac."

"They can speak with the girls on the mainland," Mrs. Wakefield told him in a voice that left no room to argue. "We're leaving as soon as we can get to the pier."

Elizabeth grabbed her father's arm. "Dad, if we can leave, Marin can leave, too! What's to stop him from getting on a boat and following us?"

"The police have talked to every boat operator on the island," said her mother. "Everyone who could give Marin passage has seen his photograph and has instructions to call the authorities if he tries to get off the island."

Mr. Wakefield turned to Joe. "Do you know what time the next channel boat leaves for San Pedro?"

Joe shook his head. "I'm sorry, sir, but you're way too late. The last channel boat of the day left before sundown."

Mrs. Wakefield felt desperate. Every instinct in her body told her to put as much distance as possible between her family and John Marin. "Does that mean we're trapped on Catalina for the night?" she asked, her voice rising.

Jessica snapped her fingers. "Maybe not! I read in a brochure that a helicopter service takes people on and off the island!"

"That's no good," said Brad as he led a second horse, a small roan, into the stable. "Helicopters can't fly in a storm like this."

Elizabeth crossed the room to the reddish horse's stall and began tenderly petting its wet muzzle. *Obviously*, Mrs. Wakefield realized, *the small horse is Fred.*

"There has to be another way to get to the mainland," Mr. Wakefield said.

"What about a charter service?" the twins' mother asked. "Someone on the island must have a boat we can rent."

"Sure," Joe answered. "There are several companies in Avalon that run charter tours or rent boats. You'll find them near the pier where the channel boat comes in. But at this time of night—"

"Then that's where we're going," Mr. Wakefield said. "I don't want my daughters to be on this island with Marin for one second longer than they have to be."

Joe nodded, a resigned look on his face. "All right," he said, coming to a decision. "Look, folks, my fiancée's mother runs a houseboat-rental service. It's almost ten o'clock, and her place has been closed for hours. But I'm sure she'll let you have a boat if I vouch for you."

"How do we get there?" asked the twins' father.

"I can take you in one of the Orizaba's electric Jeeps. But what about your luggage?"

"It's packed and waiting in our rooms," Mrs. Wakefield told him. "Can you have the hotel send it over on the channel boat in the morning?"

"No problem," Joe said. "I'll bring it to the landing myself."

The twins' mother wondered briefly why the young man with the fogged-up glasses was being so cooperative. Then she remembered his apologies and knew that he was torn by guilt about having lent Marin a horse. Mrs. Wakefield wasn't sure if she blamed him or not. At the moment it wasn't worth worrying about. The only thing that mattered was getting off the island. Getting home.

Elizabeth sat stiffly in the stern of the houseboat, feeling every chug of the engine through the wooden bench. The rain had died down to a drizzle. But in the heavy wind her damp hair slapped against her shoulders like a sheet on a clothesline.

"This boat sounds like a popcorn popper," Jessica complained. "Are you sure the motor's working OK?"

"It's fine," her father assured her from the helm. "The engine's just a little cold. And Mrs. Clayton said there's a big canister of extra gasoline, in case we need it."

"It was nice of her to stock the boat with coffee for us," the twins' mother called from the galley. "I've got a pot brewing. It'll be warm in a few minutes."

"Great!" her husband replied in a hearty voice. "Something hot to drink will do us all good. I'm glad the storm's over, but the wind has whipped up some heavy-duty waves."

Elizabeth's parents and sister went on discussing the boat, the coffee, and the storm—anything but John Marin and the reason for their hasty flight from the island. But Elizabeth's mind was elsewhere. She turned on the bench, leaning her arms on the brass railing, and cupped her chin in her palms. The lights of Catalina were receding behind the houseboat, into the fog and the distance. She knew she was leaving Marin far behind, but she felt he was nearer than ever. Something about being on a boat again brought him rushing closer, like a gale-force wind.

In a way, it was as if she'd never left the deck of Marin's sailboat the preceding Saturday night—as if everything that had happened since then was only a dream. Reality was wind buffeting her face, waves slapping against the hull, and the hollow sound of the deck beneath her feet. Even the last twinkles of landlocked lights behind the boat could have been the lights of Sweet Valley Marina the week before, mirrored in the ink-black water and the gleaming blade of Marin's knife.

She shook her head violently, as if to dispel the image. "No," she whispered, "that was last Saturday. Tonight isn't the same at all." She forced herself to focus on the differences. The wind was colder and stronger than last week, spitting hard drops of rain that felt gritty against her skin. And the chugging motor was louder—more intrusive—than the billowing white sails of Marin's yacht. Last week she'd been alone with Marin. Now she was safe, her parents and sister only a few feet away.

Still, she couldn't help feeling the same sense of heightened reality she'd felt on the deck of Marin's boat, as the coast guard's lights had cast grotesque shadows on the sail behind them while she and Marin had struggled for the knife. And she couldn't help feeling dread rising within her until she felt as if she were suffocating.

She whirled at the touch of a hand on her bare arm.

"Elizabeth!" her mother said, her blue eyes anxious. "Didn't you hear us calling you from inside?"

"No, I guess I didn't," Elizabeth said.

"The coffee's ready, honey." Mrs. Wakefield

peered down at her daughter with warm concern. "Why are you sitting out here in the rain?" she asked.

"It's not raining anymore," Elizabeth said, noticing for the first time that the gritty drizzle had stopped.

"No, I guess not. But the wind's cold, and getting stronger. I wish I had thought to borrow a couple of sweatshirts from those men at the stable. You and Jessica are dressed as if it's still eighty degrees out."

Elizabeth shrugged, trying to hide her shivering. Her mother's comment made her more aware than ever of her short-sleeved shirt and khaki shorts. Her teeth chattered.

"Come inside and get something hot to drink," her mother instructed. "Maybe we can find some blankets for you and your sister."

Elizabeth allowed herself to be led into the cabin. But she stopped in the doorway and turned for one last look at the coast of Catalina Island. She was too late. The lights of the shore had vanished behind a shroud of fog. Elizabeth felt terribly alone.

"I can't wait until tomorrow," the man insisted. "I need a boat now!"

"I'm sorry, mister," the gray-haired woman said. The porch light above showed a suspicious look on her face. "But we closed at five."

She tried to shut the door of the boat-rental office, but Marin shoved his broad shoulder into the doorway. He knew why the woman was at the office more than five hours after closing. He knew Ned Wakefield. And he was sure that the counselor would have got his family off the island as soon as he possibly could. Marin had no choice but to follow. It was the only way to make Wakefield pay for putting him behind bars—not once, but twice.

Besides, the Wakefields would certainly have alerted the authorities. The police were probably combing the island already, searching for Marin. He had to get away. He wasn't planning on ever going back to prison.

When Marin had seen the lights on inside the Clayton Boat Rentals office, he'd known exactly who had been by so late in the evening to rent a boat. Now it was Marin's turn to do the same—if the police or the coast guard hadn't already reached this woman with his description and photo. He tried to read her expression. Did she know who he was and why he wanted a boat? Or was she balking simply because of the hour?

"Even if it weren't after closing, I couldn't rent you a boat tonight," Mrs. Clayton told him. "I rented out my last houseboat this evening." She was obviously trying to keep her voice casual, but she couldn't hide the edge of suspicion in it. She glanced over her shoulder, and Marin caught sight of a flyer on the desk inside the office. He was too far away to read it.

"There's an old wooden motorboat tied up at the dock," Marin said quickly. "I'll take that one." *It's just as well,* he decided. The Wakefields must have rented that last houseboat. He would need something faster, like the sixteen-foot boat with its outboard motor, to catch them.

"That's *my* motorboat," Mrs. Clayton objected. "It's not a rental."

Marin wanted to smack the old biddy across the face. Instead he flashed her his most endearing smile. "I only need it for a few hours," he said.

"I don't care if you only need it for a few seconds," she retorted. "It's not for rent."

Marin pulled his wallet from the back pocket of his new jeans. "I'll pay you a hundred dollars."

The woman glanced around herself uncertainly, as if looking for guidance. "All right," she decided finally. "Wait here while I get the paperwork."

When she stepped into the room, Marin pretended to be inspecting the tethered boat bobbing on the waves. But from the corner of his eye, he watched her through the crack in the door. She lifted the sheet of paper from the desk, and her eyes flitted between the flyer and his face in the doorway. Realization dawned in her eyes, replaced quickly with fear.

Marin smiled. He threw open the door and crossed the room in two long strides. He swung his fist and felt a satisfying thud as it landed against the side of her head. The woman dropped like a rag doll.

Marin snatched the flyer off the floor where it had fallen. His own face stared back at him. He laughed and closed his fist around the paper, pretending it was Ned Wakefield's high-and-mighty neck. "That's what you get for sticking it out so often," he said with a chuckle. "That's what you get, Ned!"

On a hook near the door, Marin found the ignition key to the motorboat. He grabbed a pair of binoculars off a shelf. Then he broke the glass cover of the fire-extinguisher box and tore the ax from its rack. *You never know when an extra weapon might come in handy,* he thought, grinning to himself.

"Thank you, Mrs. Clayton," he said to the woman's prostrate form. "It's been a pleasure doing business with you."

As he climbed into the motorboat, Marin realized he still held the balled-up flyer in his hand. He tossed it into the sea and watched it bob on the surface for a moment, glowing ghostly white, until it disappeared into the water's blackness. Then he started the motor and steered the boat out of the dock.

Jessica poured herself a second cup of hot coffee and pulled the thin cotton blanket tighter around her shoulders. "How much longer until we get to the mainland?"

"I'm not sure how to estimate," her mother called from the ship's wheel just outside the open cabin door. "The channel boat takes only an hour or so. I'm afraid it could take a lot longer in this thing. It's dark, and the waves are rough. We have to take it slowly."

Mr. Wakefield looked up. He'd been staring at a navigation chart as if he were trying to convince his family that he really knew how to read it. Jessica knew that her parents were no strangers to boats, but they weren't experts, either. Elizabeth was a little more knowledgeable than the rest of the family, but not by much. "If this weren't an emergency," Mr. Wakefield admitted, "I'd say it's not really safe to be out here at all. But we didn't have any choice."

"No, we didn't," Elizabeth whispered. Her face was pale in the dim cabin, and she was shivering, despite the blanket wrapped around her. Jessica wondered if she was sick.

Jessica turned to the round window and looked outside. The moon had set, and the black sky was indistinguishable from the dark water. If not for the streaky reflections of their own lights in the waves close to the boat, Jessica could almost have believed they were traveling through space. Suddenly a white blur shone for an instant, then was swallowed up in a wave.

"What was that?" she asked.

Her father jumped up. "What was what?"

Jessica watched as the white blur rose on the crest of another wave and seemed to come into focus. "Dad, it's a motorboat."

"Marin!" Elizabeth whispered, kneeling beside her on the bunk to look out the same window.

Jessica saw her father's face turn white as he peered through the next window. "No!" he said in a tense voice. "It can't be him."

"Why can't it be?" Elizabeth asked.

"Marin couldn't be following us," her father said, his voice shaky. "He has no way of knowing we've left Catalina. Even if he did know, the police and the coast guard would never let him off the island. It's just not possible."

Jessica felt numb. "What if it is?" she asked. "What if he's coming for us . . ."

"No," her father repeated. He sounded more certain this time. "That can't be Marin. Look—that boat is in trouble. Marin's too methodical to get himself into a jam like that."

"What kind of trouble?" Mrs. Wakefield asked from the helm.

"It's being tossed around on the waves as if the motor's dead," Elizabeth said in a voice that sounded tense but no longer afraid.

Her father nodded. "Yes, it's foundering, all right. I want to get a better look."

Jessica tossed off her blanket and followed her

father out the cabin door. A blast of cold air enveloped her as she stepped out into the night. Behind her, she heard Elizabeth rise to join the rest of the family on the deck. Mr. Wakefield cupped his hand around his eyes to cut the glare from the houseboat's lights and stood at the railing.

"Can you tell what's happening?" Mrs. Wakefield asked. "Should I steer toward it?"

"No!" her husband said. "If the current's worse over there, we don't want to get sucked in, too."

At the wheel the girls' mother bit her lip. "Can you see anyone on the boat?"

"I can't tell," Jessica announced, leaning over the railing to peer into the gloom. "It's got one of those canvas covers pulled over the front half of it."

"Damn!" her father swore. "I wish I had thought to rent a pair of binoculars."

Elizabeth stifled a scream as a wave crashed over the smaller boat. "It's going to capsize!"

Jessica held her breath until the little white boat bobbed to the crest of another wave, streaming dark water.

"Ned, we have to do something," Mrs. Wakefield said.

"I know," her husband replied. "I'll take the inflatable dinghy and see if I can help."

"The dinghy? Ned, no! It's too dangerous in such a small boat, with the water so rough. Let's take the houseboat over to it."

"No! I'm going alone. In the meantime, see if you can raise the coast guard on the radio."

"Why don't I try that first?" his wife suggested. "You stay here, and we'll let the coast guard handle it."

"We can't, Mom," Elizabeth said, her face sad. "There's no time. Look at it. That boat won't last long out there, if its motor's down. Look how low it's riding. It must have taken on some water. There might be a hole in the hull."

Her mother nodded. "You're right. We have to try to help, if we can. Let's cast the anchor. Then you girls and I can help your father lower the dinghy into the water."

John Marin watched the progress of the mustard-colored dinghy through his binoculars. He sat inside the motorboat's canvas cover, peeking around its edge, so his body was hidden from the Wakefields. He was almost certain that they wouldn't be able to recognize him at this distance, but this was no time for unnecessary risks. It might be his last chance at Ned Wakefield and his sickeningly wholesome family. And there was always the chance that one of the Wakefields had a pair of binoculars, too.

Mr. Wakefield was heading toward the motorboat, alone in the little inflatable raft. He was rowing like crazy. The night was black, but Mr. Wakefield's yellowish boat and orange life preserver practically glowed in the dark, making him easy to spot. A pinprick of light shone momentarily, and Marin realized that the counselor was carrying a flashlight.

"Good try, Ned," Marin whispered to himself. "But you're too far away for that light to help you see what's really out here. And by the time you're close enough, it'll be too late."

Marin smiled to see that the tide was against the man. Waves crashed on the front of the little boat, spraying the counselor with sporadic showers of seawater.

"That's right, Counselor," Marin said. "I knew you couldn't stand by and let a stranger die. You heroic types are so predictable." He kicked at the water that was filling the bottom of the motorboat. It was seeping in through a small hole Marin had chopped in the hull using the fire-extinguisher ax. He laughed, watching the dinghy's progress and fingering the heavy ax blade.

As he'd been expecting, a sudden burst of static squawked from the radio in the front of the boat. Marin ducked under the canvas cover to answer Mrs. Wakefield's call for help.

"Mayday, Mayday!" came her sweet, urgent voice. "Does anybody read me?"

Marin picked up the transmitter. "This is coast guard station one-oh-nine, reading you loud and clear," he said, pitching his voice lower than usual. "What seems to be the problem?"

Mrs. Wakefield described the location of the foundering motorboat, and Marin assured her that he'd send help.

"There's just one more thing, ma'am," he added, suddenly inspired. "Because of the storm, a lot of emergency calls like yours are coming through, jamming the frequency. Now that we're aware of your situation, I'd appreciate it if you'd stay off the radio for the next hour or so—except, of course, in the case of another emergency."

The twins' mother agreed, and Marin hung up the transmitter and laughed. She was just as predictable as her husband. Then he swung the ax at the radio, and it ruptured in a shower of sparks.

Again he trained the binoculars on the houseboat. Jessica and Elizabeth stood on the deck, side by side. Against the black of the night, one twin's arms looked bone-white in the boat's deck lights. That was Jessica, Marin decided, taking note of her loose hair and bare midriff. Elizabeth's hair was pulled back; a blanket swaddled her shoulders. Still, they looked more alike than different. Two identical heads gleamed gold, and two identical hands shielded their eyes as the twins' gazes followed their father's progress.

"Don't worry, girls," Marin muttered. "First I'll take care of your precious father. Then it's your turn—you and your pretty little mother." He smiled. Wakefield's wife was standing on the deck of the houseboat, looking sexy, as always—even at this distance, and on a dark night.

"You can't escape from me this time, ladies," Marin said, running his thumb along the ax blade. "Ned Wakefield's worst nightmares are about to come true."

Marin scurried under the tarp to the front of the boat long enough to scrawl something on a sheet of paper. He attached it to the steering wheel on a clip that was meant for a map. Then he crawled back outside, into the wind, and squinted across the jagged waves at the spot of gold that he knew was Mr. Wakefield's life raft.

"Next time, Ned, don't believe everything you see," Marin told the figure approaching over the waves. "Of course, there won't be a next time for you—or your family."

He let the rush of salt-tangy wind wash over his body like a waterfall. He breathed deeply, feeling the power of the wind entering him, making him stronger. He checked to make sure the boat's ladder was hanging over the hull, like a welcome mat for an old friend. Then he slipped over the opposite side of the boat—still clutching the ax in his hand—and waited in the dark, cold water.

"Hello!" Mr. Wakefield called into the wind as he pulled the inflatable dinghy up alongside the motorboat. "Is anybody there?"

No one answered his hail. He shone his flashlight along the length of the boat, but the disk of yellow light seemed pathetic against the huge, storm-tossed darkness of the ocean at night. Something metal glinted in the weak beam of the flashlight. An aluminum ladder hung from the side of the boat.

That's strange, Mr. Wakefield thought. *Who'd leave out the ladder in a storm like this?* He began to swing his body onto the ladder, but the oversize life jacket impaired his movements. Impatiently, he yanked it over his head and tossed it back into the dinghy. Then he climbed the ladder and tied the dinghy's line to the motorboat. Water splashed around his feet as he landed on the deck.

Liz had been right, he saw. The motorboat was taking on water quickly. *There must be a hole in the hull,* he thought. *This thing won't be afloat for long.*

He poked his head under the canvas cover and peered into the darkness beneath, sweeping his flashlight in an arc. "Anybody here? I've got a boat tied up alongside. I can get you to safety," he called.

Mr. Wakefield's eyes adjusted to the darkness, and he realized that he was speaking to the empty night. Somehow the motorboat's occupants had left. He lowered himself into the driver's seat, perplexed. What had happened? Why was there nobody in the boat? Had someone fallen overboard?

Had the occupants been rescued? Maybe there had never been anyone there, he considered. Perhaps the boat had broken away from its moorings, empty, and been swept out to sea.

Then he noticed something white on the steering wheel. He shone his flashlight on a sheet of paper that was clipped to the wheel and read the hastily scrawled writing on it:

"You lose, Counselor. Alice and the girls are mine."

Bile rose in Mr. Wakefield's throat. Marin had been playing with him all along. The foundering motorboat was a setup. Marin was no doubt on the houseboat with his wife and daughters already—or on his way there.

Marin is with Alice and the twins, Mr. Wakefield's mind echoed in horror. Panic gripped him, and he rushed to the side of the boat where he'd left the dinghy. He was halfway down the ladder before he noticed that the inflatable craft was gone. He peered into the distance and caught a glimpse of brighter color on the black waves. His own orange life jacket bobbed along with the rubber boat. At this distance, and in the dark, the twins' father couldn't make out the features of the man in the life jacket. But he knew exactly who it was.

Marin. And the killer was well on his way toward the girls and their mother.

Still clutching the ladder, Mr. Wakefield peered

farther into the distance. He looked toward what would have been the horizon, if the night had been light enough to differentiate between sea and sky. And there he saw what he was looking for. The houseboat's hazy hull materialized in snatches, bouncing through the mist like a gull caught in an upwind. But something was different about the houseboat. He saw a pinpoint of dazzling yellow light, intense enough to cut through the fog. His wife must have turned it on to guide him back. Unfortunately, now it could only help Marin.

The twins' father climbed back up the ladder. *I have to find a way to save my family*, he thought desperately.

He swept the interior of the motorboat with his flashlight. A pair of binoculars lay on a seat, just inside the canvas boat cover. Without them all he could see of the houseboat was that yellow light and an occasional blur of hazy white—if he knew where to look. With the powerful binoculars, he could see his daughters on the deck, staring over the side as if trying to catch sight of his dinghy.

Mr. Wakefield examined the dark stretch of ocean between himself and the houseboat. His grip tightened on the cold, slick metal of the binoculars as he found the dinghy. A wave crashed over Marin's head as he rowed the little craft with muscular, sure strokes. Marin continued, his body pumping backward and forward, the fountain of water causing hardly a break in his strong, overhand stroke. He was gliding toward the houseboat at a steady pace, and the waves were helping to push him closer and closer.

For an instant the twins' father poised his body to dive from the motorboat and follow Marin through the water. But reason won out. Mr. Wakefield was in excellent shape for a man his age. But the waves were treacherous and the distance long. And Marin had an enormous head start. Heartsick, Mr. Wakefield realized that he didn't have a chance of overtaking the younger man before he reached the houseboat. In fact, he admitted, he had little chance of surviving at all in the rough, cold seas for more than a few minutes.

But he still had to find a way to help his family. If only he could somehow signal his wife to pull up anchor and outrun the dinghy. Then she could radio the coast guard to capture Marin and rescue her husband.

"A radio!" Mr. Wakefield yelled, sprinting to the front of the boat. Most boats that size didn't have a radio, but maybe this one did.

It did. But of course Marin had damaged it beyond repair, hacking it into a useless mass of burned-out circuits and crumpled bits of sharp metal.

"Dammit!" Mr. Wakefield swore. But his voice was lost in the howling of the wind, the thundering of the sea, and the ominous creaking of the slowly sinking boat. Suddenly one end of the canvas cover sprang loose in a gust of wind. It began to flap loudly against the edge of the windshield, sending splatters of cold water onto his already wet hair.

Impatiently, he tore off the cover and threw it onto the deck. What did it matter if he had a roof over his head? He was already soaking, and the canvas only blocked his view.

"But what good is seeing him if I can't stop him?" he demanded angrily. As he sank onto the front seat, he caught sight once again of the note still attached to the steering wheel. The bluish letters, once hard and angular, were now rounding out, becoming splotchy and growing spidery tendrils, as drops of water splattered them. But the words were still the same:

"You lose, Counselor. Alice and the girls are mine."

"*No!*" Mr. Wakefield screamed at the hazy gold dinghy that was still visible in the distance.

His foot disturbed something metallic on the floor. It was the ignition key for the boat. He shook his head. Marin was evil and warped, but he wasn't stupid. If the key was still on the boat, it was only because the boat wouldn't work. Or because Marin knew it would sink before Mr. Wakefield could take it anywhere.

The twins' father turned the key in the ignition and was greeted by the dull whine of a motor that refused to turn over. He pounded his fist against the dashboard. "Start, dammit! I have to keep Marin away from my family!"

But it seemed that the contest between the lawyer and the murderer was over, and that Ned Wakefield had lost. Twisted with hatred and vengeance, Marin was nearing the houseboat where Alice and the twins waited. Meanwhile, the girls' father was trapped on a sinking motorboat, with little hope for rescuing himself, let alone his family.

He had never felt so helpless.

Chapter 10

Jessica stepped into the houseboat's cabin, grateful to be out of the wind. Elizabeth had come inside from the deck a few minutes earlier and was seated on the edge of the double bunk. Jessica sat down next to her. She pulled the blue blanket that was wrapped around Elizabeth's shoulders around herself as well, so that it enveloped both twins.

Vaguely, Jessica remembered the oppressive heat of the forest in midafternoon, and the longing to feel the wind through her hair. The guided horseback ride seemed like ages ago; now Jessica felt as if she'd been cold and damp forever.

Elizabeth acted oblivious to Jessica's arrival. She sat on the bunk, staring at her fingers. Jessica noticed that her twin's nails had been chewed down to ragged squares. Elizabeth obviously needed some help relaxing. And Jessica knew just the right person for the job.

Jessica tweaked one of the blond tendrils that had sprung loose from her sister's ponytail. "At least our hair's finally dry!" she exclaimed in a flippant tone. "I guess mine must be as straggly looking as yours."

Elizabeth didn't look up. "Thanks a lot, Jess. It's great the way you always know exactly what to say to make a person feel better."

Jessica sighed. Elizabeth was in one of her sarcastic moods. But Elizabeth needed cheering up, and Jessica knew that nobody could do it better than she could. "As soon as all this is over," Jessica said cheerfully, "I'm going to take the world's longest, hottest shower and wash my hair. Then I'll pour about half a bottle of that mega-expensive new conditioner into it." She gave a playful tug on her sister's ponytail. "You want me to save the other half of the bottle for you?"

Elizabeth whirled. "How can you worry about your *hair* at a time like this?"

"I just—"

"Dad is out there in those terrible waves, on a flimsy little life raft!" Elizabeth interrupted. "Aren't you afraid for him?"

Jessica's good spirits vanished like mist in a strong wind. She scooted her body across the bunk, to lean against the wall.

Elizabeth sighed. "Jess," she said softly, "I'm

sorry. I didn't mean to snap at you." She slid over and rested her head against her sister's shoulder.

"Of course I'm afraid," Jessica admitted. "I thought I was trying to cheer you up. I guess I was trying to cheer myself up, too."

Elizabeth squeezed her hand. "Where's Mom?"

"She's pulling out the medical supplies from the storage compartment under the deck," Jessica said. "I asked if I could help, but she told me to come in and put on some more water for hot drinks."

Elizabeth's eyes widened. "Medical supplies? Does she think Dad's hurt?"

"No," Jessica replied, "but he might rescue some people from that motorboat. If he does, she thought they might need—I don't know, bandages or something."

"Oh, yeah. I guess so. You know, Dad's been gone so long I had almost forgotten about the people on the motorboat." Elizabeth closed her eyes. "Jessica, I'm worried about him."

"He hasn't been gone *that* long!" Jessica protested.

Elizabeth opened her eyes. "How would you know?" she asked.

"Don't get sarcastic again about that wristwatch thing," Jessica snapped. "Just because I never wear a watch does not mean I have no sense of time."

"Well, it sure doesn't mean—"

"All I'm saying is that it doesn't seem like it's been that long!" Jessica interrupted. "Remember,

Dad had to row the dinghy all the way to the motorboat, help the people he finds there, and make it all the way back here."

"Jess, it's eleven thirty," Elizabeth said sadly. "He's been gone three quarters of an hour."

"So?" Jessica countered. "The motorboat was far away, and you know what the waves are like."

"Yes, I do," her sister said. "That's what I'm afraid of."

"There's no reason to be afraid," Jessica assured her, trying to swallow her own fear. "Dad's good at rowing. Don't you have to steer the raft kind of back and forth in diagonal lines when the waves are against you?"

"Something like that," Elizabeth said. "It's called tacking."

"Well, that would take a long time," Jessica insisted. "And he's probably taking it slowly and carefully, just to be on the safe side."

"We should see him coming back toward us by now," Elizabeth said.

"I think it's foggier than it was before. We might not be able to see him until he's right up close."

Elizabeth suddenly sat up straight on the bed. *Jessica, what if he can't find us?*

"Oh, I wouldn't worry about Dad missing the boat," Jessica assured her. "Mom turned on a super-bright yellow light that he could see miles away. This thing is better than the high school's new stadium lights. Dad *can't* miss us."

"Good," Elizabeth said. But Jessica noticed that she shuddered. Too late, Jessica remembered the brilliant lights of the coast-guard cutter as it pulled up alongside Marin's sailboat the week before. They must have blinded Elizabeth on the deck, making it harder for her to see the knife Marin had held above her. Mentioning a boat's bright lights had probably not been her smartest move. The last thing Elizabeth needed was to think about John Marin on a boat at night.

"Actually, it was probably the light that fooled me," Jessica said quickly.

"What are you talking about?" Elizabeth asked.

Jessica shrugged. "Nothing, really. It's just that I thought I spotted Dad getting pretty close to us, when I was outside a few minutes ago."

Elizabeth gasped. "What did you see?"

"For a second I thought I saw a kind of goldish blur," Jessica said. "I figured it was the dinghy, but I was wrong. It disappeared, so I thought I imagined the whole thing. I bet it was a reflection of that bright yellow light on the waves."

Both twins jumped at the sound of a hollow thump. "Dad?" they asked each other in the same breath.

"It sounded like something bumping against the side of the boat," Jessica said, jumping to her feet. "Maybe it was the dinghy!"

Elizabeth shook her head slowly. "No. It

couldn't have been Dad. That noise came from starboard. Dad will be coming from the port side."

"Maybe not!" Jessica jumped to the opposite side of the cabin, where another porthole was set into the wall, between the upper and lower berths of a set of bunk beds. "It's rough out there. What if he got turned around?"

"I don't know," Elizabeth said. "Do you see anything?"

Jessica peered out the porthole. "No," she finally admitted.

The twins' mother appeared in the doorway of the cabin. "That noise was nothing, girls," she said. "The storm must have knocked tree branches and other debris into the water. I guess a stray piece of flotsam thumped against the hull as it floated by."

"You checked for the dinghy?" Elizabeth asked.

"Yes, I looked," their mother said. "It wasn't him."

"What if we're looking on the wrong side of the boat," Jessica suggested, "and he can't yell loud enough for us to hear him?"

"I looked over both sides," her mother assured her. "And there's no dinghy out there. Don't worry, I'm sure your father will be back soon."

Mrs. Wakefield spoke lightly, but Jessica saw tension in her mother's face.

"I'm sure he will be," Elizabeth echoed. Jessica knew that her not-very-convincing smile was for their mother's benefit. A moment later the smile turned into a grimace when a particularly loud gust of wind lashed the side of the boat, drowning out the various creaks, groans, and thwacks that made up the now-familiar background noise of the houseboat in rough water. Jessica fell against her sister, and their mother gripped the door frame for balance.

For a moment Jessica thought she heard an angry voice in the wind. The hair rose on the back of her neck, and she shivered. Then she shook her head, and the voice was gone. The wind was noisy—full of the sounds of moorings that vibrated like guitar strings, of floorboards that creaked and moaned, and of waves whipped to a frenzy. But it was only wind. Gradually, the boat righted itself. Jessica pulled the blanket closer around her bare shoulders.

"I have some more work to do on the deck," Mrs. Wakefield said after she'd regained her balance.

Jessica and Elizabeth dutifully rose to join her.

"No," their mother objected. "Don't even think of helping me, either of you. Besides, I'm almost finished."

"But, Mom—" Jessica began.

"Absolutely not," Mrs. Wakefield insisted. "I want you both to stay here in the cabin until your father returns and to stay warm. You've been chilled through."

"Someone should be out there watching for Dad," Elizabeth pointed out.

"Don't worry. I'll be able to keep an eye out for your father. I promise I'll yell for you as soon as I see him rowing up."

Both twins sighed heavily after their mother disappeared outside.

"I hate boats," Elizabeth said suddenly, flopping back down onto the wide bunk.

Jessica collapsed beside her. "No, you don't. You love boats."

"That was before last Saturday night," Elizabeth countered. "And before *this* Saturday night. I think it'll be a long, long time before I want to get near a boat again."

"There's only one problem with that," Jessica said, a small smile playing on her lips.

"What?" Elizabeth asked.

"We live in a seaside town with about sixty million boats in it. And we work at a marina."

Elizabeth laughed grimly. "OK, so I'm overreacting," she admitted. "But don't invite me on any moonlit sails anytime soon."

"I'm with you on that one," Jessica said. "Next Saturday night let's go bowling instead."

Elizabeth's eyes opened wide with surprise. "You hate bowling. You said it's boring."

Jessica shrugged. "I could do boring," she said.

A wave splashed over the outboard motor and spurted in Mr. Wakefield's face. He tasted salt but continued trying to pry the plastic casing from the motor. He had to get the boat running quickly; nearly a foot of water now sloshed around his calves. It was hard to see anything in the inky darkness, but the motorboat was riding so low in the water that the twins' father knew it was close to sinking. He had already tried the bilge pump, but Marin had damaged it beyond repair.

"This is hopeless!" he exclaimed aloud. "I'll never get this motor fixed before the water rises. I need more time!"

He kicked impatiently, sending a wave of icy water sloshing down the length of the boat. But his foot struck something softer than the boat's wooden floor. He shone the flashlight through the water at his feet and saw the gray canvas cover that had sheltered the front part of the boat from the rain, lying in a water-covered heap. He remembered that he'd tossed it there earlier.

Wait a minute, Mr. Wakefield thought with growing excitement. *That canvas is water-repellent. It might be exactly what I need.*

He knelt in the bilgewater, groping with numb fingers at the bottom of the boat. He had to find the hole through which the sea was slowly but surely seeping.

Marin had done his work well. The jagged gash in the wooden hull was about four inches long and less than two inches wide. A carefully wielded ax blade could have carved it, Mr. Wakefield guessed. He lifted the boat cover from the bilgewater and shook it out. He folded the canvas quickly, arranging a section that looked about the right size, and shoved it into the gash in the hull. He worked the canvas farther into the hole until he thought it would stay put for a while.

Unfortunately, it was only a makeshift solution. Some water was still seeping in around the canvas plug. In fact, he realized with dismay, the hole was actually getting bigger. The boat was old, and the boards were rotting. Marin's ax had done more than tear a gash. It had split the wood of one board, and the split was growing.

The twins' father shook his head. He couldn't worry about that now. For the moment he had managed to slow the leak. If a huge piece of the hull split open later—well, he would worry about that when it happened.

Now I have to bail out enough to keep this thing afloat, he thought. *Then I'll fix the motor and catch up to Marin.*

As he began to bail, he shook his head in wonder at Marin's careful, methodical planning. The murderer had worked out this whole, complicated scheme, right on the spot, as soon as he realized the Wakefields were escaping the island by boat.

As usual, Marin had every detail covered. The hole in the hull was large enough to ensure the boat's demise, but small enough to sink it slowly. The time lapse would have been absolutely necessary for Marin's purposes, Mr. Wakefield realized.

The slow leak gave the twins' father enough time to reach the motorboat before it went under—and had given him enough time to understand fully the fate that Marin had planned for him and his family.

Mr. Wakefield had stumbled right into Marin's trap.

John Marin submerged quickly beneath the chilling waves, holding tight to the houseboat's taut, sinewy anchor line. A surge of water had thrown him hard against the starboard hull of the houseboat. Had anyone heard him?

For a moment he had the impression of movement above him, and a glint of gold. Then it was gone. Marin relaxed and rose back to the water's agitated surface. The gold glimmer was a blond head. Mrs. Wakefield or one of the twins had looked over the side for the source of the thump, had seen nothing, and had gone away. No doubt the three assumed he was a stray tree branch or a forgotten tire, bumping harmlessly against the hull.

Marin peered into the distance one last time. Good. The fog still shrouded the dinghy, which he'd anchored thirty yards away. Its only inhabitants now were Mrs. Clayton's fire ax and Ned's life preserver. Marin was sure he could find the small raft again when the time was right. He might have a long way to swim in order to reach it, but he was a strong swimmer. He knew he could make it. For now, the important thing about the dinghy was to keep it out of sight. Unexpected guests were always the most fun.

For a moment Marin longed for the ax. It was such a powerful weapon; he felt so masterful when his fingers caressed its smooth wooden handle and his arms weighed its substantial heft. But it couldn't be helped. The ax was too big and heavy to carry as he swam from the anchored dinghy to the anchored houseboat. Besides, the ax was a massive, sloppy weapon. He had something cleaner and flashier in mind for the Wakefield women. Through his wet shirt, he felt for his knife. It was still there, hanging from his belt loop on a piece of mooring.

Everything was ready for the final stage of Operation Wakefield.

Carefully, Marin braced his feet against the side of the boat and began pulling himself up the anchor line, walking his feet up the hull while carefully holding his body steady. He couldn't move in utter silence, under the circumstances. But that shouldn't matter. The creaking of the boat and the pounding of the waves against its hull would cover any slight noise he made. He just had to take care not to be too loud.

Suddenly a powerful gust of wind slammed into Marin's body, hurling him against the houseboat's slick hull. His hands burned on the anchor rope as he slid a couple feet down the line. "Oh, hell!" he shouted.

He stopped with a sharp jerk, swinging from the rope. He clamped his jaw shut while he regained his balance. He counted in his head as he listened. *One thousand one . . . One thousand two . . .*

No, he decided after two minutes—they hadn't heard him. The wind and the subsequent pitching of the houseboat had made enough noise to cover the sounds of his near fall and careless exclamation.

Marin breathed deeply for a moment. Then, stealthily, he made his way, hand over hand, to the top of the anchor rope. He pulled himself over the brass railing that surrounded the deck. Then he dropped to the polished planks of the deck, ducking low to remain out of sight.

Somebody else was on the deck, with her back to Marin. She was kneeling a few yards away from him, over some sort of compartment in the floor. Luckily, a bright yellow light that hung between them was pointed in her direction, illuminating Alice Wakefield's golden hair like a halo. It also lit the deck beyond her and reflected off an arc of iridescent black waves on the other side of the ship's far railing. Marin, crouching near the opposite railing, behind the yellow light, was in almost total darkness. He knew that nobody in the lighted circle would be able to see him.

He gazed for a minute at the supple curve of Mrs. Wakefield's back and the grace of her movements, even on an unstable boat. Then he smiled, anticipating his revenge on Ned Wakefield, once and for all.

Mr. Wakefield willed his tired body to bend and straighten, lift and throw. He bailed water from the motorboat faster than he would have thought possible. *It must be between eleven thirty and midnight,* he thought. But he kept bailing. He couldn't take the time to grope around for the flashlight and shine it on his watch. But he guessed that the killer must have had enough time to reach the houseboat by now.

Panic washed over Mr. Wakefield. He stopped bailing. He grabbed the binoculars from the front seat and peered into the night. A sudden gust of wind nearly knocked him off his feet. But when he regained his balance, he saw that the wind had cleared away some of the mist.

He could see the houseboat, its yellow light shining like a star against a black background of water and sky. But where was Marin? The dinghy should be visible too, as a tawny blur somewhere between the motorboat and the houseboat. He scanned the area again, but the lifeboat wasn't there. Part of his mind told him he should be happy not to see the killer closing in on his family. But Mr. Wakefield felt only terror.

I'd rather be able to see him, even watch him row closer to the houseboat, he told himself quietly. *At least then I'd know what he was up to. There's nothing as bad as not knowing.*

Mr. Wakefield turned back to the motor and yanked off the plastic casing with one tug. He had to get the motor running. Now.

The twins' mother shielded her eyes from the houseboat's bright light and peered into the gloom. Her lips were chapped by the strong wind, and she could taste salt on them.

For the hundredth time that night, she wished for a pair of binoculars. *Heck, I'd take a telescope,* she thought. *A periscope. Or even a microscope. I could use it to examine my own sanity. Why in the world did I let Ned go out there by himself?*

Not only was there no sign of her husband's dinghy, but she couldn't even see the motorboat anymore. The fog was too thick, or the boat had drifted too far away. Or the motorboat had capsized.

Mrs. Wakefield felt tears of fear and frustration gathering in her eyes. She didn't want the twins to know it, but she was growing more afraid with every passing second.

She squinted at her watch. It was nearly midnight.

"That's it," she decided aloud. "I can't take this anymore. I don't care about keeping the frequency open for emergencies. This *is* an emergency. I'm calling the coast guard."

◦ ◦ ◦

Marin stood silently in the shadows, watching Mrs. Wakefield walk resolutely across the deck to the radio. He'd be damned if he was going to allow her to reach it.

Marin whipped a knife from his pocket, admiring its clean, elegant blade of gleaming metal. He raised it carefully, took aim, and deftly sliced through the line that connected the houseboat to its anchor.

The boat jumped free, at the mercy of the wind and waves. And Elizabeth, Jessica, and their mother were at the mercy of John Marin.

The twins' mother felt the boat lurch under her as she reached for the radio transmitter. Suddenly the vessel seemed untamed and dangerously unsteady.

"That's odd," she said aloud. "It feels as if we're adrift."

Mrs. Wakefield grabbed a post for balance and laid her hand on the radio.

Something rammed against the back of her head. The deck tilted up crazily to meet her crumpling body. An instant later, everything went black.

Mr. Wakefield sat at the wheel of the motorboat, the wind whipping his face over the low windshield. He felt as if he were willing the creaking old craft along, rather than driving it. By midnight he had poured so much effort into the motorboat that it seemed like an extension of his own body.

Unfortunately, the boat was as weary and stressed-out as he was. He'd found the problem with the motor as soon as he'd pried off the casing. A spark-plug wire was missing. No doubt Marin had yanked it free and tossed it overboard into the roiling ocean. It hadn't taken long for Mr. Wakefield to figure out that he could substitute a wire from the smashed radio. But like his plug in the hull, the repair was a makeshift one. The boat ran, but only slowly and haltingly.

Mr. Wakefield had never known that plain old water could be so hard—so substantial. The boat lunged forward in fits, its bow ricocheting off waves that felt like boulders under the hull. And with every bounce the motor chugged and sputtered and threatened to die.

He grabbed the binoculars from the seat next to him to check his course against the houseboat's position. It still hung there in the dark, like a pale white ghost carrying a yellow lantern. It was farther away than he'd hoped. But he was getting closer.

Suddenly the yellow light began to glide forward. Mr. Wakefield rubbed his eyes. *That can't be right*, he thought worriedly.

But it was. Somebody had pulled anchor. The houseboat was floating off into the distance.

Fear coursed through his body. His wife and daughters would never have set off alone like that. They would have waited for his return. Somebody else was in control of the houseboat.

Marin.

A minute later the white blur of the houseboat had disappeared. He could no longer see the bright point of yellow light. The twins' father was completely alone in the dark seascape of wind and water.

Chapter 11

Tears blurred Elizabeth's vision as she looked into the storage compartment at her feet. It was the same compartment where her mother had found the medical supplies. But now it was empty, and half its interior was in shadow.

"I said get inside!" Marin yelled, his knife at Jessica's throat. "Do it, Liz! Or there'll be one dead twin lying on the deck."

Elizabeth nodded, her eyes locked on to Jessica's. She stepped into the rectangular hole, which suddenly reminded her of a tiny coffin. She didn't want to scrunch her body into the dark, cramped space and let him close the door over her. "It's too small," she said, her voice broken with a sob.

"Do it," Marin ordered again. "Sit on the bottom and keep your head down. You'll fit."

He slashed the knife across Jessica's neck, and Elizabeth screamed. But Jessica was all right; Marin had held the knife an inch in front of her. He winked at Elizabeth. "Next time I'll slice her for real."

Elizabeth sat in the storage space with her knees up in front of her. Before she lowered her head, she took one last look at the deck of the boat. In reality, the houseboat was pitching wildly on the waves, like some rodeo animal. But in Elizabeth's memory, the scene would always be preserved like a snapshot in the utter stillness of an instant.

The cold yellow spotlight illuminated half the deck, plunging the rest into utter blackness. Marin stood at center stage, his own inky shadow pooled beneath and behind him on the wood planks. One of his muscular arms crossed Jessica's chest, pinning both her hands at her sides. The other held the knife, poised and ready in front of her throat. In his grasp Jessica looked small and fragile, her eyes wide with fear, tears running down her face.

Worst of all, behind Marin on the deck lay the twins' mother. Her eyes were closed; blood streaked her face. Her body lay still, and Elizabeth couldn't tell if she was breathing.

In the next instant Marin narrowed his eyes at Elizabeth, and she slowly lowered her head to her knees. Then he stepped forward, dragging Jessica with him like a rag doll. With his foot he pushed the compartment's lid over Elizabeth with a snap that echoed in her brain. All light vanished.

Something yellowish rose from the black waves ahead of the motorboat. Mr. Wakefield squinted into the night, but the shifting fog obscured the shape of the floating object. He slowed the boat to a chugging halt but kept the engine running. If he turned the engine off, he wasn't sure he'd be able to start it again. He trained the flashlight on the tawny form. It was the dinghy from the houseboat. The dinghy wasn't adrift; beside it a taut anchor line disappeared into the waves. The little boat was empty.

"Why did he leave it out here?" the twins' father asked aloud. "What was he planning?" He scanned the fog with the binoculars, but the houseboat was nowhere in sight.

He anchored the motorboat and slid down the ladder into the dinghy. His own life jacket was there, as well as a heavy, long-handled ax that looked as if it had been taken from a fire-alarm box. He eyed the ax grimly as he weighed it in his hands. It sickened him to think that he might have to use it on another human being, but Marin's acts barely qualified him for membership in the species. And the ax was the only weapon the counselor had. He took it with him when he climbed back into the still-sputtering motorboat.

Water splashed around his feet, three inches deep on the wooden deck. *That canvas plug must be working itself loose in the hole,* he thought. But he decided not to fix it. He couldn't lose any more time. He had to find the houseboat soon. If he didn't, it wouldn't matter if the motorboat sank and dragged him to the bottom of the ocean with it.

Despite the few minutes it cost him, he tied the dinghy behind the motorboat. If he managed to get the twins and his wife off the houseboat and away from Marin, they would need something to escape in, and the motorboat obviously wasn't going much farther. Then he revved the motor again, and the boat leaped forward with an awkward bound.

This has to be a nightmare. It's the only possible explanation, Jessica thought, watching the hatch close over her sister's head.

Jessica had been sure that she and Elizabeth were safe from Marin, at least temporarily. A few minutes earlier the twins had heard footsteps enter the cabin behind them. They had spun around, expecting to see their mother.

The next few seconds had played out in slow motion. Her sister must have known the truth an instant before Jessica had. Jessica remembered seeing a glass of water fall from Elizabeth's hand to the table near the bunk beds. She remembered water splashing her own bare thighs, near the hem of her cutoffs. And she remembered recoiling in horror at the sight of John Marin standing over them, his hair damp and disheveled. A straight, sharp knife had glittered in his hand.

Now Marin held that same knife cold against the front of Jessica's throat.

Two weeks earlier she would have snuggled deliciously into the powerful arm that was wrapped around her bare midriff. But now its pressure on her skin made her feel dirty.

"How did you get here?" she sobbed. "How did you follow us?"

Marin laughed. "Shut up, darling, and do exactly as I tell you," he sneered.

A cramp seared through Elizabeth's left thigh. She longed to stretch out her legs. But the toes of her sneakers were already butting against the opposite wall of the tiny compartment. Stretching was out of the question. She couldn't even massage the cramp away through her shorts; there was no way to get her hand anywhere near her thigh.

Crammed into the small space, Elizabeth had no room to move her legs, her shoulders, or even her head, which rested on her knees in front of her. Her arms, stretched around her knees, had a little more freedom, but not much. She could move them up and down, but not from side to side. As the runaway boat bounced on the waves, she was continually bumped against one side or the other. She was sure she'd have purple bruises on both arms by morning.

If I live until morning, she thought in despair.

The tight fit wouldn't have bothered her nearly as much if it hadn't been for the total darkness in the compartment. Logically, she knew she was alone. The creepy-crawly feelings that kept skating up her bare arms and legs were the products of her own imagination. *There are no bugs in here!* she reminded herself. She would have a much easier time believing that if she could check it out for herself.

Elizabeth couldn't remember ever being somewhere this dark before. She shifted her head a few inches from side to side but couldn't see even a faintly lit outline of the compartment's lid above her. The seal seemed to be absolutely airtight.

Airtight! The hairs stood up on Elizabeth's arms. "How much air is there in here?" she whispered, horrified. "How long do I have until I use it all up?"

For one panic-stricken moment she was sure she was suffocating. Her lungs felt tight, as if an iron band were squeezing the air from them. Her head spun as she gasped for breath.

No, she realized. She couldn't have used up all the oxygen so quickly. She couldn't give in to her fears, or she'd never think of a way out of this.

Elizabeth forced herself to breathe at a slow, steady pace. Once she felt calmer, she realized that she could hear every word being said on the deck above her.

"You won't get away with this!" Jessica challenged Marin, her voice quavery but resolute. "My father will be back any minute, and then you'll be sorry."

Marin laughed—a long, drawn-out cackle that raised goose bumps on Elizabeth's legs. "Your father, my dear, is out of the picture."

"He is not!" Jessica insisted. "He went to help some people on a motorboat! He's on his way back here now!"

"You Wakefields are so gullible," Marin said in a calm, reasonable voice that would have made him sound charming if he hadn't been saying such terrible things. "I suppose it's genetic. At least that's one defect that won't be passed on to any future generations—after I get through with all of you."

Elizabeth gasped. The sinking motorboat had been a setup. Her father had gone on a wild-goose chase, designed to keep him away from his family so that Marin could move in for the kill.

"By now Dad's figured out that you tricked him," Jessica said desperately. "He's on his way back here in the dinghy."

"The dinghy?" Marin said, obviously amused. "Jessica, darling, how do you think *I* got here? Your father doesn't have the dinghy. And by now he doesn't have the motorboat, either. The boat—and your father—are at the bottom of the ocean."

Elizabeth desperately tried to control her quiet sobs, thinking of her rapidly depleting oxygen supply.

"Ned Wakefield, Counselor to the Fishes," Marin continued. "It has quite a ring to it, doesn't it?"

Elizabeth heard muffled thumps and knew that Jessica was struggling with Marin. "Be careful, Jessica!" she whispered, remembering the strength of Marin's viselike arms from her own struggle with him, on the deck of another boat.

A loud *smack* cut short a scream. "You'll get a lot worse than that if you don't shut your mouth and let me tie you up," Marin threatened, his voice harsh and dangerous.

"What difference does it make?" demanded Jessica. "No matter what I do, you're planning to kill us anyway, aren't you?"

When he spoke again, Marin's voice once more had the controlled, affable tone that had fooled Jessica and Elizabeth into thinking he was a harmless, friendly guy. "Yes, I do plan to kill you." It was the same tone of voice he might have used to say that yes, he did plan to see a movie. Elizabeth shuddered. "The only question is when, and how."

"I don't care when or how," Jessica said defiantly. "If you're going to kill me, you might as well do it now."

"No, Jessica!" Elizabeth screamed as loudly as she could.

Jessica hesitated but went on. "I'm not going to cooperate with anything you tell me to do, you scumbag! What do you think of that?"

"What I think is immaterial," Marin said smoothly. "Let's see what your sister thinks, shall we? Perhaps she's willing to die quickly, too, just to satisfy your need to defy me."

"No!" Jessica screamed. "Leave Elizabeth alone! I'll let you tie me up. Do whatever you want to me."

"I thought you'd come around," Marin said with a chuckle.

Elizabeth was terrified, but now she was seething mad, as well. She never could stand by and listen to anyone hurt her sister. How dare he manipulate Jessica by threatening Elizabeth? It was the same sleazy tactic he'd used on Elizabeth earlier, to get her to climb into the storage chamber.

Elizabeth's right hand balled into a fist, and she pounded the floor with it. To her surprise she felt something cold and hard under her hand. Elizabeth groped for it and grimaced. A sharp pain slashed through her finger. She dropped the hard object with a metallic clatter. Immediately, Elizabeth felt blood running down her finger, and wiped it on her sock. Whatever she had touched was sharp. If she had the chance, maybe the object could be used on Marin. Elizabeth felt again for the piece of metal, and this time picked it up safely and turned it in her fingers.

The object was a small knife with a razor for a blade, a scalpel. It must have been among the medical supplies that had been stored in the hold before Mrs. Wakefield had taken them out. With the cold steel in her hand, Elizabeth felt stronger. She'd find a way to hurt Marin with it, she vowed.

If she didn't die of suffocation before he opened the lid.

The motorboat lurched over the dark waves, its patched-together motor sputtering and wheezing. Behind it, the inflatable dinghy bounced from side to side on its slender line. Mr. Wakefield kicked at the four inches of water around his feet and prayed that the little motorboat would keep running—and stay afloat—until he found the houseboat and his family.

He held the binoculars to his eyes and scanned the night. The fog was intermittent now, blowing over the water like ragged specters. Finally he saw what he was looking for—a ghostly form up ahead, too white to be a trick of the fog, with a piercing yellow light over it, beckoning.

But the light was moving quickly away from him; the houseboat was picking up speed. Mr. Wakefield simply wasn't sure if the old motorboat would be able to catch it.

Somebody's hand was on Mrs. Wakefield's arm. Her husband must be home. *Yes, that has to be it*, she thought groggily. Who else would have his hand on her arm? But this wasn't home, she remembered. She was too cold, and her lips tasted salty. Now she knew. She was on a boat, and her husband had gone. Was he back now? She wasn't sure. She couldn't think. Her head felt as if it were full of rocks. She tried to open her eyes, but her eyelids were too heavy.

The hand gripped her arm and jerked it behind her back, hard enough to bring tears to her eyes. *This can't be Ned*, Mrs. Wakefield thought. *My husband would never hurt me.* Somebody was tying her up, using rough, sinewy ropes that pulled too tightly and scratched her skin.

"Don't hurt her!" screamed a voice. It was the voice of one of her daughters, Mrs. Wakefield realized, though she couldn't tell which one. In terror, their voices sounded exactly the same. Her daughters were in trouble.

Mrs. Wakefield wrenched her eyes open, and a light like the sun seared her eyeballs. She snapped them shut and tried again, carefully.

Suddenly the twins' mother knew exactly where she was. She was on the houseboat, with the bright yellow light. And a man she recognized from John Marin's photograph was tying her to the deck. To her left Jessica half sat, half sprawled, fastened tightly with rope to iron rings set into the planking. One side of her face was bruised. In her scanty bikini top and short shorts, she looked particularly helpless and out of place.

"Mom!" Jessica cried.

"Keep quiet, both of you!" Marin commanded.

Mrs. Wakefield turned to Jessica. "Elizabeth?"

"She's OK—" Jessica began.

Relieved, the twins' mother let out the breath she hadn't known she was holding. Marin slapped Jessica across the face.

"Don't you dare slap my daughter!" Mrs. Wakefield shouted.

"She'll get another one—and a lot more—if I hear another word out of either of you," Marin warned.

The twins' mother had never met this man, but she would have known who he was even if she'd never seen his photograph. He was handsome, she supposed. Or he would be, if a more pleasant expression replaced the anger that now hardened the lines of his face. His eyes were midnight-blue—almost black—and his body was powerful and well toned, in an unremarkable outfit of blue jeans and a blue-and-white-plaid shirt that hung open over a white T-shirt. In fact, John Marin *looked* perfectly ordinary, not at all the way she'd imagined a convicted killer would look. But he radiated hatred the way a furnace radiates heat.

For no apparent reason except to test her,

Marin kicked Jessica in the side. Jessica groaned, but her mother could see that she wasn't badly hurt. Mrs. Wakefield clenched her teeth to keep from speaking out. *Where is Elizabeth?* she wanted to scream.

As if in answer to her unasked question, Marin turned to look at Mrs. Wakefield, grinning affably. The ogre who had kicked her daughter in a rage only a moment earlier was now replaced by an attractive young man with an easy smile.

"I suppose you're wondering where your daughter's *better* half is," he said, with an amused glance toward the seething Jessica. "To tell you the truth, I'm afraid I forgot to keep track of the time, like I'd planned. There *might* still be some oxygen in that teeny-tiny little space. Then again, there might not be."

Mrs. Wakefield's eyes widened, and she forgot to be silent. *"Where is Elizabeth?"* she yelled.

Marin strolled across the deck to the storage compartment where the girls' mother had found the boat's medical supplies. To her horror, he lifted his foot and tapped on the lid.

Beside her mother, Jessica struggled to break free of her bonds. "You let her out of there!"

"Please," was all the twins' mother could choke out.

Marin shrugged. "Well, when you put it so politely . . ." With agonizing slowness he lifted the hatch of the storage compartment.

Elizabeth's head bobbed convulsively as she gasped for breath. "I'm OK, Jess," she said as soon as she could speak. Then she caught sight of her mother, and her face filled with relief. "Oh, Mom, you're all right. I was so worried—"

"No talking in the ranks, girls," Marin said, shaking his head as if he were scolding naughty children. "Come on, Elizabeth. It's your turn to get roped. I always wanted to be a rodeo star."

He grabbed Elizabeth's arm and jerked her to a standing position. She winced, and her mother could see that she was in pain.

"Give her a minute," Mrs. Wakefield pleaded. "She's all cramped up from being stuffed into that box."

"I'll be OK in a second," Elizabeth said, still panting. She leaned over for a minute, the way a runner does after a race, and rested her hands on her shins, as if trying to catch her breath. Her mother's eyes widened as Elizabeth whipped a small scalpel from her sock and held it in her palm.

Mrs. Wakefield's eyes were on her daughter's cupped hand as Elizabeth slowly straightened up. Then Elizabeth sprang into action and thrust the knife toward Marin's stomach.

Marin's affable manner vanished. As quick as a panther, he grabbed Elizabeth's wrist and twisted. With a cry of pain she dropped her small, innocuous-looking knife. Marin kicked it away, still gripping her wrist.

"You little idiot," he said into her ear, his voice ugly with hate. "Don't you know by now that you can't get the better of me? Don't you know that I can crush you"—he twisted her wrist farther—"anytime I want to?"

Elizabeth's knees buckled, but Marin jerked her up cruelly.

"Stop it!" Jessica and her mother screamed together.

Marin only laughed. Then he threw Elizabeth to the deck next to her sister and tied her tightly.

"You know, there's something I really regret about all of this," Marin told them as he gave his final knot one last tug.

"How sad for you," Jessica remarked.

Marin just grinned at her and disappeared around the side of the cabin. He returned a moment later with a metal canister of gasoline. Mrs. Wakefield gasped, afraid that she finally knew exactly what Marin had in mind for them.

Marin continued speaking, as if he had never stopped. "The entire point of my whole plan, of course, was to get back at my old friend Ned, in a way that would be sure to get his attention." He began pouring gasoline onto the deck, in a circle around Alice and the twins. Some spattered on Mrs. Wakefield's pants leg, and the smell overpowered the scents of sea and salt that had permeated everything around her until that moment.

"No!" Jessica screamed. "How can you do this?"

"It appears that my plan has succeeded," Marin said smoothly, ignoring the interruption. "What I regret is that I've now got you all exactly where I want you, and poor old Ned isn't even here to see it."

He drained the last of the gasoline can onto Jessica's cutoff jeans. "Denim burns very nicely, you know," he confided to her, still smiling.

"Let my daughters go!" Mrs. Wakefield pleaded. "You can do whatever you like to me."

"Mom!" Jessica screamed.

At the same time, Elizabeth cried, "No!"

Marin disappeared into the cabin. He returned a moment later with a box of wooden matches in his hand. He slipped one out, lit it, and held it over Jessica's head, grinning.

"Untie my daughters," the girls' mother proposed again, trying to keep her voice calm. "You'll still have me here. That's enough revenge on my husband. He'll be devastated. Please."

Marin laughed and blew out the match. "Oh, Alice, you're so beautiful and so earnest. But I forgot—you still believe your husband is alive."

"What are you saying?" Mrs. Wakefield whispered.

"I guess you were a little indisposed earlier," Marin said with mock sadness, "when I was telling Jessica about Ned's watery grave."

Mrs. Wakefield felt blood rushing to her head and shook it so she wouldn't faint. She couldn't let herself believe Marin, not when her daughters were in so much danger.

Marin lit another match and stared into its flame. She saw fire reflected in his midnight-blue eyes, shimmering there like the fragmented reflections of the boat's yellow beacon light in the dark, treacherous waves.

Suddenly Marin shoved the lit match toward Mrs. Wakefield's face. "I do regret that Ned won't be able to watch you all die," he told her. "Oh, well, I'm sure he imagined your deaths many, many times—as the water closed in over his head. Ned had such a marvelous imagination. You know, I think I'm going to miss him."

Jessica's eyes followed Marin's hand as he gestured with another lit match.

"Life is so fragile," he mused, staring at the flame. "One minute you're alive and arguing cases in court, sending people to prison for years. . . ." His eyes hardened, and he looked, one by one, at the twins' mother, at Jessica, and then at Elizabeth, as if reassuring himself that he had their attention. "And the next minute, you're fish food," he concluded. He blew out the flame.

Marin tossed the spent match aside. "Of course, you three will die a little faster than the counselor did," he said, "though I have tried to pour the fuel a couple feet out from you. I wanted to give you a few minutes to really contemplate what's happening to you. It's so much meaningful that way, don't you think, Alice?"

He pulled another match from the box and lit it. Then he tossed it into a pool of gasoline a few feet from Mrs. Wakefield's back. With a sickening *whoosh*, flame billowed up like a sail behind her.

Elizabeth screamed.

Jessica, tied between Elizabeth and her mother, looked at them both. In their faces she saw reflected her own fear and horror. What she didn't see was the intense anger that was rising in her chest. She had never in her life wanted to kill somebody the way she wanted to kill John Marin at that moment. But the only body parts she had free were her left foot and her right elbow. Neither seemed to be of much use for harming Marin or for freeing herself and the others.

"Alice, I do wish we'd had more time together," Marin said sadly, his face orange in the glow of the fire. From the tone of his voice he could have been toasting marshmallows at Boy Scout camp.

Marin lit another match and gestured toward Elizabeth with it. "Liz, honey, I enjoyed our last sail, even if it was cut short—I'm glad *this* one won't end before I've finished showing you a really hot time." He tossed the match into a shallow puddle of gasoline a few feet away from her, where it burst into flame.

"And Jessica—brash, fun-loving Jessica—I'm sorry I couldn't put you on television sooner. I'm glad I can oblige you now. Too bad you won't be around to watch the news: 'The bodies of three women were found with the charred remains of a houseboat, et cetera, et cetera.'" He laughed. "Good-bye, Jessica. You were truly a fun date."

He pulled out another match, flicked it to life, and began to toss it toward Jessica.

Something barreled into him from one side, and Marin sprawled onto the deck. The lit match, knocked from his hand, fell toward Jessica, but the flame burned out before it brushed harmlessly by her leg.

Marin rolled a few feet. Then he jumped up and disappeared into the shadows outside the circle of light.

A second man was on board, and he was fighting with Marin in the dark. Jessica couldn't see them. "Who is it?" she screamed above the roar of the flames, praying that her mother or sister had got a better look than she had. "Was it Dad?" *It had to be,* she told herself. *Who else could it be?*

"I couldn't tell for sure!" Elizabeth screamed back, her voice hoarse with the smoke. "Jessica, the fire's getting closer to me!"

"Work your hands free, girls!" the twins' mother yelled. "One of mine is coming loose!"

Elizabeth screamed again and then fell into a coughing fit. Jessica could already feel the heat of the flames on her face and legs. The powerful gasoline smell reminded her that her clothes were drenched with the stuff. And the smell of smoke was getting stronger.

Something crashed onto the part of the deck outside the light. Jessica turned her head, but her vision couldn't pierce the darkness. A stray spark caught her attention as it floated through the air toward her. Her eyes followed it, willing it to extinguish itself in midair, as the last match had. The spark landed in the ends of her mother's hair, and a trickle of fire rose from it.

"Mom!" Jessica screamed. She reached out with her free elbow and managed to smother the flame.

Suddenly two male figures staggered into view. Mr. Wakefield swung at Marin with an ax, forcing him close to where Jessica lay tied to the deck. Mrs. Wakefield screamed. Marin, the quicker of the two men, lunged to the side. Then he stepped in to jab his knife toward the counselor's ribs.

"Dad!" Elizabeth coughed.

Jessica acted. As Marin lunged toward her father, she extended her left foot as far as she could. Marin tripped and dropped the knife, sprawling on the deck with a thud. Mr. Wakefield shifted the ax in his hands. He swung the ax in a wide arc and slammed its handle against the side of Marin's head. Marin lay still.

"Ned!" Mrs. Wakefield cried. "Free Elizabeth first!"

Hungry tongues of flame licked at Elizabeth's bare legs. As Jessica watched in horror, a fiery tendril leaped out from the main blaze, igniting Elizabeth's sleeve. Her father sprang to her side and snuffed it out with his hands. As the flames roared around him, he used Marin's knife to cut the ropes holding Elizabeth in place. Then he bounded to his wife and freed her, while Elizabeth untied Jessica's hands.

"This way to the dinghy!" he cried, motioning them away from the flame. "Hurry! The fire has spread to the cabin. The whole boat's going to blow when it reaches the fuel tanks."

Jessica grabbed Elizabeth's hand and sprinted across the deck, following their father. Just behind her, she could hear their mother's ragged breathing. She realized that the wind was tossing the flames around the deck. Everywhere the fire touched, it took hold, igniting the wood all around them. The smoke hung heavy in the air, smelling acrid and making it hard to breathe. The air was hot and gritty on Jessica's bare skin. She felt as if she were running through a tunnel of fire. Behind her, her mother began coughing uncontrollably.

Mr. Wakefield reached the brass railing at the edge of the deck and gestured over it. Jessica looked down and saw the mustard-colored dinghy below, illuminated now in the uneven, flickering light of the fire.

"Quick!" the twins' father yelled. "Grab the rope and slide over the side," he instructed, pushing

Elizabeth to a rope tied to a cleat on the railing. The dinghy was directly underneath it. "Jessica, you're next! Be ready to go over the side as soon as I tell you."

"Dad, there's another boat down there!" Jessica shouted.

"It's the motorboat we saw before," Mr. Wakefield explained. "But it's practically submerged. It'll sink completely in another few minutes."

Jessica climbed over the railing and tested the rope in her hands. A crashing roar and a flash of light made her stop. A shower of sparks erupted from the part of the deck where Jessica knew the cabin was, though a wall of flame now blocked her view.

"The boat's electricity just shorted out," Mrs. Wakefield explained between coughs. Firelight shone in her eyes.

Jessica nodded, now understanding why the night suddenly seemed darker, despite the fire's ghastly orange cast. The bright yellow light no longer shone over the deck.

"Ned, how will we make it to shore in that little boat?" Mrs. Wakefield asked, recovering her breath. "We don't even know where we are."

"Don't worry," her husband assured her. "This fire will bring the coast guard here in no time."

Mrs. Wakefield nodded. "Go on down, Jessica!" she said. "Hurry!"

"Alice, you're next," Mr. Wakefield said. "When you reach the dinghy, take it out a safe distance from the houseboat. Wait for me there. I have to go back." He gestured toward the inferno on the other end of the deck.

"Dad!" Jessica wailed.

"Jessica, go!" her father ordered.

"Ned, what are you talking about?" Jessica heard her mother asking from above her head as she shimmied down the rope. "Where are you going?"

His answer was lost to Jessica in the roar of wind, waves, and fire.

Elizabeth felt as if she'd been transported into an old movie she'd once seen about the sinking of the *Titanic*. The cold, rough sea and the black night were the same as in the movie. And the houseboat also looked like something out of a movie; it was too terrible to be real. The boat's surface was a thick carpet of flame. Soot and other debris rained into the waves around her like confetti, with an occasional fragment still burning as it fell.

Jessica was in the dinghy, too, sitting beside Elizabeth near the bow. Their mother was just lowering herself into the stern from the rope that hung from the houseboat's railing.

"Mom! What are you doing?" Elizabeth screamed as Alice cut the line that held the dinghy to the side of the larger boat. "Where's Dad? We can't just leave him behind!"

"Take an oar, Liz," her mother instructed, keeping the other one for herself in the back of the boat. "I don't like it any better than you do, but he's gone back to get Marin. He says he'll jump overboard with him and swim to us."

"*What?*" Jessica yelled. Elizabeth saw fire in her sister's eyes that had nothing to do with the fire on the houseboat. "That's ridiculous!" Jessica continued. "Marin practically killed us all! Why the heck does Dad want to save his nasty, pathetic excuse for a life?"

Elizabeth wouldn't have put it quite so bluntly, but she had to agree.

"Jessica, your father said there's a flashlight up there at the very tip of the bow. Find it and keep it focused ahead of us. Give a yell if you see any debris in the water that we need to steer around."

"But Mom! Dad is—" Jessica began.

"Jessica!" Mrs. Wakefield interrupted sharply. "I know. But there's nothing you can do for him right now. Just do as I said—please."

Jessica nodded glumly.

"Mom, I don't understand," Elizabeth ventured, trying to keep her voice reasonable. "Letting a monster like Marin live is one thing. But Dad risking his life to save him—"

"I wanted to argue with your father," the twins'

mother admitted, pumping away at her oar. "But there was no time for—"

An explosion rocked the ocean around them. Elizabeth whirled. As she stared in shock, the houseboat erupted in a fountain of flame and smoke.

Jessica screamed. Elizabeth turned to her sister and gasped, startled. The eerie orange light made Jessica's hair glow as if it were on fire, too.

"It's all right, girls," their mother said, with only a note of panic in her carefully controlled voice. "Your father had plenty of time to get off the boat. I'm sure he's in the water right now, swimming toward us."

"Why did Dad have to go back?" Jessica cried, sobbing. "It doesn't make any sense! He didn't even know if Marin was still there to save. What if Marin had already woken up and jumped off the boat himself? Then Dad would be risking his life, while Marin was already—"

She froze as she realized what she was saying. In her mind Elizabeth completed her sister's thought: *While Marin was already swimming away.* Elizabeth peered around at the dark, choppy waves, each one gilt-edged with the reflected glow of the fire. What if John Marin was under those black waves right now, swimming silently toward the dinghy?

Suddenly a male hand rose from the waves and grasped the side of the boat. Elizabeth screamed.

The nightmare isn't over, she thought in horror. *Marin is back.*

A head bobbed to the surface. "Is everyone all right?" Mr. Wakefield asked.

He was breathing heavily, but he was alive.

Elizabeth, Jessica, and their mother all sprang forward to help pull him into the dinghy. For the next few minutes they all hugged each other, weary but grateful to be together and safe.

Elizabeth wasn't sure she wanted to hear the answer to her next question, but she knew she had to ask it. She raised her head from where it rested against her father's wet shoulder. "Dad, what about Marin? Did he escape from the boat before you got to him?"

Mr. Wakefield shook his head. "Marin is dead."

Jessica's face showed disbelief, and Elizabeth was sure that her own held exactly the same expression.

"Are you sure, Dad?" Jessica asked. "Are you absolutely sure he's dead?"

"He's dead, all right," their father told them. "I saw the body. The smoke got to him before I could."

"Thank heaven he's the only casualty," Mrs. Wakefield said. "Thank heaven." She was sobbing, and her husband wrapped his arms around her.

Jessica was crying, too, a reflection of orange flames glinting in each tear as it rolled down her face. Elizabeth was startled to realize that her own face was wet with tears, but she wasn't sure if they were tears of fear or relief.

"We made it," Elizabeth whispered, patting her sister's arm. "We're finally safe."

Then she straightened her back, dipped her oar into the water, and resolved to put the burning boat far behind her.

SWEET VALLEY HIGH™

Don't miss any of this summer's fabulous Sweet Valley High Collections!

Double Love Collection

DOUBLE LOVE
SECRETS
PLAYING WITH FIRE

Summer Danger Collection

A STRANGER IN THE HOUSE
A KILLER ON BOARD

Château D'Amour Collection

ONCE UPON A TIME
TO CATCH A THIEF
HAPPILY EVER AFTER

Flair Collection

COVER GIRL
MODEL FLIRT
FASHION VICTIM

All Transworld titles are available by post from:
Bookservice by Post
PO Box 29
Douglas
Isle of Man
IM99 1BQ

Credit Cards accepted.
Please telephone 01624 675137 or fax 01624 670923
or Internet http://www.bookpost.co.uk
or e-mail: bookshop@enterprise.net for details.

Free postage and packing in the UK.
Overseas customers allow £1 per book (paperbacks)
and £3 per book (hardbacks)